GOOD
PARROTKEEPING

Robin Deutsch

Good Parrotkeeping
Robin Deutsch

Project Team
Editor: Tom Mazorlig
Copy Editor: Stephanie Fornino
Indexer: Lucie Haskins
Designer: Angela Stanford

T.F.H. Publications
President/CEO: Glen S. Axelrod
Executive Vice President: Mark E. Johnson
Publisher: Christopher T. Reggio
Production Manager: Kathy Bontz

T.F.H. Publications, Inc.
One TFH Plaza
Third and Union Avenues
Neptune City, NJ 07753
Copyright © 2009 by T.F.H. Publications, Inc.

All rights reserved. No part of this publication may be reproduced, stored, or transmitted in any form, or by any means electronic, mechanical or otherwise, without written permission from T.F.H. Publications, except where permitted by law. Requests for permission or further information should be directed to the above address.

Library of Congress Cataloging-in-Publication Data

Deutsch, Robin.
Good parrotkeeping : a comprehensive guide to all things parrot / Robin Deutsch.
p. cm.
Includes index.
ISBN 978-0-7938-0666-9 (alk. paper)
1. Parrots. I. Title.
SF473.P3D58 2009
636.6'865--dc22

2009014524

This book has been published with the intent to provide accurate and authoritative information in regard to the subject matter within. While every reasonable precaution has been taken in preparation of this book, the author and publisher expressly disclaim responsibility for any errors, omissions, or adverse effects arising from the use or application of the information contained herein. The techniques and suggestions are used at the reader's discretion and are not to be considered a substitute for veterinary care. If you suspect a medical problem consult your veterinarian.

The Leader In Responsible Animal Care For Over 50 Years!®
www.tfh.com

CENTRAL
Garden & Pet

TABLE OF CONTENTS

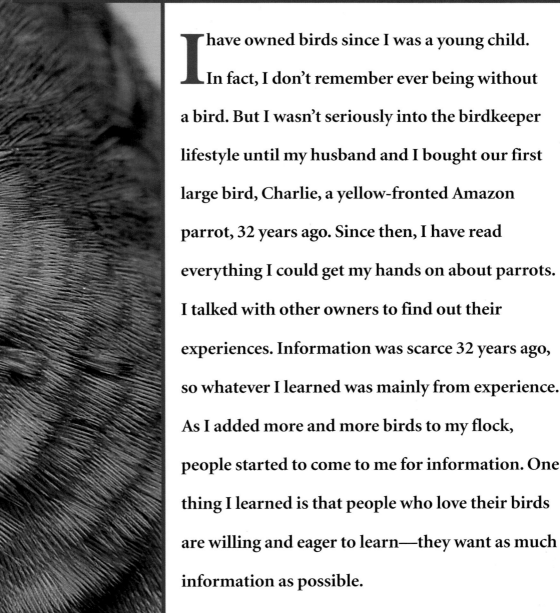

I have owned birds since I was a young child. In fact, I don't remember ever being without a bird. But I wasn't seriously into the birdkeeper lifestyle until my husband and I bought our first large bird, Charlie, a yellow-fronted Amazon parrot, 32 years ago. Since then, I have read everything I could get my hands on about parrots. I talked with other owners to find out their experiences. Information was scarce 32 years ago, so whatever I learned was mainly from experience. As I added more and more birds to my flock, people started to come to me for information. One thing I learned is that people who love their birds are willing and eager to learn—they want as much information as possible.

Good Parrotkeeping

Over the years, I have talked to brand-new bird owners as well as more experienced bird owners. There were many questions that they all had in common when it came to learning how to take better care of their birds. I listened to all of their questions—I even listened to the questions people called or wrote to me with. Then I started teaching classes on bird care, and there were even more questions.

When I taught those classes on bird care, I was surprised at all the things new bird owners really needed to learn. Over the years I talked to a lot of people and found out what they wanted and needed to learn about. Whether these owners were new or experienced, they wanted their questions answered. In this book, I answer these questions. Whether I am explaining how to select the best parrot species for you or how to keep your bird safe, you will have your questions answered. You will learn about daily bird care and what

Many Alexandrine parakeets are great talkers.

The golden conure is one of many endangered parrot species.

you should and shouldn't do. You will learn about avian nutrition. You will find out why a yearly avian veterinarian appointment is necessary. Most importantly, you will learn how to keep your bird tame and how to prevent behavioral problems.

I hope that this book will answer all of your questions and that you find it helpful.

Robin Deutsch

Chapter One

YOUR PARROT AND YOU

Owning a parrot is one of the most rewarding experiences you could ever imagine, but it takes a little work to make sure that your parrot is receiving proper care. Sometimes it may seem that they are as much work as a two-year-old human child, and they can be that way for 80 or more years, depending on the species. But above all, they will bring you so much joy and laughter that you will agree they are worth it. There is a reason why most bird owners end up adding more and more birds to their feathered family.

Parrots, such as this African grey, are social creatures who need daily interaction with their owners.

As with a human child, you need to make sure that your parrot's environment is safe and that his psychological needs are met. Caring for your bird will be easy as long as you know what to watch out for as well as what to expect. This chapter will help you learn more about your parrot and the different considerations that you need to think about.

Parrots as Pets

Parrots have been captivating people for thousands of years. Alexander the Great was known to have kept parrots as pets. While Christopher Columbus was exploring the New World, he was so fascinated by the birds that the Native Americans kept as pets that he ended up bringing some of these incredible creatures back with him. There have even been parrots in the White House!

Today, parrots are still valued for their beauty, intelligence, and companionship. Collectively, parrots are the third most popular pet worldwide. Before you run out and buy a parrot, however, first consider why you want one. You would be surprised at some of the outrageous reasons why some people buy a parrot.

CONSIDERATIONS

Before buying a parrot, consider how bringing such an intelligent and alien creature into your home will affect you and your lifestyle. You also need to consider the opposite—how coming to live in your home will affect the bird. Here are the most important things to think about as you decide whether to acquire a parrot.

COMPANIONSHIP

Do you want a companion that could be as loyal as any dog could be? Or do you want this bird because he would look great in your living room? Parrots cannot be kept in a cage and ignored. They need companionship and daily interaction. After all, these are flock creatures, and without other parrots around, you are your parrot's flock.

TALKING

Perhaps you are looking for a pet that can talk? This is probably the most common reason why people want a parrot. If you are buying one because they might talk, be forewarned now. Although all parrots are capable of some mimicry, only about ten percent of them ever develop any kind of vocabulary. Some may only imitate sounds, such as the phone ringing or that irritating sound of your spouse snoring. Some may only say those very embarrassing things. The truth is that there have been only handfuls that have developed impressive vocabularies. For example, one little budgie has made it into the Guinness World Records as the world's record holder for his ability to talk. This little guy has an incredible vocabulary of more than 1,000 words! A talker like that is extremely rare, though—do not purchase a parrot expecting him to definitely talk.

Never buy a parrot on impulse. Make sure that you have thought it over first and have carefully made a decision.

LIFESTYLE

What is your lifestyle like? Parrots are flock creatures. What this means is that they need daily interaction if they are to thrive. A parrot would not be a good choice if you are rarely home or are traveling all the time. If you are home often, then a parrot may be a good pet for you.

TIME

Are you willing to spend time every day playing with the bird? Some parrots like budgies don't require hours of your day, but they still need time with you. Cockatoos, on the other hand, would love to be surgically attached to you so that you spend every waking moment with them.

CLEANING

How much time do you have to clean a cage every day? The size of the cage will determine how long this could take. A cage for a lovebird or parrotlet won't take long to clean, but a cockatoo's cage will take longer. Don't forget that you need to change the food and water as well as clean the cage daily.

DWELLING

What about where you live? People in small apartments can have parrots as pets, but they need to choose carefully. Some parrots can be very, very loud! Okay,

11

Good Parrotkeeping

Kids and parrots can be wonderful companions, but an adult must be responsible for the parrot's care. A cockatiel and his family are shown here.

the truth is that they can be ear-shatteringly loud. Screams this loud can and will cause hearing damage. While you may not mind such loud noise, your neighbors may not appreciate it. You must also consider that the larger the parrot, the more space he will require. So if you live in a small apartment, you may need to pick a parrot who is smaller as well as on the quiet side.

MESS

You should be aware that parrots are messy. Seed, feathers, and yes, even droppings are usually all over the place. Some parrots are so good at creating a mess that they can accurately toss a seed into your shoes 50 feet (15.2 m) away. They seem to take great pride in accomplishing this feat. People who are neat freaks tend to have a hard time dealing with this mess. But neat freaks can and have lived successfully with parrots. They just sweep or vacuum ten times a day!

CHEWING

What about the damage a parrot could do to your house and belongings? The larger parrots, such as macaws and cockatoos, love to redecorate homes in their own unique style. Do you mind having window ledges with huge beak marks on them or perhaps walls redesigned with skillfully placed chew marks? Smaller birds can make tiny little nibbles on your expensive blinds. This is one reason why you need to spend so much money on toys to keep your parrot occupied.

CHILDREN

What about children? Kids and pets can be wonderful companions, but you need to realize that parrots rely on instinct and can, if frightened, bite. Very young kids could hurt some of the smaller, more fragile birds, while bigger birds could do some damage with their large beaks. If there are very young children in the household, they need to be taught respect for all pets in the household, and an adult must always supervise whenever the parrot is around. Older children can be great with parrots, but you cannot rely on them to properly take care of a bird. You must check to make sure that they are giving them fresh food and water daily and cleaning their cages.

PLAYFUL

How playful is the bird you want? Some parrots are hyperactive; others are real perch potatoes. Some play with toys constantly, and others only move them around to get by. If too much activity is more than you can handle, think about a species of parrot that is on the calmer side.

PETS

What about other pets in the household? Would a parrot get along with them? Would the other pets get along with the parrot? Even the smallest bite from a dog or cat could be lethal to your parrot. Supervision is needed whenever your bird is out of his cage.

What about other birds? A friend of mine once said that parrots are like potato chips—you can't stop at one. Although some birds do get along with each other, most often they do not. As long as there is supervision whenever they are

Although this African grey (right) and blue-fronted Amazon (left) are sharing a perch, you must provide each bird with his own cage, play stand, etc.

both out, this is not usually a problem. You may need to get different play centers for each bird and make sure that there is some separation.

LONGEVITY

How long will the parrot live? When you are buying a parrot, realize that they generally live longer than a dog or a cat. A budgie could live 15 or more years. Other parrots could live 70 or more years. There have been many documented cases of them living 100 years or more! So if you buy a bird like a cockatoo or macaw, realize that they will probably outlive you and possibly even your children. Have you thought about his care if something happens to you?

EXPENSE

Do you know how much that parrot will cost you? Parrots are not cheap. The parrot himself is often the least of the expenditures; you must also add in toys, a cage, food, and maybe a play center. And you will have to replace toys frequently, especially for larger species. Don't forget to add in the cost of an avian veterinarian exam to make sure that the bird is healthy. Can you put this into your budget? The only thing that is totally priceless is the amount of love and affection your parrot will give you.

ALLERGIES

Do you or does someone else in your household have allergies or lung disease? Some species of parrots, such as cockatoos and African greys, are known as powder birds. They produce a fine powder that gets everywhere. People with allergies or lung disease tend to have problems because of this. Even nonpowder parrots can still cause some problems. Check with your doctor before you buy a parrot if you have one of these health issues.

SMOKER

Are you are smoker? Birds have sensitive lungs, and like people, they can develop cancer. Although smokers can have parrots as pets, they need to be considerate of them and smoke outside and away from the bird.

COOKWARE

Do you use nonstick, polytetrafluoroethylene (PTFE)-coated cookware? If you do, are you willing to get rid of all of it? When overheated, PTFE produces a chemical that is fatal to parrots. Instead, you will need to use hard-anodized aluminum, stainless steel, or ceramic-coated cookware.

VACATIONS

Do you plan to go on a vacation? If you are, who will take care of your parrot when you are gone? You cannot just leave enough food and water for the time you will be gone. So many parrots have died slow, agonizing deaths because the owners left what they thought would be enough food and water for a week. They didn't take into account that water bottles could be knocked down or that food could be tossed out of the cage.

VETERINARIAN CARE

Good veterinary care is extremely important. Are you willing to take your bird in for a yearly exam? Get him care when he is sick? Even a budgie needs to be seen at least yearly by an avian veterinarian. Good veterinary care is essential to the health and longevity of your parrot.

NOISE LEVEL

Parrots can be noisy; some are much louder than others. They vocalize, and some vocalize more than others. Bourke's parakeets and other grass parakeets have soft voices and their sounds pleasing. Budgies can chatter but they aren't loud. However, some people find this noise annoying. Most African species are quieter than South American species.

WHO IS THE PARROT FOR?

Don't get a parrot for someone else who may or may not want one. This is also true for children. If you get a child a pet, she should be old enough to understand the responsibility of owning one, and you still need to ensure that she is properly taking care of the animal. Also, you may decide that you want the parrot, but the parrot may decide that he loves your spouse instead and hates you. Parrots can choose someone else other than the one who wanted them in the first place.

I Can't Hear You Over the Parrot!

The noise level of a parrot can sometimes be ear shattering. In terms of numbers, a macaw can scream at 105 decibels, a Moluccan cockatoo can scream at 135 decibels, and the little nanday conure has been recorded as high as 155 decibels. Screams this high can injure your eardrums. Some more numbers to consider are: mealy Amazon, 124 decibels; Quaker parrot, 113 decibels; mustached parakeet, 111 decibels; mitred conure, 100 decibels. At a distance of 100 feet (30.5 m), the average jet engine is 140 decibels—some parrots are louder!

SUMMING UP

I hope I have given you some things to consider before you buy a parrot. Parrots are well worth any difficulties that may occur. They are loving, funny, loyal, curious, intelligent, and just plain wonderful. They lift up your spirits whenever you are down, and they listen intently to how your day was or how you are feeling. They are always happy to see you and make you feel needed. They never judge; they only give you unconditional love.

Are Free Parrots Really Free?

If you are answering an ad in the newspaper for a cheap or free parrot, be suspicious, especially if the seller wants to meet you someplace other than where she is keeping the bird, like a parking lot. Remember, there is no such thing as a free bird. These so-called "cheap" or "free" birds may have health or behavioral issues. After visits to a veterinarian or behaviorist, these birds may end up costing you more money than a bird for whom you would have paid a normal price.

Choosing a Parrot

Now that I haven't scared you away, it's time to go out and start looking for a parrot. It doesn't matter whether you decide to go to a breeder or to a pet store. Both can be excellent places to go to buy a parrot. No matter where you decide to obtain a bird, what matters most is how the current owners take care of him.

WEANED AND UNWEANED PARROTS

If you are buying a young baby who is still being weaned, watch to see how the owner interacts with him. A properly socialized baby who is not force weaned will have fewer behavior problems when he gets older. A baby who is force weaned is made to start eating on his own even though he is not ready.

Watch to see if the owner is giving the weaning baby a wide variety of foods. Teaching a baby bird to eat different foods is easier than trying to teach an older bird to eat those foods. Be aware that certain birds, such as budgies, are not normally hand-fed. This is because budgies are usually docile enough that they are easily hand-tamed.

What is a weaned bird? A weaned bird is one who no longer requires someone to help feed him. He is eating on his own. You still need to find out how the bird was fed. Was he spoon fed, syringe fed, or tube fed? Tube feeding is just shoving a flexible tube into the baby's crop. This method doesn't allow any individual time with the feeder, nor does it allow for natural feeding habits to form. A tube-fed bird often develops more problems, both behavioral and physical, because of the tube feeding.

Is it better to use a spoon or syringe? Both are good methods, but I recommend spoon feeding to those who are uncomfortable or don't have experience in feeding a baby. Some birds may be aggressive eaters and can be injured if an inexperienced owner feeds them with a syringe. Spoon feeding, however, is messy.

So what is better to buy, a weaned bird or one who you will wean on your own? This depends on how experienced you are in feeding a bird. Weaning takes practice and patience, so it is usually for the more experienced bird owner. Some breeders or pet stores will take the time to teach you how to feed the baby so that you can wean the baby yourself. This may be a little scary once you are on your own.

Why is it so hard to wean a baby yourself? To begin with, the temperature of the formula has to be correct. Formula that is too thin or too thick can cause problems, and you have to make sure that the bird doesn't aspirate (inhale) the formula. Some babies are slow eaters and others eat rapidly. There are many things to think about when you are feeding a baby. Most important of all is that you want to make sure that the baby is doing well and is growing properly.

If you decide to wean the baby yourself, find out what he was being fed, what times he was eating, and how he was fed, either with a spoon or syringe. When you bring the baby home for the first time, he will already be stressed. By sticking to the same time, the same formula, and the same feeding method, you will help reduce this stress. By changing these things, you can cause digestion problems, such as a slow-emptying crop or a crop that doesn't empty at all.

Hand-fed, properly socialized parrots make the best pets. This Quaker parakeet is being fed by syringe.

If you are looking for an older bird and not a baby, where you get him is still an important consideration. Unfortunately, there are always unscrupulous people out there who will try to sell a sick or diseased bird to unsuspecting customers. Remember, we live in a buyer-beware world. If the price of a bird is too good to be true, there is usually a reason. If the current owner won't provide a health document or allow you to take the bird to the vet to make sure that he is healthy, then don't buy him.

What to Look For

Below are some things to look for in either a weaned baby or an older one.

ACTIVITY AND BEHAVIOR

Check to see if the bird is listless or if he is active and alert. Some birds are higher

If the person selling you a parrot can't answer your questions or direct you to someone who can, she may not be the person from whom to buy the bird. As a new bird owner, you will probably have plenty of questions. This is why it is important to buy the bird from someone who knows what she is doing and doesn't mind you asking these questions.

energy than others. For example, a budgie is usually more active than an Amazon parrot. Look at the bird and see if he is watching you with as much interest as you are watching him. Baby birds won't be as active as an older bird, but they should seem interested in what is going on.

Observe the bird to see if he plays at all or if he just sits there. Likewise, look to see if he is overly hyper. A bird who sits low on the perch all fluffed up is often ill. Watch the bird's tail. Does it bob up and down each time the bird breathes? If it does, the bird might be ill. If he is way too hyper and can't sit still for more than a few seconds, there could also be something wrong with him. However, it is normal for a weaning baby to not play much—most babies are still trying to figure out perching. Birds who are senior citizens also do not play much due to old age.

PHYSICAL CHARACTERISTICS

NARES

Look at the bird's nares. The nares are the two little holes right above the beak; in other words, these are the bird's nostrils. Are the nares dry, or are they wet or stained? If they are wet or stained, he could have an upper respiratory infection or other problems. Are the nares clogged up, or do they appear free of material? Clogged nares are an indication that the bird is sick. A bird who has chronic sinus conditions may have a vitamin A deficiency, which may indicate a poor diet. Also while checking out the nares, look at the cere. The cere is the rasied area right above the beak where the nares are located. Is it crusty looking or have growths on it, or is it normal for that species?

BEAK

Look at the beak. Is the beak chipped, very flaky, or broken? Does it align correctly, or is it crooked? A beak that is misaligned could prevent the bird from eating properly or even climbing the bars of the cage. Sometimes baby birds are hatched with a beak problem or develop one because of poor feeding techniques. With today's advances in avian medicine, many beak problems can be corrected. However, you may not want to take on the expense of fixing this problem when you are just starting out with a new bird. Is the beak shiny, or it is dull looking? Birds such as African greys and cockatoos will have a dull, almost powdery-looking beak. If the beak is shiny, it can indicate a health issue. A healthy beak should appear smooth and symmetrical and have a gleam to it.

FEATHERS

Look at the feathers. In most birds, the feathers should have a healthy sheen and not appear dull or chewed up. Birds who should have feathers that appear powdery or duller in color are cockatiels, cockatoos, and African greys. These are powder birds, so dull-looking feathers are normal. If these birds have feathers that are bright and shiny, then there is a problem. Birds like eclectus have feathers that appear more hair-like than like feathers. Feathers that are chewed on are signs that the bird could be a feather plucker. These birds could have other behavioral problems as well. It could also be a sign of an illness.

If the bird is an adult housed by himself and he has feathers missing from his head, he could have psittacine beak and feather disease (PBFD). It is normal for cockatoos and cockatiels to have a bald patch when they raise their crests. This is not the same thing as missing feathers. Baby birds may have feathers starting to come in for the first time, and they may not look as they would in an adult bird.

EYES

What about the eyes? Do you see any discharge coming from them? Are they crusted over? Does the bird hold them open, or do they appear "sleepy" or droopy? Do they appear swollen or puffy? Does the bird have both eyes? Check carefully for warts, lumps, or growths around the eyes. Eyes should appear bright and not dull or cloudy. Eyes can also be an indication of age. Baby budgies have a solid dark color that will develop a yellowish ring around the pupil as they age. African greys have dark eyes when they are younger that get lighter as they age as well.

Check the parrot's eyes, cere, and beak carefully before you buy him. This is a healthy-looking Fischer's lovebird.

Legs, Feet, and Toenails

Next, examine the feet. Check the bottoms of the feet for any cracks or sores. Birds' feet are sensitive and can become infected if not properly cared for. Does the bird have four toes on each foot? A parrot has a zygodactyl toe arrangement, meaning that two toes point forward and two toes point backward. Does the bird favor one foot over the other? Do they seem as if they are painful to the bird?

What about the nails? Are they so long that they are curling into the bird's feet, or are any of them missing? Nails should not be too short, either; nails that are too short could prevent the bird from getting a proper grip on things.

While checking the bird's legs, make sure that the joints are not swollen or red. This would normally indicate a serious medical problem.

Keel

Check the keel, the bone that runs down the center of the bird's entire chest

Jenday conure with a metal leg band. Most birds sold as pets within the United States should have leg bands.

area. You should be able to feel this bone but not to hold it between your fingers. If you can hold it between your fingers, the bird is probably too thin, indicating poor diet or illness. If you can't find the keel bone, you may just have a little porker on your hands. However, this also could indicate a poor diet or an illness. A bird who is of a good weight will have muscles on either side of the keel. While weight is not always an indication of a health problem, it is something to consider when determining the health of any bird you are buying.

Never attempt to remove a bird's leg band yourself because you run the risk of seriously injuring him.

VENT
Finally check the vent. The vent is under the tail and is where the droppings come from. Is the vent stained? If the vent is stained or has dried fecal matter on it, the bird could be ill.

LEG BANDS
Check for leg bands, which can be made of plastic or metal. There are two kinds of leg bands: open and closed. A closed band is put on the leg when the bird is a baby. These bands are flattened and come in various colors and sizes that are appropriate for each species. Closed bands indicate that the bird was bred in captivity and that he was not removed from the wild and imported into the country. These bands typically have the breeder's ID number, the bird's ID number, and sometimes the year the bird was hatched. These bands cannot be put on an older bird because they will not slip over an adult bird's foot.

Open bands are applied to a bird who was imported through a quarantine station. The bird may have been legally imported from another country or confiscated from smugglers who illegally took the bird from the wild. These bands are round and have an opening on them. These gray-colored bands are inscribed with the identifying marks of the quarantine station they came through and the lot number they were in.

All bands have the potential to cause problems, but open bands tend to be more dangerous. Check the legs to make sure that these bands, if present, are not causing sores or pain. They can only be removed by a skilled avian veterinarian, and it can be tricky. You have to weigh the pros and cons of having the band removed. Even with a skilled avian veterinarian removing them, you run the risk of cutting the bird's skin or breaking his leg.

CAGE AND SURROUNDINGS
Pay attention not just to the parrot but to his immediate environment as well. How many birds are kept in one cage? Is the cage overcrowded? Are there many

cages right next to each other? How clean are these cages? Overcrowding can lead to stress, which could lead to illness. Cages that are close together or that have many birds in them could have a sick bird who may go unnoticed until the other birds start showing signs of illness.

Look at the perches in the cage. Are they clean or are they covered with fecal matter? A parrot not only needs clean perches, but he also needs various sizes. Is there only one kind of perch, or are there different types? Are they all at one level or at different levels? Keep in mind that baby birds may not be perching yet, so there may not be any perches in their cages.

Look at the bottom of the cage and the droppings. In normal adult parrots, their droppings are a greenish color outside and a white or a whitish green inside. Birds who are fed foods with a high water content will typically have droppings that are more watery. It is normal for lories and lorikeets to have more liquid droppings because of their diet. But if you constantly see watery droppings in a bird who is only given a seed or pellet diet, he could either be extremely stressed or sick. Baby birds who are not weaned will also have looser droppings, which is normal.

Rescued parrots are likely to have bad habits, such as biting or screaming. A screaming lutino ring-necked parakeet is shown here.

OTHER CONSIDERATIONS

Even after checking the bird out yourself, it is always wisest to take any bird you buy to see an avian veterinarian because parrots are good at hiding illnesses. The sooner you do this, the better—not just for the bird but also so that you can address the situation with the seller.

Wherever you buy your bird, find out about the return policy and/or health guarantee. Return policies can save you a lot of money if the bird is sick. Find out how much time you have to take the bird to the vet, making sure that there is enough time for tests to be performed.

Some birds are currently vaccinated against polyomavirus and other diseases. This is becoming more common in certain areas where there have been outbreaks, although most pet stores and breeders do not do this. If the bird isn't vaccinated, discuss it further with your avian veterinarian.

Rescue Birds

Rescue birds need to be treated differently than baby or young birds. Many rescue birds have been abused physically, emotionally, or even nutritionally. Some have health-related issues, and others may have behavior issues—many will have both!

Whenever you deal with a rescue bird, make sure that you don't make direct eye contact at first. This is because direct eye contact could be taken as a sign of aggression in some parrots. A bird who has been abused may take this as aggression and become terrified or frantic. Always talk calmly and softly to him, and allow him to trust you at his own pace. Rescue birds can be wonderful pets if you don't push them or try to force them to accept you. Remember to take baby steps toward helping a rescue bird trust you. Some of these birds have been in abusive homes for years (sometimes decades), so trust doesn't come easily. A rescue bird will need more time to adjust than a baby bird, and you may find that he is more paranoid about certain things. Go slowly. Show him that he can trust a human again.

Rescue birds who come from reputable rescue groups have had an avian veterinarian checkup to make sure that there are no health issues. If there are, the bird will be treated and checked again after treatment.

Problems arise with rescue groups that aren't reputable. Ask around; call your local bird club or an avian veterinarian to find out which rescue group is considered best.

Coming Home

You have decided that you wanted to become owned by a bird. You even have decided what species is right for you and have purchased or adopted the individual bird you want. What do you do next?

It is important to take your new bird to an avian veterinarian as soon as possible. Regardless of any health guarantee the former owner gave you, you still need to have an avian veterinarian determine if the bird is truly healthy. For details on avian veterinarians, see Chapter 7.

BEFORE YOUR BIRD COMES HOME

Before you actually bring your bird home, you need to have his cage set up. This includes having the perches, food bowls, bottom covering, and some toys ready to go inside the cage. Don't overwhelm your new bird with toys right away; just have a few until he gets used to them and starts to play normally. Even if you intend to move the cage eventually, start with it in a corner. This will help prevent your bird from being startled by people coming up on him unexpectedly. At first, use newspaper on the bottom of the cage so you can check his droppings. Loose droppings are a sign of a stressed bird and a bird in a new environment is a stressed bird. This can be normal, but you need to watch them closely for other abnormalities as well as overly loose stools.

One perch will need to be higher than the others, because birds prefer to roost in high places at night. However, this highest perch needs to be low enough so the bird can sit on it without being all hunched over. For baby birds, place the perches almost on the bottom of the cage. Babies do not perch well, and you do not want the parrot to fall off from high up in the cage. You can always move the perches higher up once he starts climbing more.

BRINGING YOUR BIRD HOME

You will need to bring your bird home in a carrier. Do not put the bird on your lap or on the car seat without a carrier. Not only is it illegal in many states to drive with an animal loose in the car, it can be deadly to your bird if you are in an accident or even if you just have to stop sudden. Use a safe carrier with either a perch built into it or a towel on the bottom so the bird won't slide around. For a baby bird, the towel is best because babies do not perch very well. Never place the carrier in the trunk of your car. Put the carrier on the seat and secure it with the seatbelt or place it on the floor of the car. You can read more about carriers in Chapter 2. When you pick up your bird, go right home. Don't make any unnecessary stops.

When you get home, carefully put the new bird into his cage. Talk calmly to him as he settles in. After making sure that he is fine, walk away and let him settle down alone for a short time.

SETTLING IN

Parrots—depending on age, species, and past experiences—vary in how long they will take get acclimated to a new environment. Very few settle in immediately. Rather, it can a few days or even months before your parrot starts acting normally. The new environment will be scary for your parrot and he will miss his familiar surroundings and people. Some birds may not eat the first day or two and may not move a lot or make much noise.

While you may want to show off your new bird, this isn't the time for this. Your bird is already stressed and doesn't need the additional stress of meeting strange people. this includes your family. Explain to them how scared the new bird is and that they shouldn't crowd around the cage, make a lot of noise, or try to handle him just yet. Keep loud noise and bustling activity to a minimum.

Talk to your bird calmly and move slowly when you are around him and his cage—and instruct your family to do the same. When you try to handle him, take it slowly and be gentle. Don't expect him to trust you right away. It takes time to build a relationship with a parrot.

It can take some time for your new bird to start trusting you. Be patient.

The information about the different parrot species in this chapter is only a generalization. I am using the most common traits of each species. The bird you have is an individual and may or may not exhibit these behaviors. I have broken down the information into several categories based on the type of experience needed for each of the different species. Note that because most parrots are so small, their weights are given in grams rather than other units for better accuracy. For more specific information on cages, accessories, and diets for parrots, see the chapters in this book devoted to those topics.

Birds for Beginners

BOURKE'S PARAKEETS

Bourke's parakeets (*Neopsephotus bourkii*) are excellent pet birds, and they make wonderful companions for the elderly. Although they are hardy, they are still more delicate than budgies and other parrots, so they aren't a good bird for young children. These parakeets make a great addition to nursing homes and rehab centers because they are so gentle and quiet. In fact, they are considered to be one of the quietest of the parrots. Even though they are also considered to be the gentlest of the parrots, they become stressed easily. This is why they don't do as well in households with very young and active children.

PHYSICAL CHARACTERISTICS

Bourke's parakeets are around the size of a budgie, being only 7 to 8 inches (17.8 to 20.3 cm) in length and weighing around 40 to 50 grams (1.4 to 1.8 oz). About half of their length is their tails. These birds are too small to microchip. Bourke's parakeets have a life expectancy of around 12 to 15 years, provided they are given proper care.

Their heads are small for their bodies, and they have very large eyes for their head size. They are most active at dusk and at dawn. Their voices are soft and sweet sounding, and while they aren't good talkers, some may be able to imitate noises.

These birds are sexually dimorphic. The males have a blue band above their ceres, while the females have a white band. At around eight to nine months of age, they become mature and develop their full adult coloration.

TEMPERAMENT AND BEHAVIOR

Bourke's parakeets do not use their feet to eat with or to play or manipulate toys. They enjoy swings and ladders, although they don't play with their toys like budgies or cockatiels do. While some people feel that they are boring birds, I have not found this to be the case at all. My Bourke enjoyed a little slide that was in his cage. This little daredevil would not only climb

Bourke's parakeets are gentle and quiet birds.

up the ladder, but he soon found that running up the slide and then turning around and going down was even more fun.

Bourke's parakeets do not normally like bathing, but they may rub up against wet lettuce placed in their cages. They are not chewers, nor are they destructive. Although not normally messy, if your Bourke wants your attention, he may throw some seed at you just like a little brat. Some Bourke's parakeets are cuddlier than others, but most of all they enjoy sitting on your shoulder close to you. Most do not tolerate excessive cuddling well.

CAGE AND ACCESSORIES

Cage size should be a minimum of 18 x 18 x 18 inches (45.7 cm), although because they are straight flyers, cages that are wider are better. Bar spacing should be 3/8 to no more than 1/2 inch (1 to 1.3 cm). Use a bottom grate with them because they enjoy going on the ground to forage.

Their perch size should be around 1/2 inch (1.3 cm) in diameter, with perches of varying diameters being best. Safe tree branches, such as apple, are excellent provided they weren't treated with any chemicals. You should use a therapeutic perch for at least one of the perches. If you can find a therapeutic perch with varying diameters, get one that is 1/2 to 1 inch (1.3 to 2.5 cm).

DIET

Bourke's parakeets need a rich and varied diet appropriate to their size. They do not seem to drink as much water as other species their size.

BUDGIES

Budgies (the full name is budgerigar; the scientific name is *Melanopsittacus undulatus*) are the most popular parrot in the world today. When John Gould brought the first budgies back to England from Australia with him in 1840, the love affair with these lively 7-inch (17.8-cm) birds began. The normal coloration is green with a yellow head, but today there are more than 1,000 color mutations, including the very common blue with a white head. In

Budgie Versus Parakeet

In the United States, budgies are usually called parakeets. However, this can cause confusion with the numerous other parrot species that are typically called parakeets, such as ring-necked parakeets. To avoid this problem, this book will always use the term "budgie" when referring to this species.

It is important for an avian veterinarian to perform procedures such as wing trims and cutting the nails of Bourke's parakeets because they are a high-stress bird. When stressed, they may shed many feathers all at once. A simple procedure such as taking a little blood can cause them to go into shock and die.

Budgies are available in a dazzling array of colors.

fact, the only color that budgies don't seem to come in is red. These birds are commonly bought as a first bird. Because of their size, they are excellent parrots for apartment dwellers.

PHYSICAL CHARACTERISTICS

Budgies are one of the smallest parrots. They typically weigh around 30 to 55 grams (1.1 to 1.9 oz) and are 7 inches (17.8 cm) in length. Budgies are too small to be microchipped.

The males are capable of talking, and some have even developed impressive vocabularies. Females are less likely to talk and in fact rarely do so. Most budgies are sexually dimorphic, which means that you can tell the difference between the males and females. The cere of the mature male is blue in color, while the female's cere is either brownish or pink in color. This may not be the case in certain color mutations and is not true of young birds, who have pinkish ceres.

There are two types of budgies: the American and the English. English budgies are a little larger than American budgies, especially in the head. The English budgie has a slightly shorter life span than the American, but both make good pets. American budgies, if given the proper diet and other care, can live up to 30 years!

TEMPERAMENT AND BEHAVIOR

Generally, both sexes possess a loving, playful, and gentle nature. They are excellent birds for someone wanting a family bird or even an individual wanting a bird of her own. While not loud, they do make chirping sounds. Most people find these chirps pleasant.

Budgies are extremely intelligent, although this is usually underestimated by many people. They can be little escape artists, so make sure that the cage door can be securely closed or they may figure out how to escape.

CAGE AND ACCESSORIES

Get as large a cage as you have room for, but the bars must be no more than 3/8 to 1/2 inch (0.9 to 1.3 cm) apart. If the bars are farther apart, your budgie may escape or get his head stuck between the bars. The minimum size is 18 x 18 x 18 inches (45.7 cm) (length x width x height).

Perches with varying diameters from 1/2 to 5/8 inch (1.3 to 1.6 cm) in diameter are the best. Budgies love natural wood branches, especially from untreated apple trees or from other safe trees, because they enjoy stripping the bark from them. A therapeutic perch will help keep the nails trimmed. The therapeutic perch should be 3/4 inch (1.9 cm) in diameter. If you can find a therapeutic perch with varying diameters, get one that is 1/2 to 1 inch (1.3 to 2.5 cm).

Toys are necessary for a budgie's well-being. These birds love swings, ladders, mirrored toys, and toys with bells. While they are not destructive, they still enjoy chewing, although this is more like little nibbles. One thing a budgie can't do is use his feet to eat with or to play or manipulate toys. His beak is his only tool for carrying and moving objects.

DIET

Budgies need to be on a diet that contains more pellets than seed. They also require vegetables, fruits,

Mature male budgies have a blue cere.

Young Budgies

When choosing a budgie, buy one who is young because he will be easier to train and tame. Young budgies, in most color mutations, have stripes that cover the head and continue down to the cere. The cere will typically have a pinkish hue to it. Young budgies also have dark eyes without a yellowish ring around them. The cere typically changes color when they are six months old.

and grains if they are to thrive. They require a typical diet for a parrot of their size.

COCKATIELS

Cockatiels (*Nymphicus hollandicus*)—or "tiels" as they are commonly called—are the second most popular pet parrot around the world. Like budgies, they are normally friendly and outgoing with delightful personalities, and they are also originally from Australia. Buying a hand-fed cockatiel is best because they make the best pets. Make sure that the baby was properly socialized, or he may develop behavior problems later on as he matures. Cockatiels are a good choice for people in an apartment because they are not very noisy, nor do they require a lot of space.

Cockatiels are great family pets. Although they may pick a favorite person, they will still go to all of the members of the family—they are not "one-person" birds.

Male cockatiels have yellow faces and bright orange cheek spots. The females' faces are gray with less vibrant spots.

PHYSICAL CHARACTERISTICS

Cockatiels are a little bigger than the budgies, being around 12 inches (30.5 cm) in length. They weigh between 75 and 125 grams (2.6 and 4.4 oz). Because of their small size, cockatiels can't be microchipped. Cockatiels can live a long time if given the proper diet. They have a life expectancy of around 35 years.

The normal color is gray with white on the sides of the wings and an orange cheek patch. They are usually sexually dimorphic, although in the lutinos and albinos (two color varieties), it is harder to tell the difference between the male and female. Males will have a solid yellow head (with the orange cheek patch), while the females stay mostly gray or have a small amount of yellow on their heads.

Cockatiels are powder birds, which means that their skin produces a powdery substance that can be a problem for people with allergies or lung problems.

TEMPERAMENT AND BEHAVIOR

Tiels are far more intelligent than they are generally given credit for, and like all parrots, they are entertaining. They need a lot of attention, however. Most love their heads scratched and may even bang their heads against your hand, demanding head scratches. Cockatiels do not use their feet to eat with or to hold or manipulate toys.

Cockatiels are very good at imitating sound, especially whistles, and some individuals have even learned how to whistle entire songs. Males are more vocal than the females are, although both make excellent pets.

A common behavior among tiels is beak grinding—moving the beak to produce a grinding noise. This usually occurs when they are getting ready for bed, and it is completely normal and should not be any cause for concern. Another common behavior is yawning. For some reason, tiels tend to yawn more often than other parrot species.

CAGE AND ACCESSORIES

Cockatiels must have a cage that is at the very least 24 x 18 x 24 inches (60.1 x 45.7 x 60.1 cm), although bigger is better. The bar spacing should be at 1/2 inch (1.3 cm).

Perches should be of various sizes and vary from 1/2 to 3/4 inch (1.3 to 1.9 cm) in diameter. Provide safe tree branches for your tiel to shred and chew. The therapeutic perch should be 3/4 inch (1.9 cm) in diameter. If you can find a therapeutic perch with varying diameters, get one that is 1/2 to 1 inch (1.3 to 2.5 cm).

Cockatiels love toys, especially ladders, swings, and toys that they can manipulate or chew. They are not strong chewers but appreciate soft wood to nibble. Otherwise, they might start nibbling away on your magazines or books.

DIET

Feed your cockatiel a balanced diet with not only seed or pellets but also vegetables, fruits, and grains. Feed him a balanced, varied diet appropriate for a parrot of his size.

LINEOLATED PARAKEETS

These little dynamos (scientifically known as *Bolborhynchus lineola*) are not well known, but they make wonderful pets and are well worth the search. They are excellent with children and adults. Although they are quiet, they are also energetic, and they love human interaction. Both males and females are capable of talking, sometimes as young as 12 weeks. Their voices are soft and childlike, and they tend to amaze people by being such a small bird with a great talking ability. Their chirps and calls are soft, so linnies make excellent apartment birds.

PHYSICAL CHARACTERISTICS

Lineolated parakeets are a little smaller than a budgie, being only 6 inches (15.2 cm) long and weighing around 50 grams (1.8 oz). These birds are too small to microchip. Linnies can live for 15 or more years provided they receive a proper and balanced diet. There are a few color mutations available, such as lutino, aqua blue, cobalt, and mauve.

There is only a slight difference between male and female. The females will sometimes have less black at the end of their tails, as well as less black on the shoulder area. They should be sexed either by DNA or surgically for accuracy.

Although not as common as some other parrots, lineolated parakeets are ideal birds for the first-time owner

TEMPERAMENT AND BEHAVIOR

If you are looking for an affectionate bird who loves being with people and has a pleasant voice, try to find a lineolated parakeet. This species is so gentle and easygoing that you can approach them even in the wild. In captivity, parents will unconcernedly let you handle the babies as long as you move slowly.

These birds are not as messy as some other parrots, which is a plus. They do tend to forage on the ground, so a grate is a must to keep them off the bottom of the cage.

Keep things out of reach of their cages. Even though they are small, they use their feet to grab things. As mentioned earlier, they are energetic, and besides this they are also acrobatic and seem to prefer being upside down instead of right side up. Even when they stop to look at something, it isn't unusual for them to hang upside down to check it out. Linnies enjoy bathing, and most prefer being gently misted. However, some may also enjoy a shallow dish of water in which to splash around.

Some linnies have an odd behavior when sitting on their perches. It is not unusual for them to sit clinging to the perch with their heads pointing downward and with their tails pointing straight in the air. Breeders refer to this as their "bat" posture.

Bird of Many Names

Although usually called lineolated parakeets, you may find them for sale under the names barred parakeet or Catherine parakeet. Bird hobbyists often shorten their common name, referring to these little birds as "linnies."

CAGE AND ACCESSORIES

Pick a cage that is longer instead of higher. A good choice is a cage 30 x 24 x 24 inches (76.2 x 61 x 61 cm). Bar spacing should be around 3/8 to 1/2 inch (1 to 1.3 cm). Choose a cage that has plenty of horizontal bars because linnies are high energy and love to climb and keep busy.

Perches should be of varying diameters from around 1/2 to 5/8 inch (1.3 to 1.6 cm). Wooden dowels or natural branches work best. A therapeutic perch will help keep the nails trimmed. The therapeutic perch should be 3/4 inch (1.9 cm) in diameter or with varying diameters of 1/2 to 1 inch (1.3 to 2.5 cm). They enjoy ladders, swings, and toys of all kinds. They are not strong chewers, but if you don't want little linnie nibbles all over your magazines and books, keep them out of sight.

Provide your linnies with several food dishes. This is because besides loving to play, they love to eat. Gram for gram, they probably eat more food than other parrots. Many owners describe them as having hollow legs.

They love to sleep in little hanging huts or beds, although if you don't have one, your linnie will also sleep on a high perch.

DIET

Like other parrots, linnies require a varied and balanced diet of pellets, seed, grains, fruits, and vegetables. Avoid seed mixes that contain sunflower seed, which has too much fat for these parrots. Be aware that linnies drink a lot of water, and this is usually normal for them. When given soft foods, they seem to immediately wipe their beaks on their perches or on whoever is holding them.

LOVEBIRDS

Lovebirds (*Agapornis* species; several are popular pets) can also be a good first-time pet with the right owner. They can be a great choice for older children but may be nippy with younger children. Lovebirds are a good pet for people who live in an apartment. They can be wonderful with all members of the family provided they were hand-fed and properly socialized.

There are ten different species of lovebirds, although the most popular and readily available is the peach-faced lovebird (*Agapornis rosiecollis*). Other species of popular lovebirds include Fischer's and masked lovebirds (*A. fischeri* and *A. personata*, respectively). Some species of lovebirds are endangered in the wild. There are also several different color mutations available in the various species.

Buy a young lovebird rather than an older one because the younger ones are easier to tame. Most juvenile lovebirds have some black on their beak, which usually disappears by four months of age; thus, the blacker the beak, the

Young lovebirds—peach-faces in this photo—have black coloration on their beaks.

younger the bird. This may not be true in certain color mutations.

Physical Characteristics

Lovebirds are only around 4 to 7 inches (10.2 to 17.8 cm) in length and weigh up to 50 grams (1.8 oz). Because of their small size, lovebirds cannot be microchipped. Although some species of lovebirds are sexually dimorphic, this is not true of the popular pet species. These must be sexed either by DNA or surgically. Lovebirds can live a long time given their size, especially if they are provided a proper diet. The life expectancy is more than 20 years.

Temperament and Behavior

It is important that lovebirds be kept singly so that they won't bond to each other and lose their tameness. If another lovebird is introduced into the household, they will bond with each other and not to you. If not properly or consistently handled, lovebirds can become nippy when they mature. With proper training and consistency, though, this usually doesn't happen. The males generally seem to be less temperamental than the females.

Lovebirds not so Loveable

The name "lovebird" was given to these birds because in the wild, they were always seen cuddling and engaging in mutual preening. However, their name can be misleading. Lovebirds who are not properly socialized or handled by all family members daily can become nippy and sometimes aggressive. Lovebirds also rarely get along with other birds or other types of pets.

Lovebirds are extremely curious and have a boundless amount of energy. They are often more independent and strong willed than other smaller parrots. Their talking ability is limited, and both sexes are similar in this ability. Lovebirds do not use their feet to eat with or to play or manipulate toys.

Cage and Accessories

Because they are such active birds, lovebirds must be kept in a larger cage than you might guess. A minimum size is 18 x 18 x 18 inches (45.7 cm). Bar space should be around 3/8 to 1/2 inch (1 to 1.3 cm). Lovebirds can also be little escape artists, so make sure that you properly lock the cage.

Perches should have varying diameters from around 1/2 to 5/8 inch (1.3 to 1.6 cm), and at least two should be provided. A therapeutic perch will help keep the nails trimmed. The therapeutic perch should be 3/4 inch (1.9 cm) in diameter. If you can find a therapeutic perch with varying diameters, get one that is 1/2 to 1 inch (1.3 to 2.5 cm).

Lovebirds love swings, bungee cord toys, toys with bells, and soft wood that they can chew. They are not strong chewers but are more like nibblers. If you don't want little beak marks on your magazines or books, keep them out of reach of a lovebird. Also, they really enjoy going inside things, so provide your bird with a hanging hut or hanging bed. If he becomes more aggressive because of the hut, you will need to remove it.

DIET
A proper diet should consist of not only seed and pellets but also vegetables, fruits, grains, beans, and small amounts of cooked lean meat.

ROCK PEBBLERS
Rock pebblers (*Polytelis anthopeplus*) are a perfect choice for a family and for those living in an apartment. They have sweet, easygoing personalities and will go to everyone. Mainly kept as an aviary bird, they can make great pets nonetheless. Although not a cuddler, this bird will enjoy sitting on your shoulder as you go about your daily activities. Rock pebblers can be hard to find, especially as hand-fed babies. This is because they are difficult to wean and are usually bred to be aviary birds.

Rock pebblers adapt well to being pets or aviary birds.

PHYSICAL CHARACTERISTICS

They are around 16 inches (40.6 cm) in length and weigh around 170 to 180 grams (6 to 6.3 oz). These birds are large enough to be microchipped. They have an unusual body shape that is stubby and stocky; their heads seem way too small for their body size. Rock pebblers are sexually dimorphic, and the males develop their bright yellow-green coloration at around 18 months of age. The females are a darker olive green. These parrots have a life expectancy of around 20 to 30 years when provided excellent care.

By any Other Name

Rock pebblers go by several other names. These include black-tailed parakeet, smoker, Marlock parakeet, regent parrot, and regent parakeet. Regent parrot and rock pebbler seem to be the most common names.

TEMPERAMENT AND BEHAVIOR

Although they are not the sharpest parrot around, rock pebblers do possess some intelligence. They just tend to be slower at learning things. For example, my rock pebbler took a week to realize that when he continued walking on top of his cage to the edge, he would fall off. Even though they are a larger bird, they do not use their feet for playing.

Both sexes are capable of talking. In fact, they are excellent talkers, and some even start talking as early as three to four months of age. Their voices are soft and childlike, and even their normal chatter is soft.

They are natural ground feeders, so it is normal for them to spend time on the floor of their cage. This is why it is important to use a bottom grate and to clean the cage daily.

Rock pebblers are not destructive, nor are they strong chewers. They also do not play with their toys as much as other parrot species do—my rock pebbler only seems to notice his toys when he bumps into them. Still, they enjoy ladders, swings, and rope toys.

CAGE AND ACCESSORIES

These birds have long tails, so they need a larger cage. A cage around 30 x 36 x 30 inches (76.2 x 91.4 x 76.2 cm) is excellent for them. Bar spacing should be around 1/2 to 5/8 inch (1.3 to 1.6 cm).

Perches should vary from 5/8 to 1 inch (1.6 to 2.5 cm). A therapeutic perch should be 1 inch (2.5 cm) in diameter. If you can find a therapeutic perch with varying diameters, get one that ranges from 3/4 to 2 inches (1.9 to 5 cm).

DIET

Rock pebblers require a nutritious and varied diet for a parrot of their size. They love to eat and seem to consume anything given to them. It is amazing how much food they can put away.

PARROTLETS

The various species of parrotlets are extremely entertaining birds and are a wonderful choice, especially when space is limited. They are the smallest of the parrots sold as pets, measuring only 4 to 5 inches (10.2 to 12.7 cm) in length and weighing only around 30 grams (1.1 oz). Because they are quiet, they make good pets for people living in apartments. Most people describe them as being comical and clownish. Parrotlets are not among the best talkers, although the males have a better chance of talking than the females.

There are 3 genera and 17 species of parrotlets with around 20 subspecies. The most commonly kept parrotlet in the United States is the Pacific or celestial parrotlet (*Forpus coelestis*). Also available are the green-rumped (*Forpus passerinus*) and the Mexican parrotlet (*Forpus cyanopygius*). The green-rumped is considered to be the most gentle. There are several different color mutations available.

Pacific parrotlets and other parrotlets are fearless and sassy little birds.

PHYSICAL CHARACTERISITCS

Parrotlets are small, stocky parrots. They have rounded heads and short, stubby tails. They have a life expectancy of 20 to 30 years provided they are given a proper diet. These birds are too small to microchip.

Parrotlets are sexually dimorphic and can be visually sexed when they are around three weeks old. The male has cobalt blue flight feathers, which the female lacks.

Parrotlets need open food and water dishes because they will not stick their heads into a hooded food dish.

TEMPERAMENT AND BEHAVIOR

While extremely smart, outgoing, curious and affectionate, parrotlets can sometimes be moody, nippy, and territorial. They like to playfully nip at fingers and earlobes when they are younger, and if not taught otherwise, they can become nippy as they mature. Unlike other parrots, parrotlets do not bond with the person hand-feeding them. Rather, bonding takes place between six and nine weeks old.

Parrotlets can make a good family pet provided everyone interacts with them often. Otherwise, they can bond strongly to one person, becoming aggressive toward others. This usually tends to occur with the females more often than with males. Males usually make better family pets. When properly handled, they can be loyal and affectionate with all members of the family. It is important to give them daily interaction or they may lose their tameness.

Parrotlets are closely related to the Amazons, and you need to train them in a similar fashion as you would an Amazon. By setting boundaries and rules early on, you will end up with a wonderful pet. They are a great pet for someone with some experience. Even though it is so easy to spoil them, resist this temptation. If they are spoiled without boundaries and rules, they will become little monsters.

Fearless and curious, these parrots can be aggressive toward other birds, even those bigger than they are. They can also be extremely inquisitive and will get into all kinds of mischief if not properly supervised. Never leave a parrotlet out if you aren't around to keep him safe.

CAGE AND ACCESSORIES

A cage around 18 x 18 x 18 inches (45.7 cm) is a good size because these are active birds. Bar spacing should be around 3/8 to 1/2 inch (1 to 1.3 cm). The best cages have mostly horizontal bars on which the bird can climb.

Perch sizes should be of varying diameters from 3/8 to 1/2 inch (1 to 1.3 cm). For optimal foot care, use a perch with varying widths.

Meet the Poicephalus

Other members in this genus kept as pets include the un-Caped parrot (*P. fuscicollis*; often considered a subspecies of the Cape parrot, *P. robustus*), the Meyer's parrot (*P. meyeri*), Jardine's parrot (*P. gulielmi*), and the red-bellied parrot (*P. rufiventris*). All are excellent pets that share similar behaviors with the Senegal. Red-bellies are comical and have sweet dispositions, while the Meyer's are curious but can be nippy at times. Jardine's parrots are little acrobats with a mischievous and curious nature. The un-Caped are the gentle giants, sweet and cuddly.

DIET

Parrotlets thrive on a varied diet appropriate for a parrot of their tiny stature.

SENEGAL PARROTS

The Senegal parrot (*Poicephalus senegalus*) is the most popular pet species of the genus *Poicephalus*—the group is commonly called the poicephalus parrots by bird hobbyists and breeders. They are extremely intelligent, although unlike some other parrots this size, they are not as mischievous or curious. They have a great sense of humor and will keep you entertained for hours.

These parrots can make a good family pet and are also good for people living in an apartment. All members of the family need to handle a Senegal often to make sure that he doesn't become a one-person pet. These birds do require an owner with some experience because they go through a nippy stage when they are testing their boundaries. If properly handled at this time, this stage will pass quickly and they will once again become loving companions.

PHYSICAL CHARACTERISTICS

Senegals are around 8 to 10 inches (20.3 to 25.4 cm) in length and weigh around 110 to 140 grams (3.8 to 4.9 oz). These birds can be microchipped. With proper care, a Senegal may live 20 to 30 years. To tell a younger Senegal from an older one, look at their eyes. A juvenile has dark eyes that will turn to a yellow color at around six months of age.

TEMPERAMENT AND BEHAVIOR

Senegals vary in temperament depending on how well they were socialized. They are more likely to develop phobias than other parrots. They may react strongly to changes in routine or in their environment. The key is to make sure that they are properly socialized as babies and that they are introduced to things slowly. Some Senegals are very cuddly and affectionate, especially toward their favorite person. If properly raised and handled they will allow this cuddling with all members of the family.

They are only fair talkers and seem better at imitating sounds rather than words. Don't be surprised to hear your Senegal imitate an alarm clock or the telephone. They are playful and will even play on their backs with foot-held toys. Senegals enjoy chewing, so make sure that you provide your bird with toys he can destroy.

CAGE AND ACCESSORIES

Poicephalus parrots need a cage around 24 x 30 x 24 inches (61 x 76.2 x 61 cm), although the un-Caped needs a larger cage. Bar space should be around 1/2 to 5/8 inch (1.3 to 1.6 cm).

Perches should be natural wood with various diameters—3/4 to 1 inch. (1.9 to 2.5 cm) is a good range. A therapeutic perch with varying diameters between 3/4 to 2 inches (1.9 to 5 cm) or one with a diameter of 1½ inches (3.8 cm) works well. They love swings, ladders, and chewable toys.

DIET

Senegals fare well on a varied diet for a parrot of their size. They may also enjoy a chicken bone from a cooked wing, which they will crack open to eat the marrow. Most Senegals tend to love peanuts, so offer them as special treats.

Senegal parrots (left) are relatively quiet birds. Meyer's parrots (right) are popular parrots closely related to the Senegal.

What's It Mean?

The name brotogeris means "voice of a man," even though these species are not the best talkers. In Ecuador, they are called *pericos*, which means "little parrot" in Spanish.

Birds for Experienced Owners

BROTOGERIS

Brotogeris is another case where the scientific name for the genus has become the common name used by breeders. These are South American (one species in Central America) parakeets, and species and subspecies kept as pets include the grey-cheeked (*Brotogeris pyrrhopterus*), yellow-chevroned (*B. chiriri*), white-winged (*B. versicolurus*), canary-winged (also *B. versicolurus*)cobalt-winged (*B. cyanoptera*), orange-chinned (*B. jugularis*), and golden-winged (*B. chrysopterus*) parakeets. Although this genus also contains the Tui (*B. sanctithomae*) and plain (*B. tirica*) parakeets, these two species are rarely found in the United States. The canary-winged, white-winged, and yellow-chevroned parakeets are sometimes considered subspecies of each other and sometimes considered separate species; there needs to be more research on their status.

The most well-known brotogeris is the grey-cheeked. These little gems are hard to find because they are not being bred as often as they used to be, and they are rapidly becoming endangered in nature. Grey-cheeks are commonly called pocket parrots because they enjoy riding around inside a person's pocket.

PHYSICAL CHARACTERISTICS

Brotogeris have a life expectancy of around 15 years or a bit more, provided they are given a proper diet and excellent care. These species are not sexually dimorphic and must be sexed genetically or surgically. Brotogeris are small, mostly green birds with narrow, protruding bills. The species range in size from just over 6 inches to about 9½ inches (15.2 to 24.1 cm). These birds are too small to microchip.

TEMPERAMENT AND BEHAVIOR

As with almost any parrot, it is best to get a hand-fed, properly socialized baby brotogeris. This will help prevent behavior and health issues from developing in the future. Their chatter can be loud at times for their size. Even so, all brotogeris still make

Canary-winged parakeets can be good talkers.

a good choice for apartment dwellers.

These parakeets are extremely intelligent, adventurous, and stubborn. They will figure out a way to get what they want no matter what, and it takes an experienced owner to stay a step ahead of them. Brotogeris will scream when they don't get their way or if they want attention. This screaming can also occur if strangers come over or if they hear certain sounds. They can be very much like a two-year-old throwing a temper tantrum. Because they are so cute and cuddly, it is easy to spoil a brotogeris, no matter the species. Beware of this trap; set boundaries early and stick to them.

It isn't unusual for these species to become more aggressive during breeding season or when they reach sexual maturity. This is another reason why they are better for an experienced owner than for a first timer.

All species of brotogeris love to eat. In fact, their favorite social activities seem to surrounding mealtime. They often want to share your dinner with you by eating it right off your plate. If you have one like this, provide him with his own little plate, which should have healthy food on it. Brotogeris can also be messy, throwing seed and food on the floor of their cages and in the surrounding area.

All brotogeris species have been described as fearless and will get into trouble if not watched. They can also be accident prone. Keep a close eye on your bird because he may like to burrow in tight places and can easily get stuck in things. Supervision is really needed if other pets are present because these little guys are so fearless that they will even challenge macaws, cats, and dogs.

Grey-cheeks are very tame, and

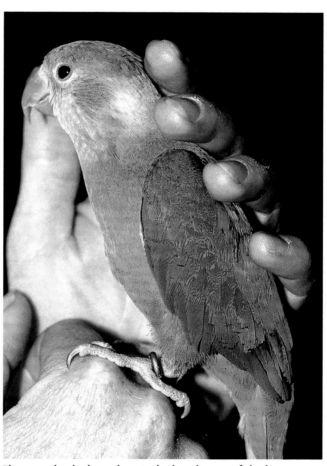

The grey-cheeked parakeet is the best known of the brotogeris, although the species is becoming rare.

Birdie Escargot

Golden-wings have been observed in nature eating freshwater snails. They hold onto the shell with one foot and use their upper beak to get to the snail. They have also been seen eating algae.

these loving birds form strong bonds with their owners. If they are properly socialized, they will form strong bonds with all members of the family. But beware: They are territorial as well. Some owners refer to them as little "watch birds." Whenever anyone comes near the house, these feisty little birds will sound a warning call. Canary-winged parakeets make excellent pets. They are friendly, although they can show some jealousy toward other pets. Canary-wings are slightly better talkers than grey-cheeks. When they are threatened, they raise their wings and clap them together, making quite a loud noise. Yellow-chevroneds are friendly and tame, but they can be jealous of other pets. Golden-wings can be shy and a little quieter, but they are also friendly, active, and love to climb. Cobalt-wings possess a more passive nature than the grey-cheeks, but they can be a little more vocal.

CAGE AND ACCESSORIES

A cage around 18 x 18 x 18 inches (45.7 cm) is a good size for brotogeris. Bar spacing should be around 3/8 to 1/2 inch (1 to 1.3 cm). Perch diameters should vary from around 1/2 to 3/4 inch (1.3 to 1.9 cm). The therapeutic perch should be 3/4 inch (1.9 cm) in diameter or a varying diameter of 1/2 to 1 inch (1.3 to 2.5 cm).

Because all brotogeris are active birds, make sure that you provide yours with swings, ladders, and rope toys. These birds love to play and stay busy.

Brotogeris like to sleep in a hanging bed or hut because it makes them feel more secure. All species of brotogeris love bathing, so make sure that you either mist your bird daily or offer him a shallow dish of water in which to splash around.

DIET

Brotogeris need a varied, nutritious diet, but it is important to feed them a diet lower in protein than other parrot species. Use a low-protein pellet—no more than 11 percent protein content. Too much protein will cause kidney damage in these species.

CONURES

Conures are active birds who need a more experienced owner. Most conures do not make a good choice for those living in a small apartment because they can be quite loud. However, there is one species that can be a good first bird, the green-cheeked conure (*Pyrrhura molinae*). There are more than 40 different species of conures, and they each have their own unique traits and behaviors. At least a dozen species are fairly common in the bird hobby. Conures naturally range from Mexico south to the tip of South America; several species are found in the Caribbean Islands.

Conures, while capable of talking, are not known for their talking ability. Most have the reputation of being very loud. Some species also have the reputation for being nippy. This is usually due to the fact that the owner is not experienced or the baby was not properly socialized.

Physical Characteristics

Conures vary in size from 9 to 21 inches (22.9 to 53.3 cm), depending on the species. They also vary in coloration, from being mainly green with just a small dash of color on their heads to an overall brilliant yellow. Conures have a ring of bare skin around the eye that varies in size and color by species. These birds are not sexually dimorphic and so must be sexed surgically or genetically. They can be microchipped.

The green-cheeked conure (left) probably makes the best pet out of all of the conures. Sun conures (right) are playful and fun but also very loud.

Good Parrotkeeping

California Conures

Flocks of feral conures live in California. The most famous of these are the parrots of Telegraph Hill. This flock is made up of mitred and cherry-headed conures. There is an acclaimed book and documentary about the Telegraph Hill flock, both titled *The Wild Parrots of Telegraph Hill*.

Conures have a life expectancy of around 30 years, depending on the species. Some can live for more than 50 years!

TEMPERAMENT AND BEHAVIOR

Conures have personality plus. They are very intelligent and curious, so they need supervision whenever they are out of their cage. Many are quite acrobatic and comical.

Whatever conure species you decide on, he will require daily interaction and training. Some conures are more affectionate and cuddly than others, but they all enjoy attention and head scratches. Conures tend to be one-person birds, but they may accept other members of the family when well socialized.

These parrots need an experienced owner who is consistent and sets proper guidelines and rules. Lacking this, they can develop problem behaviors, such as screaming, biting, and feather plucking.

Some conures have unusual behaviors. One of these is head bobbing. This is a normal behavior in baby birds because it alerts their parents that they are hungry, but many conures carry this trait over into adulthood. It is a way of getting attention. Like many other parrot species, they have a habit of beak grinding, which they do when they are getting ready for sleep or are content.

CAGE AND ACCESSORIES

Because conures vary greatly in size by species, the size of the cage you will need for your bird will depend on the species. A cage for the larger conures should be around 36 x 40 x 36 inches (91.4 x 101.6 x 91 cm) with bar spacing between 5/8 and 3/4 inch (1.6 and 1.9 cm). For the smaller species, a cage measuring 30 x 36 x 30 inches (76.2 x 101.6 x 76.2 cm) with bar spacing between 1/2 and 5/8 inch (1.3 and 1.6 cm) will be fine.

Perches should be of varying diameters from 3/8 to 1¼ inches (1 to 3.2 cm) depending on the species. Put one high up in the cage because conures love to roost high above the ground. The therapeutic perch should have a diameter of 3/4 inch (1.9 cm) up to 1½ inches (3.8 cm) for a large conure. If you buy a therapeutic perch with varying diameters, choose one that is ½ to 1 inch (1.3 to 2.5 cm) for the smaller conures and 3/4 to 2 inches (1.9 to 5 cm) for the larger conures. They also enjoy rope perches.

Some conure species, such as the green-cheeked, enjoy sleeping in hanging beds or huts. Keep in mind that it may cause nesting behavior in some individuals and make them more aggressive. If this happens, remove the hanging bed.

Conures are active and they are chewers, so provide plenty of toys to keep yours busy. Give him bungee cords and rings and he will be happy. Also, provide toys that your conure can chew and destroy or else he may chew on your furniture.

Diet

As with all birds, it is important to feed conures a varied, balanced diet. Like some other species, conures will eat the meat off a chicken wing and crack open the bone to get at the marrow.

Species

The most popular and well-known conure is probably the nanday (*Nandayus nenday*). They have a reputation of being nippy and moody at times, but with proper guidelines and boundaries, they are affectionate and loyal birds. Nandays get their beautiful coloring—green overall with a black head and bright red

Nanday conures can be good talkers but also loud screamers.

Although not the most colorful of the conures, the Patagonian conure is often an affectionate and loyal companion.

legs—by the time they are two years old. They love bell toys, and the more noise the bell makes, the more they seem to love it. They need a lot of attention and a large play area. Some will even play on their backs.

The beautiful sun conure (*Aratinga solstitialis*) can be a great bird for the right owner. As juveniles, they look similar to the jendays. They can be loud, however, and they have the highest-pitched screams of all of the conures. They can be cuddly and playful. Sun conures require experienced owners because once they reach maturity, they can be nippy.

Jenday conures (*Aratinga jandaya*; also called janday conures and jandaya conures) are playful birds who have a reputation of being even noisier than the sun conures. Like the suns, they can be nippy at times, but they are cuddly and affectionate with their favorite person. Some jendays have a habit of sleeping on their backs, which has scared many an owner into thinking their parrot had died.

Perhaps the best conure is the little green-cheeked. These are such wonderful birds that even someone with very little experience can own them. They are not destructive like the other conures, nor are they noisy or demanding. They possess a sweet, affectionate nature and make a good family pet, rarely bonding to just one person. Green-cheeks are entertaining and playful. You can tell a young green-cheek from an adult by looking at his eyes; a juvenile's irises are darker than in a mature bird.

The Blue-Naped Parrot

The blue-naped parrot (*T. lucionensis*) is closely related to the great-bill and may be easier to find in the pet trade. This species is a bit smaller than the great-bill. The coloration of the two species is similar, except the blue-nape has a bright blue patch on the back of his neck and head. Blue-napes tend to be more social than great-bills.

The Patagonian conure (*Cyanoliseus patagonus*) is the largest of the conures. They may also be the loudest of the conures, but their playful personalities make up for this problem. Patagonians are very affectionate and loyal, although they can also be demanding. They are capable of talking, and some have even developed a nice vocabulary.

GREAT-BILLED PARROTS

As the name suggests, great-billed parrots *(Tanygnathus megalorynchos)* have large beaks. It seems as if their bills are too big for their heads. These interesting Indonesian birds are rare in aviculture. One reason great-bills are so uncommon is that the babies often die during the weaning stage.

They are capable of talking, and some individuals have developed large vocabularies. Many owners describe a great-bill's voice as sounding a bit like a windup toy. Although they are not screamers they can be loud at times, so they aren't a good choice for those living in apartments. Great-bills make great pets and are definitely worth seeking out. Females seem to be more available than males.

PHYSICAL CHARACTERISTICS

Great-billed parrots are around 15 to 16 inches (38.1 to 40.6 cm) in length and

Great-billed parrots are curious, intelligent, and mischievous birds who do best with an experienced owner.

weigh around 260 to 360 grams (9.2 to 12.7 oz). Great-bills have a life expectancy of around 30 years. They are not sexually dimorphic and must be sexed either by DNA or surgery.

Great-bills and their relatives appear to be top heavy because of their small tails and large beaks. The tail is narrow and rounded at the end. In coloration, great-bills are mostly green. The feathers near the shoulder are black and edged with yellow or green, while the flight feathers are blue and black. The enormous beak is bright reddish-orange.

TEMPERAMENT AND BEHAVIOR

Great-billed parrots make good family pets because they normally do not bond to just one person when properly socialized. However, a great-bill does need a more experienced owner. They are highly intelligent, curious, and mischievous parrots. A great-billed parrot can be opinionated and may become a bit nippy when asked to do something he doesn't want to do. An owner who is consistent and knowledgeable will be able to deal with this problem.

Although these are not normally cuddly birds, they do enjoy attention and head scratches. They love to play and need plenty of toys to destroy, but they are not very destructive parrots. Great-bills tend to be messy and throw food everywhere.

CAGE AND ACCESSORIES

Great-bills need a cage around 30 x 36 x 30 inches (76.2 x 91.4 x 76.2 cm). Bar spacing should be around 5/8 inch (1.6 cm). The diameter of the perches should vary from 1/2 to 1 inch (1.3 to 2.5 cm). To help keep his nails trimmed include a therapeutic perch of 1¼ inches (3.2 cm) diameter in your great-bill's cage. If you use a therapeutic perch of varying diameter, the diameter should range from 3/4 to 2 inches (1.9 to 5 cm).

Because great-bills are so messy, you should use a water bottle instead of a water bowl. This will cut down on your cleaning chores.

DIET

In nature, great-billed parrots eat a lot of fruit. You should feed yours a varied parrot diet, but include a high percentage of fruit. Great-bills will even eat lory food on occasion. Mangos and coconuts are the favorite treats of most great-bills.

It has been reported that there have been kakarikis who suddenly died for no apparent reason. These sudden deaths were sometimes associated with nail or wing trims or some stressful event. This is why it is important that you have an avian veterinarian perform these tasks.

Red-fronted kakarikis (along with the other species) are very active birds who need plenty of time out of their cages.

KAKARIKIS

There are a few species of parakeets from New Zealand called kakarikis (or kaks). The most commonly kept species is the red-fronted or red-crowned parakeet (*Cyanoramphus novaezelandiae*). These birds have wonderful personalities and are very intelligent. They are extremely active birds, and they also possess short attention spans. They are constantly on the move, exploring their environment. Although they generally dislike being cuddled, they love to be on their people. In fact, they tend to be all over their people, rarely sitting still for long. Because they are active, they need plenty of time outside of their cages. Play centers are a must!

I don't recommend these birds for households with young children. These are active, busy parrots, and young children might hurt them accidentally. Kaks can get into mischief easily, and they need to be watched closely because are curious and will explore their entire environment, even getting under sofas, chairs, or cabinets.

These parrots are capable of talking, and the males seem to be better talkers than the females. Their voices have an unusual quality to them. Some owners have described it as being similar to the bleating of a goat.

PHYSICAL CHARACTERISTICS

Kakarikis are slender green parrots who reach a size of around 10 to 11 inches (25.4 to 27.9 cm) in length and 60 to 80 grams (2.1 to 2.8 oz). With proper care, they can live from 20 to 30 years. They tend to mature early, at around five months of age. They are too small to microchip.

Kaks are sexually dimorphic. The males tend to have a larger beak (thus a harder bite), larger body, and larger head. Of course, this isn't 100 percent accurate. To be sure of the sex, kaks must be sexed genetically or surgically.

TEMPERAMENT AND BEHAVIOR

Kaks are good apartment birds because they are not noisy, nor are they very destructive. However, many owners have told me that once they become adolescents, the females tend to become nibblers, and the males become territorial. Make sure that you keep things away from the cage because kaks will reach out with their feet and pull the item into the enclosure.

Buy a kakariki as a hand-fed baby who was properly socialized to ensure he won't become aggressive when he reaches maturity. Even then, many still become nippy. For this reason, this parrot requires a more experienced owner versus a first-time owner.

If you are going to wing-clip your kak, clip his wings before he takes his first flight. These birds tend to do better with future wing trims then. Obviously, don't clip the wings if you are keeping kaks in an aviary.

Kaks have excellent body language, and you will know if they are going to bite. First watch their eyes. They will suddenly become less round and take on an almost mean glare. They will start pinpointing (making their pupils very small, a common sign of aggression in parrots) their eyes as well. The head will seem to become flatter, and they will lower them. Then the little beak will open. At this point, take the warning and back off because the next step is lunging and biting you.

Kakarikis love to walk hanging upside down bat fashion from the top of their cages. What is unusual about this is that they do so without using their beaks, as most other parrots do. They also frequently hang from one foot.

Another unusual thing about some kakarikis is that

Boys or Girls?

So do male or female kaks make better pets? While the males normally don't like a lot of physical contact, they seem to be more people oriented. And even though they are better talkers, they can also be better biters! They can really bite hard. The females, on the other hand, can talk, but they do not bite hard at all. They may also be more acrobatic than the males. However, the females tend to chew more than the males, while the males can be more territorial. So think carefully about which sex would be better for your situation.

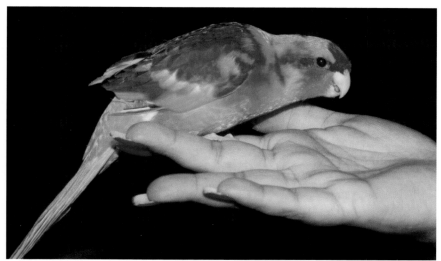

Red-fronted kaks are available in a few color mutations.

they prefer to eat and drink from crocks on the floor rather than higher up. If the one you have is like this, you must check his food and water more often to make sure that he didn't spill it or poop in it. Kaks also have a habit of throwing all of their food to the bottom of the cage and then scampering down, eating all they can find like they are starving. While I would normally recommend a bottom grate to prevent this from happening, kakarikis are very terrestrial, and they like to scratch on the bottom of their cage, just like a chicken does. This behavior is important to their well-being. You will need to clean the bottom of the cage in the morning and then again at night to prevent bacteria from growing.

CAGE AND ACCESSORIES

Kakarikis are normally kept as an aviary bird because they need a large flight cage and because they are so active. The minimum cage size for these birds is 36 x 30 x 36 inches (91.4 x 76.2 x 91.4 cm). Because the kak is a smaller bird, ensure that the bars are not so far apart that he could get stuck trying to escape. Bar spacing should be around 1/2 inch to no bigger than 3/4 inch (1.3 to 1.9 cm). Kakarikis are excellent escape artists, so lock the cage carefully. Remember, they are intelligent and can open their cages themselves. Buy a cage that has several locks on it, or buy a couple of locks for it.

Perch size should be of varying diameters from around 5/8 to 3/4 inch (1.6 to 1.9 cm). A therapeutic perch should be used to help keep the nails trimmed. The therapeutic perch should be around 1 inch (2.5 cm) in diameter.

Provide plenty of toys for your kak to play with because they love playing and tend to play roughly. Cardboard boxes in which they can hide and play are fun toys for them. They spend a lot of time on the ground scratching around, so make a little scratch box for your bird. Using untreated pine wood chips, place them in a cardboard box a few inches (about 7 or 8 cm) high. Hide little toys or food, such as cereal or air-popped popcorn, for him to find. This will keep him busy.

DIET

Because kaks are so active, they love to eat and will eat almost anything. In the wild, they have been seen eating seaweed, brine shrimp, and even mussels. Feed your kak a well-balanced, varied diet appropriate for an active parrot of his size. Many kaks relish mealworms.

PIONUS

The pionus parrots (named for their genus, *Pionus*) look like small Amazons, and the two have some similar traits. However, pionus tend to be a little quieter and less aggressive than Amazons. Males tend to be more aggressive than females, especially during the breeding season. Unlike the Amazons, they do not tend to bond to just one person but rather the entire family. If properly raised and socialized, these birds make great family pets because they will go to everyone. Pionus are capable of talking, although their vocabulary is nowhere near that of some of the Amazons. Their voices have more of a raspy quality to them, and they tend to talk softly. In nature, pionus are found from Mexico south to Paraguay and northern Argentina.

PHYSICAL CHARACTERISTICS

Pionus are medium-sized parrots who range in size from 8 to 11 inches (20.3 to 27.9 cm). They can weigh from 180 to 280 grams (6.3 to 9.9 oz), depending on the species. These birds are large enough for microchipping. Pionus can live 35 or more years.

The blue-headed pionus has a reputation for being a shy parrot.

These parrots have short, squared-off tails and an area of bare skin around the eyes. Most are predominantly dark green with brighter colors on the head and wings, but there are also species that are dark blue and bronze in color. The colors tend to be subdued but are iridescent under good lighting. They need to go through at least two full molts before they get their adult plumage in at around one year of age.

TEMPERAMENT AND BEHAVIOR

Because they are quieter than the Amazons are, a pionus can make an ideal pet for someone who lives in an apartment but still wants a larger bird. They are friendly and outgoing for the most part, although some individuals can be shy or nippy. Pionus are also not overly demanding. They need daily interaction, but they are also content to play on their own.

They have one peculiar trait: When frightened, they make a wheezing noise that sounds like someone with asthma. This is normal and shouldn't be confused with an upper respiratory infection. They may also growl when feeling threatened.

Pionus love to bathe, just like Amazons do. Mist your bird daily, and the quality of his feathers will improve. Pionus love being gently misted or even put into the shower on a shower perch.

CAGE AND ACCESSORIES

The cage should be a minimum of 36 x 36 x 30 inches (91.4 x 91.4 x 76.2 cm). Bar spacing should be around 5/8 to 1 inch (1.6 to 2.5 cm). The best cages have at least two sides that are predominantly horizontal bars on which the bird can climb.

The perches should be natural woods such as manzanita or untreated apple branches. The diameter of the perches should vary between 3/4 to 1 inch (1.9 to 2.5 cm). A therapeutic perch is also needed to help keep the nails trimmed; it should be around 1½ inch (3.8 cm) in diameter.

Pionus are intelligent and do best when given toys that challenge their intellect. Choose toys that they can take apart or that have parts they can manipulate.

Pionus parrots can make great family pets. This is a white-capped pionus.

Diet

Like Amazons, pionus are prone to obesity, so providing a proper diet is important. They should get a high-quality seed mix without sunflower seed, or better yet, use a good pelleted diet. Nuts should be fed only in moderation and mainly used as a treat. Balance this out with plenty of fruits, vegetables, grains, and the occasional piece of cooked, low-fat meat.

Species

Although there are eight species of pionus, only five are sold in the United States. Of these, the bronze-winged (*Pionus chalcopterus*) is the most common, and hand-fed babies make exceptional pets. The next readily available pionus is the Maximilian's parrot (*P. maximiliani*), or maxi for short. This species is sometimes called the scaly-headed parrot because the feathers are scalloped, making them look a bit like snake scales. They are extremely outgoing and curious, and they love to explore their environment. Maximilian's are also considered the best talkers of the pionus species; they are probably the species with the most desirable pet traits. The little white-capped pionus (*P. senilis*) can be a little more difficult if they were not properly hand-fed and socialized. One word can sum up the white-capped: feisty. The blue-headed pionus (*P. menstruus*) is a beautiful bird with a great personality. They tend to be shy, but that isn't to say that they aren't entertaining. The dusky pionus (*P. fuscus*) is hard to find. Although they have the reputation of being the most outgoing and mischievous of the pionus, they are also the noisiest. They are generally laid-back, however, not in the least bit high strung.

Globe-Trotting Quakers

Quaker parakeets are adaptable birds. This trait has enabled them to form feral populations outside their natural range when they either escape or are released from captivity. Some places that Quakers have invaded include Bermuda, Israel, the United Kingdom, Spain, Puerto Rico, and many places within the United States, including Chicago, Cincinnati, Brooklyn, coastal Rhode Island, and more.

QUAKER PARAKEETS

Quaker parakeets (*Myiopsitta monachus*) are active and vocal birds who can be loud at times, so they do not make a good choice for those living in an apartment. Because of their ability to adapt easily in almost any environment, they are banned in many states. Before buying a Quaker (also called monk parakeets), check with your state to see if they are allowed. You should also check to see if any special permits or requirements are needed. They are naturally found in Argentina, Bolivia, and Paraguay.

Quakers have very clear voices for their size. Some Quakers are good talkers and will pick up words quickly, while others may only say just a few things, if anything at all. Many start talking at around six months of age. Aside from the budgie, Quakers are the best talkers of the small birds.

While they make wonderful pets, Quaker parakeets are illegal to keep in some states because they are considered an invasive species.

PHYSICAL CHARACTERISTICS

Quakers are around 11 to 12 inches (27.9 to 30.5 cm) in length and weigh around 90 to 150 grams (3.2 to 5.3 oz). Despite their size, these birds can be microchipped. Quakers are small to medium parrots, with large heads and rounded beaks. There are several color mutations of Quakers available, including cinnamon and blue. Quakers can live between 15 to 20 years, although many are now living up to 30 years because more owners are providing proper diets. The differences between the sexes are small; they need to be sexed either genetically or surgically.

Quakers have an unusual feather adaptation: They have "barbs," or notches, on the second, third, and fourth flight feather. These notches are believed to help with slow flight, hovering, and even backward flight.

TEMPERAMENT AND BEHAVIOR

Quakers are intelligent and sensitive parrots, and if their needs are met, they are wonderful pets. If not, they can be real terrors. Hand-fed, properly socialized

Quakers are the best ones to buy. If they aren't properly socialized and raised with consistent rules, they tend to bully their owners like feathered brats. However, those who were raised properly tend to be wonderfully affectionate and loyal pets.

Personality really varies among individuals. Some Quakers bond to just one person and are nippy to everyone else, while others are definitely family birds. They enjoy affection and love to be preened. Quakers are curious and sometimes mischievous, but they are highly entertaining. These parrots can be stubborn, especially when they want something. They can also be escape artists, so you must make sure that your parrot's cage is securely locked.

Quakers can sometimes be territorial and protective of their environment. If there are other pets around, your parrot may even terrorize them and chase them around, so a more knowledgeable owner is needed to prevent this from happening. This behavior usually occurs more often during breeding season. Quakers are also prone to problem behaviors, such as feather plucking, which usually occurs then their needs are not met. Given plenty of attention, training, and toys, a Quaker will not have such problems.

While not destructive, Quakers still enjoy chewing and need to have a variety of toys they can destroy. (They actually prefer disassembling things to destroying them.)

In the wild, Quakers build huge complex nests that have many different chambers or rooms in them. Quakers are the only parrot species that builds these communal nests, which they make of twigs, branches, straw, leaves, and just about anything else they think is suitable for nesting. The nests sometimes become so large and heavy that they topple small trees or utility poles. Single Quakers do not tend to build nests.

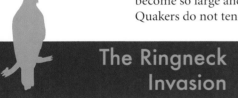

The Ringneck Invasion

Like the Quaker parakeet, ringnecks and other psittaculas have become established in places well outside their natural ranges. There are feral populations of Indian ringnecks in California, Florida, Japan, Belgium, France, South Africa, and other places.

CAGE AND ACCESSORIES

Cage size should be a minimum of 24 x 30 x 24 inches (61 x 76.2 x 61 cm). Bar spacing can range from 1/2 to 5/8 inch (1.3 to 1.6 cm). Provide several different perches of varying diameters from 3/4 to 1¼ inches (1.9 to 3.2 cm). A therapeutic perch will help keep the nails trimmed. The therapeutic perch should be 1 inch (2.5 cm) in diameter; a therapeutic perch with varying diameters should range from 3/4 to 2 inches (1.9 to 5 cm).

Quakers love climbing, so a play center should be provided. Make sure that it has ladders to occupy them. They favor rings that they can go through, as well as bungee cords. These parrots can play for hours and are always entertaining. Juveniles tend to be on the clumsy side and

can sometimes fall when playing. To prevent accidents, keep your Quaker's toys low to the ground until this stage passes. Many Quakers enjoy sleeping in hanging beds, so provide
yours with something in which he can hide or sleep.

They love bathing, so either mist your bird or provide a shallow dish of water in which he can splash around. A shower perch is ideal for a Quaker.

DIET

Because they need a lower-fat diet than other parrots, I recommend using pellets and feeding very little seed. Of course, Quakers need a varied diet that includes fruits, vegetables, legumes, and grains, just like other parrots.

RING-NECKED PARAKEETS

"Ring-necked parakeet" is a general term for the dozen or so species in the genus *Psittacula*. Many bird owners and breeders call them psittaculas as well. They are mostly Asian species, although some can be found in Africa as well. The most commonly kept ringneck is the Indian ringneck (*Psittacula krameri*), also called the rose-ringed parakeet. This section is specifically about the Indian ringneck, with material on the other species at the end.

A pair of ring-necked parakeets nests on the side of a building in India.

Indian ringnecks were probably one of the first parrots kept as a pet. They were once considered sacred beings in their native country of India when religious leaders recognized their ability to mimic human speech. Ringnecks are also good talkers, although their voices are not as clear as those of Amazons or African greys. Both the males and the females are equally good talkers.

Good Parrotkeeping

PHYSICAL CHARACTERISTICS

Ringnecks are beautiful, slender, bright green parrots with long turquoise tails. Males have a black chin with a black line extending from the chin back to the nape, sometimes making a complete ring around the neck. This black ring is bordered by a bright rose pink. Females lack these markings. The males develop this color between two and three years of age.

Ringnecks are 14 to 16 inches (35.6 to 40.6 cm) in length and weigh around 110 to 120 grams (3.9 to 4.2 oz). These birds can be microchipped. They have a life expectancy of around 25 to 35 years, but there have been some who have lived more than 50 years—undoubtedly due to an excellent diet.

TEMPERAMENT AND BEHAVIOR

Ringnecks can be loud at times, so they may not be a good choice for a small apartment. If properly socialized, they are affectionate, loving pets. Some can make good family pets as long as they are handled by everyone in the family. However, they need to have an experienced owner to make sure that they stay tame. They must be handled daily and in a consistent manner. Although all ringnecks may not be cuddly birds, they enjoy sitting on your shoulder while you go about your day. They especially enjoy eating meals with you.

Ringnecks can be sensitive birds. If unhappy or in an environment that is unsuitable, they are likely to develop behavior problems, such as screaming or feather plucking.

These parrots are active and love to play, although some play so hard that they break their long tails. Some owners have remarked that they haven't seen the long tail in years. They love to chew, so provide toys that your ringneck can destroy.

It can be easy to confuse moustached (left) and Derbyan parakeets (right). Moustached parakeets have rosy pink breasts, while Derbyans have gray to purple breasts

CAGE AND ACCESSORIES

For most psittaculas, a cage with dimensions of 30 x 36 x 30 inches (76.2 x 91.4 x 76.2 cm) is a good choice. However, an Alexandrine should have a cage of 40 x 48 x 40 inches (101.6 x 121.9 x 101.6 cm). Bar space should be around 1/2 to 5/8 inch (1.3 to 1.6 cm).

Natural wood is the best perch material as long as it has varying diameters. Ringnecks also enjoy rope perches. A perch should be of varying diameters from around 3/4 to 1 inch (1.9 to 2.5 cm). An Alexandrine should have perches with diameters around 1 to 1¼ inches (2.5 to 3.2 cm). A therapeutic perch will help keep the nails trimmed. The therapeutic perch should be 1 inch (2.5 cm) in diameter or a varying diameter of 3/4 to 2 inches (1.9 to 5 cm).

Ringnecks are highly intelligent and may figure out how to escape from their cages. Make sure that the cage is always securely locked, or your bird will get into all kinds of mischief. They enjoy bungee cord toys, swings, ladders, and leather toys. Give your bird safe natural branches that he can shred and he will be happy.

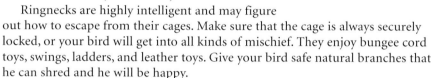

Chicken Scratching

Going to the bottom of the cage and scratching on the floor is a normal behavior of African greys. It is part of a natural behavior that they do in the wild, where they often forage on the ground.

DIET

Psittaculas need a varied diet appropriate for a parrot of their size. These species seemingly eat more food than a teenage boy!

OTHER SPECIES

A number of psittaculas are kept as pets besides the ring-necked parakeet. These include the Alexandrine (*P. eupatria*), the Derbyan (*P. derbiana*), and the moustached (*P. alexandri*) parakeets. Less well known are the plum-headed (*P. cyanocephala*), blossom-headed (*P. roseata*), and slaty-headed (*P. himalayana*) parakeets. The latter three species are normally kept as aviary birds. The other members of *Psittacula* are very rare, and sadly, some are even extinct.

Alexandrines are the largest of the ringnecks, being up to 23 inches (58.4 cm) long. They are friendly and loving, although they can be destructive and loud. They are also good talkers. Derbyans are around 20 inches (51 cm) in length, and they are the best talkers of this group. Moustached parakeets are excellent pets who love to play. Unfortunately, they can also be a little stubborn at times. They are also considered to be one of the quieter psittaculas. They grow to be around 13 inches (33 cm).

Birds for Advanced Owners

AFRICAN GREY PARROT

The African grey is not only the most intelligent of the parrots but is also considered to be the best talking of the parrots. It is believed that greys are capable of developing vocabularies of far more than 1,500 words! Greys are one of the few species that has been proven to use cognitive speech—meaning that greys have some idea of what they are saying. For example, a friend of mine has a grey as well as an older dog. The grey calls the dog in a man's voice, and the dog goes to the sliding glass door and waits to be let out. The bird has also learned to make the sound of the glass door sliding open, and every time the poor dog crashes into the door. The bird always laughs at this.

African greys have a reputation for being high strung and nervous. However, a properly socialized and raised African grey can be a wonderful pet, provided the owner is very experienced with parrots. Generally, greys are not screamers, so they can make a good pet for someone living in an apartment.

There are two popular greys: the Congo African grey (*Psittacus erithacus erithacus*) and the Timneh African grey (*P. erithacus timneh*).

There are two types of African greys in the pet trade, the Congo (left) and the Timneh (right).

Congos are the more popular of the two, but I really feel that the Timneh makes a better pet. Timnehs are smaller and darker in their gray coloring than the Congos. Congos have a reputation of being more high strung and nervous than Timnehs, but this could just be a result of how they were hand-raised.

A grey is probably not the best choice for households with young and active children, but they can make good pets if there are older children. It is important that everyone in the household handle the grey right from the beginning. A grey will sometimes choose one person and not want to go to anyone else, but if everyone handles him in a consistent manner, this does not need to happen.

Different Clips for Different Folks

Greys usually require a different wing clip than other species. Full wing clips can cause them to become clumsy or even start plucking. Check with your avian veterinarian to see which clip is best for your grey.

PHYSICAL CHARACTERISTICS

The African grey is fittingly named; both types are predominantly gray in color. The Timneh is a dark charcoal gray, while the Congo is a light silver gray. A Timneh's tail is dark red to maroon in color, and his upper beak is reddish tipped in black. Congos have bright red tails, and their upper beak is black. Greys are not sexually dimorphic and need to be sexed genetically or surgically. African greys are stocky parrots, and they have an unfeathered cere and large area around the eye. The tail is very short and squared off.

Congos are around 12 to 14 inches (30.5 to 35.6 cm) in length and weigh around 400 to 650 grams (14.1 to 22.9 oz), while the Timnehs are around 11 to 13 inches (27.9 to 33 cm) in length and weigh 275 to 400 grams (9.7 to 14.1 cm).

African greys are long-lived birds, and they can live to be 50 to 80 years old. You can tell a young grey from an adult by looking at the eyes. In a juvenile, the eyes are a solid black, and in an adult, they have a yellowish outer ring. Their eyes change in stages, which can also help give a rough estimate of their age. At around 6 months of age, their eyes will start to lighten, and by the time they are around 18 months to 2 years old, their eyes will become a pale gray color. When they reach around three to four years of age, the eyes will have the yellowish outer ring. Greys mature when they are around four or five years old.

Like cockatoos and cockatiels, greys are a powder bird. People with allergies, asthma, or lung conditions should check with their doctor before buying a grey.

TEMPERAMENT AND BEHAVIOR

Although all parrots require someone who is willing to be gentle, patient, and attuned to their needs, greys need this even more. As a grey owner, you must

Good Parrotkeeping

Hot Amazon

The Amazons are one of the groups of parrots in which the most popular species are the most difficult to deal with and therefore require an owner with a lot of experience. These top three Amazons—the double yellow-headed, the yellow-naped, and the blue-fronted—are usually referred to as the "hot" Amazons. This is a reference to their volatile temperament. However, some of the lesser-known or less flashy Amazons make good pets for experienced owners.

understand your bird's emotional state and special needs. This doesn't mean that you should let him get away with everything; instead, raise him with nurturing guidance. Males can sometimes be more aggressive than females.

Make changes slowly with a grey, including introducing toys. This will vary with your bird, of course. My grey literally jumps into the bag to see what new toys I brought home, while a friend's grey needs to see the toy for days before she can move it closer to the cage. Greys also need to settle in slowly, and they require an area where they feel safe and secure. To aid in this, put the cage in a corner and cover the top and two or three sides. Gradually remove more and more of the cover until you can keep the cage uncovered during the day. Greys can become feather pluckers, even overnight. They can pluck for a variety of reasons, from boredom to artificial coloring in their pellets. If this happens to your grey, you and your veterinarian must address the problem right away.

Greys are good at hiding in plain sight. Some think that this is a game to play, kind of like hide-and-seek. They will hide in among their toys, standing completely still, and may blend in with their background. A grey I know will hide in his owner's shoes and then pop out at her right before she picks up the shoe to put it on.

CAGE AND ACCESSORIES

Greys need a large cage, roughly 3 x 2 x 4 feet (91.4 x 61 x 121.9 cm). Bar spaces should be 3/4 to 1 inch (1.9 to 2.5 cm) for Congos, and Timnehs do better with bar spaces around 3/4 inch (1.9 cm).

There should be at least two perches, and all perches should have varying diameters from 3/4 to 1¼ inches (1.9 to 3.2 cm). Natural wood perches are best. The therapeutic perch should have a diameter around 1¼ to 1½ inches (3.2 to 3.8 cm) or a varying diameter of 3/4 to 2 inches (1.9 to 5 cm). They do best when their cages are against a wall, which makes them feel more secure.

Toys are important to a grey's well-being. Because they are extremely intelligent, they need puzzle toys and toys they can manipulate. They are not strong chewers but should still be provided with toys they can chew up.

DIET

Greys require a nutritious and varied diet for a parrot of their size. They often have calcium and vitamin A deficiencies, points you will need to keep in mind when feeding your bird.

AMAZONS

The Amazon parrots (all in the genus *Amazona*) vary greatly between species. Some make good family pets, while others will just bond with one person and may even attack other members of the family. There are close to 30 different species of Amazons, although only a handful is kept as pets. Many of the other species are highly endangered in the wild. Amazons range from northern Mexico to northern Argentina, including many islands in the Caribbean. The island species tend to be the most endangered.

Amazons are capable of talking, and some species are so good at mimicry that they can sing entire songs or even opera! Their tone quality and clarity are excellent. On the other hand, some species may only mimic sounds or a few words.

PHYSICAL CHARACTERISTICS

Amazons range in size from 9 inches up to 18 inches (22.9 to 45.7 cm) in length and can weigh 200 to 800 grams (7.1 to 28.2 oz), depending on the species.

The double yellow-headed Amazon is a feisty species and one of the so-called "hot" Amazons.

Amazons can be microchipped. They live 50 or more years, and there have been accounts of them even living for more than 90 years.

Amazons are stocky—frequently called "chunky" by owners and breeders—with rounded tails. They have a bare area around the eye and an unfeathered cere. The ones in the pet trade are mostly green with splashes of other colors on the head, wings, and tail. Amazons are not sexually dimorphic and must be sexed either by DNA or surgery.

TEMPERAMENT AND BEHAVIOR

Amazons vary greatly in personality. Some species tend to be more outgoing and full of energy, while others tend to be perch potatoes and are shy and quiet. Most Amazons are normally loud at dawn and at dusk, but some tend to be much more vocal than others. Because of this, they do not usually make good apartment pets.

Amazons are very loyal, as loyal as any dog can be. They are also highly intelligent and entertaining and can be headstrong and stubborn. Amazons like to chew.

These birds have the best body language of all of the parrots, making them easy to read. An Amazon who is displaying by fanning his tail feathers, ruffling the feathers on the back of his head, and dilating his eyes is an Amazon who is best left alone. If you don't take this warning, he will bite you.

When content or happy, an Amazon makes a particular sound that is similar in many ways to a cat purring; it is a happy sound. When stepping up on a hand, Amazons have a habit of reaching out with their beaks to balance themselves first. It takes an experienced bird owner to know that this is normal and not to pull your hand away. If you do, he may bite.

CAGE AND ACCESSORIES

Amazons need a large cage; 36 x 40 x 36 inches (91.4 x 101.6 x 91.4 cm) is the minimum size, and bigger is better. Bar spacing should be around 5/8 to 1 inch (1.6 to 2.5 cm). Perches should have varying diameters from 3/4 to 1¼ inches (1.9 to 3.2 cm). Larger Amazons may need a slightly larger-sized perch. Include a therapeutic perch with a diameter around 1¼ inches (3.2 cm) for smaller Amazons and 1½ inches (3.8 cm) for larger Amazons. If you can find a therapeutic perch with varying diameters, one that is 1¼ to 2 inches (3.2 to 5 cm) in diameter will be fine.

The blue-fronted Amazon (right) is another of the hot Amazons, while the lilac-crowned (left) is more easygoing.

Some Amazons are more active than others are. Regardless, they need toys to occupy them. Toys that they can chew and manipulate are excellent. The toys should keep their bright brains busy. Most Amazons love swings and ladders.

DIET

Because Amazons are prone to obesity, they should get only a small amount of a high-quality seed mix with no sunflower seed, and their main food should be pellets. Nuts should be limited and fed only as a treat. In addition to a good pelleted mix, Amazons need fresh fruits, vegetables, legumes, and grains. Feed vegetables that are high in vitamin A because Amazons tend to develop vitamin A deficiencies. Like many other species, they enjoy meat occasionally and will break open bones to eat the marrow.

SPECIES

There is an ongoing debate about how many species of predominantly yellow-headed Amazons there are. There could be one species with several subspecies or as many as three species, with some of those species having their own subspecies. For the purposes of the bird owner, it is easiest to treat them as three separate species because they have their own traits and because they are not often crossbred in captivity. These yellow-headed Amazons include the yellow-fronted (also called the yellow-crowned), the yellow-naped, and the Mexican double yellow-headed (*Amazona ocrocephala*, *A. auropalliata*, and *A. oratrix*, respectively). All of these parrots are great talkers, mimicking with excellent clarity and tone. The double yellow-headed is considered the best talker among the Amazons. They also tend to choose one person to bond with and are aggressive toward other members of the family. Therefore, none of these parrots make a good choice as

The spread-out tail feathers of this yellow-naped Amazon indicate that he's feeling aggressive.

Orange-winged Amazons are relatively calm and sometimes shy.

a family pet. They are not cuddly birds, but they enjoy head scratches. Once they mature, they may be more aggressive, especially during breeding season. The yellow-fronted seems to be the mellowest of this group. They are extremely intelligent and need to be given toys to help stimulate their intellect. They tend to be louder than other Amazons.

Blue-fronted Amazons (*A. aestiva*) are also excellent talkers. They are similar in behavior to the yellow-headed Amazons, and like those species, they can become nippy once they reach maturity. The males tend to be moodier than the females. They tend to pick one person and are aggressive toward others. To tell a young blue-fronted from an older one, just check his eyes; in a juvenile, the eyes are brown, while in an older bird, the eyes are an orange-yellow color.

Orange-winged Amazons (*A. amazonica*) aren't as good at talking as some of the other species, but they aren't as noisy either. They are a little more laid-back. A recent study using orange-winged Amazons was rather interesting. There were two groups of the birds. One was hand-fed and properly socialized, and the other was parent raised but handled and socialized. What was most interesting was that the group that was parent raised and handled and socialized turned out to make better pets, becoming less nippy than the other group. The study is continuing to understand this better. Orange-wings can be shier than some of the other Amazons.

Lilac-crowned Amazons (*A. finschi*) make great pets. They are small and sometimes shy, but they are easygoing with sweet natures. They are not known for their talking ability, but if hand-fed, they may develop a nice vocabulary. They are not very noisy either, although they are as capable of screaming as other parrots.

Red-headed Amazons (*A. viridigenalis*; also called the green-cheeked Amazon) are normally shy and mellow. Usually they do not develop some of the problem behaviors seen in other Amazons. While not known for their talking ability, they tend to mimic sounds rather well.

CAIQUES

The two species of caiques are little bundles of energy with personalities to match. Although they are capable of talking, this ability is limited. They are best at mimicking the sounds in their environment. Their speaking voices tend to be soft and childlike, so you may be missing most of what they have to say.

These guys can be noisy at times, so they aren't a good choice for those living in small spaces. They are also not a good choice for a first-time bird owner. They require more experience because they are prone to becoming nippy without an owner who gives them consistent rules and boundaries. Also, a more experienced owner will know how to keep one out of most mischief.

There are two species of caiques, with the black-headed (*Pionites melanocephala*) the more common pet of the two. The other species is the white-bellied caique (*Pionites leucogaster*). Both are similar in disposition, behavior, and size. Their colors are similar; the most visible difference is that the top of the black-headed caique's head is black, while the head of the white-bellied caique is solid yellow. Both speices have white to yellowish white bellies. Both species are found in the Amazon Basin.

Physical Characteristics
Caiques are around 9 to 10 inches (22.9 to 25.4 cm) in length and weigh around 145 to 170 grams (5.1 to 6 oz).

Both species of caique are active, playful, comical parrots. However, they can be very stubborn.

They have short, squared-off tails and unfeathered ceres. Their beaks are narrow, and the upper beak has strong ridges. Caiques can be microchipped. They are not sexually dimorphic and must be sexed either by DNA analysis or surgery. Caiques take longer to mature than other birds of their size, not reaching sexual maturity until around five years of age. They have a life expectancy of a little more than 30 years. An interesting fact about caiques is that while most parrots are left footed, caiques tend to be right footed.

TEMPERAMENT AND BEHAVIOR

Caiques are totally fearless and will even bully a macaw if given the chance. They will rule over all of the other pets in the household as well. Make sure that you get a caique as a properly socialized, hand-fed baby. They tend to be stubborn, and once they make their minds up to get into something, it is hard to distract them. This tenaciousness and headstrong temperament, combined with their high intelligence, tend to get them into trouble. But they often have short attention spans, so sometimes a distraction will get them out of trouble.

Although it varies from bird to bird, most caiques will go to everyone in the family. However, some will pick a favorite human and may be nippy with everyone else.

Caiques are mouthy birds and love to taste their environment or play with their owner's fingers. They also love to play on their backs. Give them a foot-held toy such as a ball, and they can spend a long time playing hard with it, attacking it and flipping over on their backs to play. They also love to hop. They birds are comical, especially when they hop along their way. When they are happy or content, they make a soft trilling sound.

CAGE AND ACCESSORIES

Being very active birds, caiques need a large cage for their size. A minimum size is 30 x 36 x 30 inches (76.2 x 91.4 x 76.2 cm). Bar spacing should be 1/2 inch (1.3 cm).

Perch size should be of varying diameters from 1 to 1¼ inches (2.5 to 3.2 cm). Natural wood perches are best. One of these perches should be a therapeutic perch, which will help keep the nails trimmed. The therapeutic perch should be 1 inch (2.5 cm) in diameter or have a varying diameter between 3/4 and 2 inches (1.9 and 5 cm).

Most caiques love to sleep in hanging beds or in other places in which they can hide. They also enjoy bathing. Give yours a shallow dish of water and he will bathe enthusiastically in it. Favorite toys include swings and bungee cords. They will sometimes play so hard with bungee cord toys that they will exhaust themselves. Make sure that your caique's toys are safe, and inspect them frequently because he is likely to break them.

DIET

Caiques require a varied and nutritious diet appropriate for a parrot of their size. Feed a good mix of pellets, seed, fruits, vegetables, grains, legumes, and the occasional piece of lean meat on the bone.

COCKATOOS

The cockatoos are the love sponges of the parrot tribe. In spite of this, they do not generally make good pets unless their owner is extremely experienced. Out of all of the parrots kept as pets, cockatoos are the most difficult. They want your attention 24/7—they don't understand things such as you having to go shopping or to work or just generally having a life. They love being snuggled by the entire household and will even snuggle up under your chin and fall asleep.

Cockatoos are loud, and they love to scream. The Moluccan cockatoo can scream at 135 decibels, one of the loudest of parrots. Screams this loud can cause hearing problems.

There are 5 genera of cockatoos and 18 species, and most are endangered. Most are found in Australia, but there are species in Indonesia, New Guinea, the Philippines, and the Solomon Islands. Australia has strict export laws, and because cockatoo habitats are being ruined,

The palm cockatoo is the largest species and has several unique attributes.

Cockatoos love to cuddle with people for hours at a time. This is a Moluccan cockatoo.

these parrots have started destroying crops. They are sometimes shot as pests. Instead of capturing these birds for breeding programs, they are being needlessly slaughtered.

PHYSICAL CHARACTERISTICS

Cockatoos vary considerably, but they are all medium to very large parrots. Unusual for parrots, cockatoos are primarily either black or white in color—the one exception being the stunning pink and gray rose-breasted cockatoo. All species have large, powerful beaks. All of the cockatoos are large enough to microchip. Cockatoos are powder birds. This can cause problems for people with allergies, asthma, or other lung conditions.

One of the most distinctive features of cockatoos is the crest on the head. This crest is made of highly mobile feathers and is used to indicate mood. The palm cockatoo has a unique crest that gives him a punk rocker look. When all cockatoos raise their crests, you will see a bald spot on the top of their heads underneath it.

Although most cockatoos aren't sexually dimorphic, you can sometimes tell males from females by the coloring of their eyes. Females have a reddish brown eye, and males have a black eye. This is not 100 percent accurate, so it is best to sex them by DNA or surgery. Some species have more reliable sexual dimorphism, but most are rarely kept as pets, such as the gang-gang cockatoo.

TEMPERAMENT AND BEHAVIOR

Cockatoos become extremely attached to their owners; they really want to spend every waking minute with their person. While they are probably the most affectionate and cuddly of all of the parrots, they are also demanding and sensitive. If a cockatoo's needs are not met, he will likely develop behavior problems, which can include excessive screaming, aggression, and feather plucking. Feather plucking can even develop into more serious forms of self-mutilation.

Cockatoos can become aggressive, biting for no apparent reason. There really is a reason for it, but sometimes it is hard to figure out what it is. They get their feelings hurt easily, and when they do, they let you know. Many an owner has received severe bites because she did something her cockatoo didn't like. Never allow a cockatoo on your shoulder because sooner or later, you will get bitten. Males are more prone to aggression than females.

Cockatoos love to play, and they can sometimes play hard. They can also get overly excited from playing and may start screaming or even biting. You may need to talk calmly to your cockatoo to calm him down. They are extremely curious, and they love mischief. Even when caught in the act, a cockatoo will usually act like he is innocent and it was some other bird who did that awful thing. Cockatoos are expert escape artists who can open almost any cage door. You must put locks on your bird's cage doors, but don't be surprised if he either learns to open the combination lock or pick a padlock.

Cockatoos love to chew, and they are very destructive. Never leave a cockatoo out of his cage when you aren't around. He will redecorate your house, destroying the furniture, chewing on wires, taking apart the computer, and generally destroying anything he can get his beak on—and he'll do so in under an hour.

Cockatoos also love being on the floor, so use a bottom grate in your bird's cage to keep him out of droppings or food that falls to the bottom. These parrots will also throw food to the floor and go down to retrieve it. A cockatoo on the floor is an accident waiting to happen; not only could he be stepped on, but he could get into all kinds of mischief.

CAGE AND ACCESSORIES

A cockatoo not only needs a big cage, but he also needs a well-built cage. If the cage isn't sturdy enough, he can dismantle it. The cage should be a minimum of 48 x 48 x 40 inches (1.2 x 1.2 x 1 m). Bar spacing should be around 1 inch (2.5 cm).

Include at least two perches with varying diameters from 3/4 to 1¼ inches (1.9 to 3.2 cm). Include a therapeutic perch with a diameter around 1¼ inches (3.2 cm) or that has a varying diameter from 1¼ to 2 inches (3.2 to 5 cm).

This sulphur-crested cockatoo has erected his crest as a sign of alarm or excitement.

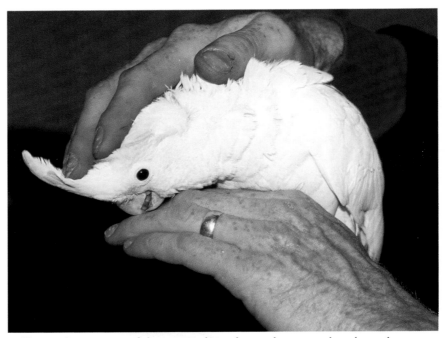

Goffin's cockatoo is one of the more independent cockatoos, making him a better pet for the average bird keeper.

DIET

Cockatoos require a varied and nutritious diet suitable for a large parrot. Be sure to include some nuts such as almonds, Brazil nuts, walnuts, filberts, or pecans in the diet. Like many other species, cockatoos will eat lean cooked meats and extract marrow from bones.

SPECIES

The umbrella cockatoo (*Cacatua alba*) is probably the most popular of all of the cockatoos. They can be hard to wean because they seem to be of the opinion that one is never too old to be hand-fed. Umbrellas go through many different stages in their lives, very much like a human child. If an umbrella is not socialized well when he goes through his "terrible twos" stage, he is likely to become an aggressive bird who cannot be handled. An unusual thing about umbrellas is that they are sometimes "hot" birds, referring to their temperature rather than their temperament. When cuddled, an umbrella may begin panting and reacting as if he is overheated. He should be allowed to cool down before being cuddled again. Umbrellas can be picky eaters, and they can also be dainty eaters, but that doesn't mean that they won't leave a mess. Umbrella cockatoos are around 18 inches long (45.7 cm) and 435 to 675 grams (15.3 to 23.8 oz). This is a solid white bird with an enormous crest.

The triton cockatoos (*Cacatua galerita triton*; one of several subspecies of the sulphur-crested cockatoo) were once popular because of their fame on the television show *Baretta*. These birds are real show-offs and they love to entertain, so they are commonly seen in bird shows. Extremely intelligent, they are wonderful escape artists, rivaling Houdini. They are not as cuddly as the umbrellas, but they still need interaction and attention. Tritons usually bond to one person rather than the entire family. They are around 20 inches (50.8 cm) in length and can weigh up to 1,000 grams (35.3 oz). They are white with yellow crests and tails. Other sulphur-crested cockatoos are the Eleonora cockatoo (*C. galerita eleonora*) and the lesser sulphur-crested (*C. sulphurea*), which is a different, smaller species. They have traits similar to the triton.

The Moluccan cockatoo (*Cacatua moluccensis*; also called the salmon-crested cockatoo) is a salmon-colored cockatoo. They are as demanding as the umbrellas, if not more so. Their beaks are also extremely strong, and they love to use them to destroy everything they can. They are more sensitive than other cockatoos, and their feelings are easily hurt. If you don't acknowledge a Moluccan when you pass his cage, he may end up biting you because of this oversight. They will cuddle with anyone who is willing to sit and snuggle for hours. They require a lot of time and patience, or they will develop behavior problems. They also love to scream. Moluccans are long-lived birds— they can live up to 100 years. They are around 21 to 22 inches (53.3 to 55.9 cm) in length and weigh around 700 to 1,045 grams (24.7 to 36.9 oz).

Major Mitchell's cockatoo may have the most beautiful crest of all of the cockatoos.

Jealous Bird

If you have other pets in the house, a cockatoo can become jealous of any attention you give to that other pet. The same goes for children. If there are young children in the house, you should probably not get a cockatoo. If you give attention to the child, your cockatoo could become jealous and may even try to attack the child.

Goffin's cockatoo (*Cacatua goffini*) is one of the smaller cockatoos. He has a salmon coloring as well, but it is not as pronounced as in the Moluccan. They are entertaining, with lots of personality. Many owners rate them as being the most curious of all of the cockatoos. These smart birds can take toys apart in minutes, as well as dismantle their water bottles. Goffin's are considered by many as being the easiest and best of the cockatoos to own. They love being cuddled, but at the same time, they can be content to play by themselves. They are around 12 to 13 inches (30.5 to 33 cm) and around 250 to 350 grams (8.8 to 12.3 oz). Their crests are smaller than the other cockatoos.

The little bare-eyed cockatoo (*Cacatua pastinator*) looks similar to the Goffin's except for the patch of blue skin around the eyes. Like the Goffin's, they can make good pets.

Major Mitchell's or Leadbeater's cockatoos (*Cacatua leadbeateri*) have beautiful crests of white, orange-red, and yellow, thus making them what most people agree are some of the most beautiful of the cockatoos. Unlike other species of cockatoos, Major Mitchell's tend to be shy and nervous around strangers or in unfamiliar surroundings. In temperament, they can be sweet one moment and holy terrors the next. When they mature, they tend to become more aggressive, and there will be a fight for dominance. This occurs more often with males than females. They reach maturity around three to four years of age. They are around 14 inches (35.6 cm) in length and weigh around 350 to 450 grams (12.3 to 15.9 oz).

The palm cockatoo (*Probosciger aterrimus*) is the largest of the cockatoos and is also the rarest in the United States; there are less than 200 known to be in this country. These punk rock-looking birds also possess the largest beak in the parrot kingdom. Even the structure of their beak is different than other cockatoos—it doesn't completely close, so the two-toned, red and black tongue is visible from the side. Their beaks are so strong that they can actually bite through a chain-link fence. They have a red patch of bare skin on the cheek, and this cheek patch will become even redder when they get excited. They can weigh between 500 and 1,300 grams (17.6 and 45.9 oz) and are around 22 to 28 inches (55.9 to 71.1 cm) in length. There are two subspecies, *Probosciger aterrimus aterrimus* and *Probosciger aterrimus goliath*, which is the larger of the two.

Palms are some of the few parrots in the world that use tools in the wild. During courtship, the males and females take hold of sticks and beat them against hollow logs like some kind of drum duet. Despite their fierce look, they are docile and shy. They also have an unusual behavior of stamping their feet, a behavior that is seen in babies who are only a few weeks old.

ECLECTUS

Eclectus parrots (*Eclectus roratus*) are oddballs in the parrot family in several ways. First, they are truly sexually dimorphic. The males and females are so different that at first they were thought to be two different parrot species. The males are bright green in color with a peachy-orange beak. The females are the more colorful of the two, being a beautiful red and purple with a black beak. As soon as the feathers come in, you can tell whether an eclectus is male or female. Eclectus parrots are different in other ways besides their coloration; their feathers appear to be more hair-like rather than feather-like.

Eclectus also don't form strong bonds like other parrots do, but that doesn't mean that they don't make good pets. They require a diet higher in vitamin A and calcium than most other parrots do. It is because of this more specialized diet that they require an owner with a lot of experience to care for them.

Male (left) and female (right) eclectus are so different in color that they were originally thought to be separate species.

The Many Eclectus

There are several subspecies of eclectus in nature, and some of these are available as pets. The most common is the Solomon Island eclectus (*E. roratus solomonensis*). They tend to be the best family pet. The red-sided (*E. roratus polychloros*) is more outgoing and boisterous and has a wonderful sense of humor. The Vosmaer's (*E. roratus vosmaeri*) matures more slowly than the others, and they are considered to be the quietest and gentlest of the eclectus.

Eclectus need interaction on a daily basis if they are to thrive. They can be a good family pet and are normally good with children who have been taught how to respect and treat a bird. They do not fare well in a household where there is too much commotion.

In nature, eclectus are found in Indonesia, New Guinea, the Solomon Islands, and the extreme northern tip of Australia.

PHYSICAL CHARACTERISTICS

Eclectus are around 375 to 550 grams (13.2 to 19.4 oz) in weight and are around 14 to 15 inches (35.6 to 38.1 cm) in length. They can be microchipped. This species has a life expectancy of around 50 to 80 years, assuming excellent care. Maturity usually comes around two years of age. Eclectus are fairly large parrots with stocky bodies. The tail is short and squared off at the end. The cere is feathered.

TEMPERAMENT AND BEHAVIOR

Eclectus are very outgoing, curious, cuddly, loving, entertaining, and intelligent, although many can be shy and standoffish. They enjoy playing, and it is not uncommon to find broken tail feathers on a juvenile because they play roughly and actively. They are not very destructive but do enjoy safe branches on which to chew.

Many are sensitive to noise and will react to sounds like thunder or fireworks. These noises can lead to feather plucking. Eclectus are prone to feather plucking generally. This can be due to their diet, a cage that is too small, stress, humidity changes, or improper placement of the cage. If yours starts to pluck, address the problem immediately.

Males tend to be mellower than the females, although both are equally intelligent. The female tends to be more moody, although this will vary among individuals. Females are more likely to be outgoing, while the males seem almost slow and shy.

They tend to go through a nippy stage anywhere from three months to two years of age. This will vary among birds. If handled properly, when this stage passes, the bird will become a loving and wonderful pet. This is also why it is important to make sure that the bird was a hand-fed baby who was properly socialized.

Eclectus are capable of talking, and they can even learn entire songs. They have an excellent tone quality, as well as clarity that has been compared to an

African grey. But beware: They love to imitate sounds, such as microwave ovens, telephones, alarm clocks, and alarm systems being turned on. They can also be loud, although they are not typically screamers. They are not usually a good choice for people living in an apartment. Those who have learned to fly tend to be louder than those who never fly.

CAGE AND ACCESSORIES

The cage should be 36 x 36 x 30 inches (91.4 x 91.4 x 76.2 cm). Bar spacing should be around 3/4 to 1 inch (1.9 to 2.5 cm). They do best when their cages are against a wall, which makes them feel more secure.

Although manzanita perches are great for most parrots, they tend to be too slippery for an eclectus. Instead use other natural wood perches that are around 5/8 to 1 inch (1.6 to 2.5 cm) in diameter. Therapeutic perches will help keep the nails trimmed. Use a therapeutic perch around 1¼ to 1½ inches (3.2 to 3.8 cm) in diameter.

Most eclectus love swings, rope toys, and bungee cords. Because they are so intelligent, they require toys that are interactive in nature. There are excellent puzzle-like toys made for birds, and these are great for eclectus.

Eclectus enjoy bathing, so either mist yours or provide him with a shallow dish of water. They really benefit from full-spectrum lighting and also need more humidity than other species do. If they do not have high humidity, their skin can dry out, possibly leading to feather plucking.

DIET

Eclectus are good eaters and will eagerly try new foods. It is important to feed them properly, or they will develop medical problems. They should get only a good-quality seed or pellets. Supplement this with fresh fruits, vegetables, legumes, grains, and occasional meat.

The eclectus especially loves grapes. However, it is best to avoid raisins because they are higher in iron, and eclectus have a problem with iron storage. They tend to store too much, which leads to a serious medical condition. Try limiting your bird's iron intake to prevent this problem.

HAWK-HEADED PARROT

The hawk-headed parrot (*Deroptyus accipitrinus*) is unusual and uniquely beautiful. He can raise the feathers on his head and nape, making him appear larger and more intimidating and giving him a hawk-like appearance.

Hawk-heads make wonderful pets that can be loyal, affectionate, curious, playful, entertaining, and comical. There are also individuals who can be moody, shy, or even nippy. Like most parrots, it is important that they were bought as hand-fed babies who were properly socialized. When this occurs, they normally make good family pets. Hawk-heads have an undeserved reputation for being aggressive, but this is because of owner inexperience.

PHYSICAL CHARACTERISTICS

Hawk-heads are the size of an Amazon, being around 12 to 15 inches (30.5 to 38.1 cm) in length and 250 to 325 grams (8.8 to 11.5 oz) in weight. They are not sexually dimorphic and must be sexed either genetically or surgically. Hawk-heads have green wings and gray heads and tails. The feathers of the body and crest are scarlet marked with bright blue. These birds can be microchipped.

TEMPERAMENT AND BEHAVIOR

Hawk-headed parrots raise the feathers of the nape and head to make them appear larger and more threatening.

Once called the hawk-headed caique, this parrot does possess some caique traits. One of these is their clown-like behavior. They also play hard, much like a rambunctious two-year-old, just like the caique. They will even roll around on their backs while they play.

Hawk-heads can be good talkers, and some can develop a nice vocabulary. They are intelligent and have a good sense of humor. They can be loud at times, so they do not make a good choice for people living in apartments.

When hawk-heads are going through the "terrible twos" stage—usually starting around six months of age—they like to play a game where they try to intimidate the people around them. If you let yours do this, he will figure out that he is the boss. Many will hang upside down and strike out at you as if they were going to bite you, but instead they tap you with their beaks. By reacting to this game, you are encouraging them to really bite. A hawk-head needs an owner who sets consistent rules and boundaries.

CAGE AND ACCESSORIES

Hawk-heads require a large cage; a minimum size is 36 x 40 x 24 inches (91.4 x 101.6 x 61 cm). Bar spacing should be around 5/8 to 1 inch (1.6 to 2.5 cm). Perches should have varying diameters from 3/4 to 1¼ inches (1.9 to 3.2 cm). A therapeutic perch should be used, and it should be around 1¼ inches (3.2 cm) in diameter or have a varying diameter of 1¼ to 2 inches (3.2 to 5 cm).

DIET

Hawk-heads love to eat, and they will eat just about anything. However, they should be fed a varied and nutritious diet of pellets, seed, fruits, vegetables, grains, and legumes.

They also need nuts, such as almonds. Like several other species, they will eat lean meat and crack open bones to consume the marrow.

LORIES AND LORIKEETS

The showy lories and lorikeets (just called lories hereafter for brevity) are beautiful and unique parrots. There are around 56 different species. Only about a dozen are kept as pets. They are different from other parrots because they are nectar and pollen eaters rather than seed eaters. This reliance on soft foods has caused their gizzard to become much less muscular that that of other parrots.

Lories have an unusual tongue and are sometimes referred to as the brush-tongue parrots. Their tongues have tiny hair-like structures called papillae that form a little brush at the end. They use the papillae to harvest pollen from flowers. In the wild, lories play an important ecological role in the pollination of hundreds of different plant species.

Lories range from Indonesia to New Guinea, south to Australia (including Tasmania), and east to many islands in Oceania, including Fiji, New Caledonia, and Tahiti. They tend to live in rain forests and mangrove stands—places with enough flowers to support their specialized diets.

They need a special diet and because of this, they have been overlooked as pets. Although personality-wise these birds are excellent pets, their care makes them difficult and recommendable only to bird experts.

PHYSICAL CHARACTERISTICS

The most popular lorikeet is the rainbow lory (*Trichoglossus haematodus*), an incredibly vibrant bird with a bluish head, red to orange breast, green and yellow legs, and orange to yellow nape. Rainbow lories are around 11 inches (27.9 cm) in length and weigh around 120 to 150 grams (4.2 to 5.3 oz). They can live to be around 30 to 35 years old. Most lories must be either genetically or surgically sexed.

Lories tend to taste their environment more than other parrot species do. For this reason, be careful when cleaning any area your lory has access to, and use nontoxic cleaning products.

83

Good Parrotkeeping

Rainbow lories, like the other lories, primarily feed on nectar, pollen, and fruit.

TEMPERAMENT AND BEHAVIOR

Lories are friendly, outgoing, and very active, with a reputation for being clownish and acrobatic. Hanging upside down seems to be a favorite pastime for them. They are curious and will definitely get into trouble if not supervised. Lories love to play, which they do with great enthusiasm. Give them a foot-held toy such as a little ball, and you will find them rolling on their backs kicking the ball in the air.

They are not loud, so a lory can make a good apartment bird. They are capable of talking and can develop good vocabularies. Their voices are high pitched but clear. Lories also make great whistlers. Some can be real chatterers, which can be somewhat annoying if you don't like that kind of thing.

While lories are a good choice for a family, they are not a good choice for a first-time bird owner because they tend to require more care than other parrot species. They also tend to be aggressive toward other bird species. They are not likely to bond with any one person and seem to love everyone.

A Lory or a Lorikeet?

What is the difference between lories and lorikeets? There is no real scientific difference between the two. Lories (shorter name) have shorter tails, while lorikeets (longer name) have longer tails.

CAGE AND ACCESSORIES

These birds are extremely active, so they need a large cage for their size. The best size is probably 24 x 36 x 24 inches (61 x 91.4 x 61 cm). Bar spacing should be between 1/2 and 5/8 inch (1.3 and 1.6 cm). Perches should have varying diameters from around 3/4 to 1 inch (1.9 to 2.5 cm). Because their nails tend to grow quickly, it is recommended to use a therapeutic perch for at least one of the perches.

Because they have a more liquid diet, they are much messier than other parrots and also tend to "squirt" their droppings. For this reason, most owners put Plexiglas around their cages and plastic on the floor, which makes cleanup must easier. Because of the high sugar content in their droppings, clean your lory's cage in the morning and then again in the evening to prevent bacteria from growing.

These birds are excellent climbers and enjoy ladders and toys over which they can climb. Bungee cord toys are also much enjoyed. Some lories love to sleep in hanging beds or huts. Another favorite pastime is bathing; give yours a pie tin filled with water, and watch him dive in. They also enjoy misting.

DIET

Providing lories with a proper diet has long been a challenge to bird keepers. Now there is a dry powder available that mixes with water, making feeding so much easier. Even with this easier-to-use diet, the food must be changed often, especially during warm weather. Change it every four hours to prevent spoilage.

Besides their special diet, lories should also receive a wide variety of fruits. As a special treat, feed your bird fruit cocktail in natural juices. They also enjoy green leafy vegetables, yams, sweet potatoes, and orange-colored squashes

Lories will eat some soft grains, so you can provide baby cereal or oatmeal mixed with some honey and/or molasses. You can even provide whole-grain breads. As a special treat, feed your lory hibiscus flowers, rose petals, bottlebrush, and other edible flowers (only those not treated with pesticides; flowers from the florist are usually chemically preserved and are not safe for a lory).

MACAWS

Although macaws are thought of as the big boys of the bird world, they actually come in two size categories. There are mini macaws, which range in size from 12 to 18 inches (30.5 to 45.7 cm), and larger macaws, which range from 19 to 40 inches (48.3 to 101.6 cm) in length. As much as they vary in size, they vary in personality. These birds can be very loud,

Never allow a macaw to be a shoulder bird. His beak can do serious damage, so you don't want him near your head and face.

some screaming at more than 105 decibels, so they are not a wise choice for people living in an apartment.

Macaws are definitely a bird for someone with a lot of experience. They have big personalities, and many of them have a tendency to challenge their owner almost daily. This isn't as bad with the mini macaws, but with the larger macaws, you need to know how to deal with them or they could cause real damage. (Remember, a big beak means a big bite.) Macaws range from Mexico to Bolivia and northern Argentina.

PHYSICAL CHARACTERISTICS
The large macaws are long-lived species. They can live 50, 60, or even 100 years! You must make sure that you provide for your bird in case you become ill, pass away, or are otherwise unable to care for one for his full life span. The mini macaws are also long lived; they have a life expectancy of around 50 to 80 years.

Both the large and the mini macaws can be microchipped. Macaws are not sexually dimorphic, except for the hyacinths. Even with the hyacinth, the dimorphism is not 100 percent accurate, and surgical or genetic sexing is the only way to be sure of his sex.

TEMPERAMENT AND BEHAVIOR
Macaws are highly intelligent, possessing the intelligence of a child between the ages of three and eight. Unfortunately, they have the emotional range of a two-year-old, and they will remain that way forever. They have a unique sense of humor and are not above teasing you or members of your family. They will even tease other pets.

The hyacinth macaw is the largest of all of the parrots.

Tongue Tales

An interesting fact about hyacinth macaws is that they have a bone in their tongues. Also, their tongues are two toned. In an adult hyacinth, the tongue is black with a yellow stripe, and in a juvenile, the tongue is black with a white stripe.

Macaws require a lot of attention and can be very demanding. If they don't get the attention they want, they may have a temper tantrum, screaming and banging their toys like a little two-year-old. You must keep your macaw busy with toys, attention, and training.

These birds are strong chewers. They can go through a 2 x 4 in a few hours and will then look for something else to tear up. Toys need to be strong enough to stand up to such strong beaks. Although the smaller macaws may take a month to go through a toy, a large one can go through a toy in a day or two!

Many macaws blush; their white cheek patches turn a bright red when they are excited.

CAGE AND ACCESSORIES

Larger macaws should be in a cage that's a minimum of 60 x 60 x 48 inches (152.4 x 152.4 x 121.9 cm). Use manzanita perches because they can stand

The blue and gold macaw (left) is the most popular species of macaw in the pet trade. The similar blue-throated macaw (right) is much rarer.

up to a macaw's strong beak. The perches should be of varying diameters from around 1 to 2½ inches (2.5 to 6.4 cm), depending on the size of your bird. A hyacinth macaw can use a perch that is 1½ to 3 inches (3.8 to 7.6 cm). The therapeutic perch should be 2 to 4 inches (5 to 10.2 cm) in diameter. Bar spacing should be 1 inch (2.5 cm). Make sure that these bars are strong enough to stand up to his beak.

Mini macaws need a cage with dimensions of at least 36 x 36 x 24 inches (91.4 x 91.4 x 61 cm). Perches should be around 3/4 inch (1.9 cm), and the therapeutic perch should be of varying sizes, around 3/4 to 1½ inches (1.9 to 3.8 cm).

Besides a large cage, macaws love play centers, so purchase one to keep your bird occupied. Toys that work best for macaws are those they can manipulate or the puzzle- type toys. Don't forget the wood toys! Macaws need to chew and destroy thing, and toys are cheaper to replace than your walls and furniture. They may also enjoy bungee types of toys, as well as rope toys.

Macaws are definitely water birds. They love to be misted or taken into the shower with you or just put on a shower perch. Although the mini macaws may like to splash around in a large, shallow bowl of water, it is hard to find

The green-winged (left) and scarlet macaws (right) can be difficult to tell apart. Scarlets never have green feathers on their wings.

something into which the larger macaws can fit. I use a small plastic kiddie pool for my macaw.

Macaws can figure out how to take their water bottles apart and throw them to the ground. My macaw has learned hundreds of ways to dismantle his water bottle. He is so good at it that it is now a game to him.

DIET

Macaws require a varied, nutritious diet suitable for a very large parrot. All macaws should receive a good-quality seed mix or pelleted diet. They also need nuts, such as almonds (one of the best nuts to feed), Brazil nuts, walnuts, filberts, pecans, and macadamias. Hyacinth macaws need more nuts in their diets than other macaws.

SPECIES

The largest of the macaws are the hyacinths (*Anodorhynchus hyacinthinus*). These are gentle giants reaching a length of 40 inches (101.6 cm) and a weight of 1,200 to 1,500 grams (42.3 to 52.9 oz). Despite their size, they are normally sweet and gentle and will even lie in your arms like a baby. Many are good family birds, provided they were properly raised and handled by all members of the family. I don't recommend them in a house with young children. Hyacinth macaws are a vibrant violet-blue color. The bare area around the eyes and a bare patch of skin adjacent to the bottom bill are canary yellow in color. The huge beak is black. They are not as noisy as some of the other macaws, but they can scream when they want to. They form strong bonds with their owners and are very loyal birds. Hyacinths require a higher-fat diet than other macaws.

Blue and gold macaws (*Ara ararauna*; also called the blue and yellow macaw) are the most popular of the large macaws. They are beautiful birds whom owners describe as clowns. They are active and need plenty of toys with which to play. They can be loud, screaming at the crack of dawn and then again at night, and tend to scream on and off throughout the day as well. Many develop a good vocabulary, with clear voices. They are high energy and love to cuddle one moment and then roughhouse the next. A favorite game is tug-of-war, or beak wrestling. Blue and gold macaws grow to around 32 to 34 inches (81.2 to 86.4 cm) in length and weigh around 900 to 1,200 grams (31.7 to 42.3 oz). As their name suggests, blue and gold macaws are primarily

Scarlet or Green-wing?

Scarlet macaws and green-wings are sometimes confused with each other, but if you look at their wings and faces, you won't have any trouble telling them apart. Scarlets have yellow on their wings and white facial feathers. Green-wings have green on their wings and red facial feathers. Green-wings are also a bit larger than scarlets.

Mini macaws available in the pet trade include the Illiger's, yellow-collared, and Hahn's macaws (left to right).

bright blue on the back and wings, with rich yellow bodies and undersides of their tails. They have small black feathers in the bare area around the eyes and mouth.

Another popular species is the green-winged macaw (*Ara chloroptera*). These are the second largest of the macaws and have a personality between the hyacinths and the blue and golds. Green-wings are around 34 to 39 inches (86.4 to 99.1 cm) in length and weigh around 1,200 to 1,600 grams (42.3 to 56.4 oz). They are mostly bright red with green and blue wings. They have small red feathers in lines on the bare area of their faces. They are considered to be the most intelligent of the macaws and can figure things out very quickly.

Scarlet macaws (*Ara macao*) have received an unfair reputation for being nippy and even aggressive. This is mainly due to how they were socialized and raised. Scarlets do not do well in a household with children, and they can sometimes be aggressive. They can also be opinionated, stubborn, and strong willed, so it really takes an experienced owner who will be consistent with them. They are not as cuddly as some of the other macaws, but they love head scratches and having their feathers preened. These birds weigh between 900 and 1,100 grams (31.7 and 38.8 oz) and are around 32 to 36 inches (81.3 to 91.4 cm) in length.

The military macaw (*Ara militaris*) is one of the smaller of the large macaws, growing to around 24 to 27 inches (61 to 68.6 cm) in length and weighing around 850 to 1,000 grams (30 to 35.3 oz). They are mostly green to olive on the back and wings and have a patch of red feathers right above the beak. They have received an unfair reputation for being nippy, but when properly socialized, they do not usually get that way. If handled consistently by a knowledgeable owner, they make wonderful pets.

Illiger's macaws (*Primolius maracana*; sometimes called the blue-winged macaw) are delightful birds. They are sweet and outgoing, yet they can be sensitive. They are also very playful. Be warned: They can be mischievous and curious, wanting to explore—and chew—everything in sight. Illiger's macaws fly like daredevils. It is not unusual to see them flying high in the air and then drop like a stone, and in the space of a breath, see them change direction close to the ground. Illiger's are difficult to hand-feed, so unless you really know what you are doing, leave this to the experts. They are around 15 to 16 inches (38.1 to 40.6 cm) in length and weigh around 300 to 350 grams (10.6 to 12.3 oz).

Other popular mini macaws are the Hahn's and the noble macaws—they are both subspecies of the same species (*Diopsittaca nobilis nobilis* for the Hahn's and *D. nobilis cumanensis* for the noble). They are full of energy and can develop quite the attitude if not handled properly. Even though they are only around 12 to 14 inches (30.5 to 35.6 cm) in length, they are still very loud. They can weigh between 160 to 200 grams (5.6 to 7.1 oz). Like all macaws, they are extremely intelligent. These birds are mostly green with a bright red patch at the top of the wing.

The Neophemas, Scientifically Speaking

Blue-winged grass parakeet, *Neophema chrysostoma*
Elegant grass parakeet, *Neophema elegans*
Orange-bellied grass parakeet, *Neophema chrysogaster*
Rock parakeet, *Neophema petrophila*
Scarlet-chested grass parakeet, *Neophema splendida*
Splendid parakeet, *Neophema splendida*
Turquoisine grass parakeet, *Neophema pulchella*

Several species of rosellas are kept as aviary birds, including the crimson, the mealy, and the Stanley.

Aviary Parrots

Some parrot species don't make good pets but can provide entertainment and joy in an aviary setting. These types of parrots generally cannot be handled.

ROSELLAS

The rosellas (*Platycercus* species) are beautiful birds originating in Australia. There are eight different species. Although some people have tried to keep them as pets, they were difficult to handle once they matured, becoming very nippy. They are happiest in a large flight where they are able to fly. They are strong chewers. Typically ground feeders in the wild, rosellas are prone to internal parasites, so the flight must either be kept clean or the food dishes must be elevated. Species of rosellas include green, crimson, Adelaide, eastern, western (or Stanley), mealy, yellow, and northern. The crimson (*Platycercus elegans*) is probably the most commonly kept.

PHYSICAL CHARACTERISTICS

Rosellas range in size from 10 to 14.5 inches (25.4 to 36.8 cm) and weigh between 90 and 170 grams (3.2 and 6 oz), depending on the species. While they are not good talkers, they can learn to whistle. They are moderately noisy birds. They have a life expectancy of around 30 years.

All of the rosellas share three features: They all have patches of color on their cheeks that are different—often brighter—than the rest of their faces; the feathers on their backs have a scalloped appearance; and all rosellas have fairly long, pointed tails.

There is some sexual dimorphism, especially in the Stanley (*Platycercus icterotis*). Male Stanleys have a very yellow cheek patch, while the yellow on the female's cheek is faint and mottled with green. In the other species of rosellas, the females have bars under their wings. In some species, you can sometimes tell the difference in sex by their beaks; the male's beak is broader, although this isn't a foolproof method of sexing. For accuracy, genetic sexing is recommended

CAGE AND ACCESSORIES

Rosellas should be in as large a flight as you can afford and have room for. They are good birds for the beginner aviculturist. They are not very loud, so they can be kept in an apartment aviary. Give them toys they can chew, and make sure that they have plenty of perches.

DIET

As with all parrots, rosellas need a healthy and balanced diet if they are to thrive. Feed them a diet appropriate for their size and activity level.

NEOPHEMAS

The neophemas (*Neophema* species) are also called grass parakeets. At one time Bourke's were included in this genus but have since been moved to their own genus. The neophemas are hardy and easy to care for, although they are not as easygoing as the Bourke's. Neophemas are a good bird for a person's first aviary. If kept in an aviary, the males can become intolerant of other males. Some neophemas are also kept as pets. They are quiet and docile, especially if hand-fed.

There are seven different species of neophemas, and the splendid, elegant, blue-winged, and turquoisine are the species most commonly kept in an aviary. Rock parakeets do not do well in captivity, and the orange-bellied is endangered and so is rarely seen.

Good Parrotkeeping

PHYSICAL CHARACTERISTICS

Neophemas range in size from 7.7 to 9 inches (19.6 to 22.9 cm) in length and can weigh between 35 and 60 grams (1.2 and 2.1 oz), depending on the species. They have a life expectancy of around six to eight years. Neophemas are sexually dimorphic, and the males are the more colorful of the two. Neophemas have long, tapering tails and long wings. They are strong and swift fliers.

CAGE AND ACCESSORIES

The flight should be a minimum of 3 x 3 x 3 feet (91.4 cm), although bigger is better. Neophemas are quiet, so they are a good choice for an apartment aviary. They are high-stress birds, so they don't do well in active households. They are ground dwellers, so their aviary must be kept clean.

DIET

Feed neophemas as you would other parrots of their size and activity level.

HANGING PARROTS

The hanging parrots get their name because of their unusual sleep habit: They sleep hanging upside down. They will also feed this way. They are small, quiet birds with a gentle and pleasing nature. Their voices are soft and pleasant, so they make good apartment aviary birds. Although kept mainly as aviary birds, some people have found them to be excellent pets. However, as pets they need constant attention and interaction. It is critical that hanging parrots kept as pets be well socialized.

The most commonly kept hanging parrot is the blue-crowned (*Loriculus galgulus*). Other species include Philippine, Bonaparte's, Sulawesi, Moluccan, Sclater's, Wallace's, green, yellow, orange-fronted,

Turquoisine parakeets are one of the more popular neophemas.

and Bismarck's hanging parrots. Most of these are extremely rare in aviculture. They range from southern India and Sri Lanka to Indonesia, New Guinea, and the Philippines.

PHYSICAL CHARACTERISTICS

Hanging parrots are around 4 to 6 inches (10.2 to 15.2 cm) in length and weigh around 28 to 40 grams (1 to 1.4 oz). They are small parrots with short, rounded tails. The bills are slender and very pointed. The hanging parrots resemble lovebirds, and the two groups are probably closely related.

CAGE AND ACCESSORIES

The flight should be 6 x 3 x 6 feet (1.8 x 0.9 x 1.8 m). These birds are not as fond of bathing as some other parrots are. They mainly enjoy a wet diet with plenty of fruits. Because of this, it is important to keep their flights clean.

DIET

In the wild, hanging parrots mainly eat fruits and nectar, with some insects and seed. In captivity, you must provide a diet as close to this as possible. They need to eat a lot of fruits and vegetables and be given flowers for their nectar. Their diet is similar to that of the lorikeets.

Aviary Parrots

Along with the parrots discussed at greater length, there are other species that make good aviary pets. These include the Port Lincoln parrot, twenty-eight parakeet, king parrot, hooded parrot, and the various fig parrots. Even some parrots normally kept as pets will thrive in an aviary setting, including rock pebblers, Princess of Wales parakeets, and lories.

The fig parrots, like this double-eyed fig parrot, do not make good pets but are wonderful aviary birds.

The chart below summarizes information about parrot species that is useful to prospective owners of a given species. In the Mess and Noise categories, the greater the number of check marks, the messier or noisier that species tends to be. In the Talking category, species that are considered good talkers have more checks than those that tend to be poor talkers. The Dwelling category indicates whether that species is quiet and/or small enough for owners living in apartments. Remember that each bird is an individual, and see the description within the main text of the species in question for more details.

Species	Mess	Noise	Talking	Dwelling
African Grey (Congo and Timneh)	✓✓	✓	✓✓✓	Apartment
Alexandrine Parakeet	✓✓	✓✓	✓✓	House
Blue and Gold Macaw	✓✓✓	✓✓✓	✓	House
Blue-Fronted Amazon	✓✓	✓✓	✓✓✓	House
Blue-Headed Pionus	✓✓	✓	✓	Apartment
Blue-Crowned Conure	✓✓✓	✓✓✓	✓	Apartment
Bourke's Parakeet	✓	Minimal	Rare	Apartment
Bronze-Winged Pionus	✓✓	✓	✓	Apartment
Brotogeris	✓✓	Minimal	✓	Apartment
Budgie	✓✓	Minimal	✓✓✓	Apartment

CHARACTERISTICS

Species	Mess	Noise	Talking	Dwelling
Caiques	✓✓	✓	✓	House
Cockatiel	✓✓	Minimal	✓	Apartment
Derbyan Parakeet	✓✓	✓✓	✓	House
Double Yellow-Headed Amazon	✓✓	✓✓	✓✓✓	House
Eclectus	✓✓	✓	✓	House
Galah (Rose-Breasted Cockatoo)	✓✓✓	✓✓✓	✓	House
Goffin's Cockatoo	✓✓✓	✓✓✓		House
Great-Billed Parrot	✓✓	✓	✓	House
Green-Cheeked Conure	✓✓	✓	✓	Apartment
Green-Winged Macaw	✓✓✓	✓✓✓	✓	House
Hawk-Headed Parrot	✓✓	✓✓	✓	House
Hyacinth Macaw	✓✓✓	✓✓✓	✓	House
Indian Ring-Necked Parakeet	✓✓	✓✓	✓✓	House
Jenday Conure	✓✓✓	✓✓✓	✓	House
Kakarikis	✓✓✓	Minimal	✓	Apartment

Species	Mess	Noise	Talking	Dwelling
Lilac-Crowned Amazon	✓✓	✓	✓	Apartment
Lineolated Parakeet	✓	Minimal	✓✓	Apartment
Lories and Lorikeets	✓✓✓	✓	✓	Apartment
Lovebirds	✓✓	Minimal	✓	Apartment
Major Mitchell's Cockatoo	✓✓✓	✓✓	✓	House
Maximilian's Pionus	✓✓	✓	✓	Apartment
Meyer's Parrot	✓✓	✓✓	✓	Apartment
Military Macaw	✓✓✓	✓✓✓	✓	House
Moluccan Cockatoo	✓✓✓	✓✓✓	✓	House
Moustached Parakeet	✓✓	✓✓	✓✓	House
Nanday Conure	✓✓✓	✓✓✓	✓	House
Noble Macaw	✓✓✓	✓✓✓	✓	House
Parrotlets	✓✓	✓	✓	Apartment
Patagonian Conure	✓✓✓	✓✓✓	✓	House
Quaker Parakeet	✓✓	✓✓	✓✓	House

Species	Mess	Noise	Talking	Dwelling
Red-Bellied Parrot	✓✓	✓✓	✓	Apartment
Red-Headed Amazon	✓✓	✓	✓	Apartment
Red-Lored Amazon	✓✓	✓	✓	Apartment
Rock Pebbler	✓	Minimal	✓✓✓	Apartment
Scarlet Macaw	✓✓✓	✓✓✓	✓	House
Senegal Parrot	✓✓	✓		Apartment
Severe Macaw	✓✓✓	✓✓✓	✓	House
Sun Conure	✓✓✓	✓✓✓	✓	House
Triton Cockatoo	✓✓✓	✓✓✓	✓	House
Umbrella Cockatoo	✓✓✓	✓✓	✓	House
Un-Cape Parrot	✓✓✓	✓✓	✓	Apartment
White-Capped Pionus	✓✓	✓	✓	Apartment
White-Fronted Amazon	✓✓	✓	✓	Apartment
Yellow-Fronted Amazon	✓✓	✓✓	✓✓✓	House
Yellow-Naped Amazon	✓✓	✓✓	✓✓✓	House

Chapter Three

CAGES AND OTHER EQUIPMENT

O wning a bird involves so much more than just getting a bird and a cage. Owning a bird can be expensive, but it doesn't have to put you in the poorhouse. There are also many safety issues when it comes to the accessories for the bird, including the cage itself.

Your bird's cage should be rectangular or square in shape.

THE CAGE

A bird's cage is his castle, a place where he will spend most of his time. This means that you must make it as safe and comfortable and entertaining as you can. Cages can cost anywhere from under a hundred dollars up to several thousand dollars. Spending a lot of money is not a guarantee of getting a good cage; you still need to check out any cage to make sure that it is both species appropriate and safe.

SIZE AND SHAPE

The cage needs to be as large as you can afford and have room for. The bar spaces need to be right for that species so that a bird can't escape or get his head stuck between the bars. The bird also needs to be able to open his wings without hitting the sides. For recommendations on the cage size and bar spacing for various parrot species, see Chapter 2: The Species.

Cages come in a variety of shapes; some are tall, square, rectangular, rounded, and even triangular so that they can fit into a corner. Once again, buy the largest cage you can afford and have room for and that is right for your species. Keep in mind that some birds need cages that are longer versus higher. Avoid round cages or complicated, multi-level cages. Any cage with bars that taper in places are probably best avoided; a parrot can get a toe, tongue, or other part stuck in the tapering area.

Antique cages need extra scrutiny before you buy one. They may be coated in toxic paint. They could have lead solder or even rust on them. There could even be fittings made from zinc, which is extremely toxic to birds. These fancy antique cages also tend to have intricate designs, which can end up catching toes or even tongues, resulting in injury.

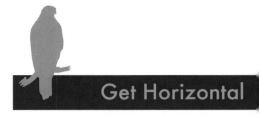

Get Horizontal

A cage with all vertical bars isn't good because vertical bars can be slippery and may prevent your parrot from climbing properly. A cage with horizontal bars allows more area for your bird to climb more naturally. Very few cages are designed with only horizontal bars, so look for a cage that has at least two sides of horizontal bars.

MATERIALS

Cages can be made out of many different materials. Some materials are good, some are bad, and others are somewhere in the middle. The best material for a cage is stainless steel. Stainless steel doesn't rust, is safe, and is very strong and durable. Powder-coated cages are excellent provided they are properly powder coated. Check to see if the powder coating is easily scraped off. If it is, don't buy the cage.

Some cages are made with pet-safe wire, which isn't very strong. These cages are generally made for smaller birds. Some cages may be fancy and made from bamboo; these types shouldn't be used with parrots or parakeets because they can chew right through them.

Some cages are painted, and the paint can chip off easily. The paint used may or may not be safe for parrots. Make sure that any paint on a cage is parrot safe and isn't chipping.

Also, check the joints and anywhere the cage was welded. Your bird will climb all over his cage, so if any of these areas aren't smooth, he might become injured. You don't want him eating the soldered areas, either.

Whatever cage you get, make sure that it is safe for your species of parrot.

DOORS

Check the door to the cage and see what works best for not only you but also for your bird. Some openings are so small that it is hard to get the bird out of his cage. Some doors swing out, some lift up (like a guillotine), and some just drop down (like a drawbridge). For doors that lift up, make sure that your bird can't just lift the door and escape. These doors can also injure your bird if he tries to escape; you will need to put some kind of clip or lock on them. Doors that swing open make it easy to get a bird out of the cage and are usually harder for him to open. However, some doors

The best cages have more horizontal bars than vertical ones, which makes it easier for your parrot to climb around his cage.

leave no spacing between the door and the cage, and toes can become trapped. You can prevent this from happening if you have something to attach to the door to prevent it from swinging shut.

If possible, buy a cage that has several openings for food and water dishes. I don't think that two is ever enough. If you only have two openings, you will need to buy another food holder that can be attached to the cage.

OTHER FEATURES

Cages also come with seed catchers, which will save you some work with the messier birds. Just be aware that you need to clean the catcher each time you clean the cage. Even though they cut down on some of the mess, they do not cut down on all of the mess. They come in metal matching the cage color; plastic; and even cloth. The smaller birds may chew on the cloth ones, but these can be washed in the washing machine, making for easier cleanup.

Most cages come with a bottom grate. Make sure that this grate is removable for easy cleanup and that it has the right bar spacing for your bird. (See Chapter 2 to determine the right bar spacing for your bird.) Be aware that birds who are prone to night fright, a condition in which the parrot will suddenly panic during the night and start flapping and banging around in the cage, can get a wing caught in this grate. If you have a bird who suffers from night fright, just remove the bottom grate if possible. Obviously, don't remove it if it allows the bird to escape. If you can't remove it, make sure that you place enough paper on top of the grate so that he can't get his wings caught in the bottom grate.

Some cages come with a bonus: a play center. If you find one like this, make sure that the play center has food cups or holders built in because this is where your bird will most often be whenever he is out. Check this area for rough spots or areas where he could get hurt. Most play centers are on the top of the cage, but there are some that are attached to the side of the cage.

Bottom Coverings

You will need to cover the bottom of the cage with some type of material. This will make cleaning easier and cut down on mess and odor. There are many materials that you can use on the bottom of the cage; some are inexpensive and others can be pricey. Never use cedar chips because these can be toxic to birds. Also, never use kitty litter, gravel, or sand, which are unsafe for parrots.

Remember that no one product is 100 percent safe. There can be problems with any product because parrots can shred and ingest anything. This is why the use of a bottom grate is important—it may keep your bird from ingesting this material. You will need to clean the bottom covering when you clean the cage.

Some coverings allow you to easily examine your bird's droppings, which are usually a good indication of his health. With other bedding materials, you won't be able to do this.

Some cages come with play stands on top of them. Check these for safety before purchase.

Natural branches make great perches. The irregular diameter and texture keep your parrot's feet in good shape.

NEWSPAPER

The cheapest and easiest material to use is newspaper. It can be cut to fit any size cage, and it will allow you to see the droppings easily. However, some birds do enjoy shredding it and tossing it outside of their cages. Although it is extremely rare, if the bird does ingest the newspaper, crop impaction could occur. Newspaper bedding is considered to be the safest of all bedding material by most parrot authorities.

CORNCOB

Corncob bedding is also easy to clean, it looks good, and it is not very pricey. It must be kept clean because it can readily develop mold from either wet food or droppings. It is lightweight, and some birds realize that by flapping their wings hard enough, it will cause the stuff to go flying. It is also difficult to see a bird's droppings on corncob, and if ingested, corncob can cause crop impactions and intestinal blockages. Several avian veterinarians have even informed me that corncob could stay in a bird's system for as long as five years!

PINE WOOD SHAVINGS

These look nice and aren't very expensive. They are absorbent and are normally good for baby birds or for sick birds (not birds with wounds). (Ask your breeder or avian veterinarian her views on this.) On the downside, they are lightweight, so when your bird flaps his wings, the shavings will go flying. Birds usually like tossing them everywhere. It is also difficult to see droppings.

PAPER PULP BEDDING

This bedding is made from recycled paper, and it contains no chemicals. This natural pulp bedding is very absorbent, and according to the manufacture, will easily break down in the crop and pass through the system if ingested. (Once again, check with

Safe and Unsafe Woods for Perches

Here are some of the reportedly safe natural woods you can use for perches:

acacia
almond
apple
arbutus
ash
aspen
bamboo
beech
bois d'arc
bottle brush
butterfly bush
citrus
cactus wood
cork
cottonwood
crabapple
date
dogwood
douglas fir
elm
fig species
fruitless mulberry

ginkgo
goat willow
grape vines
guava
hackberry
hawthorn
hazelnut
hibiscus
hickory
honeysuckle
horse apple
larch
lilac
liquidambar
mandrone
magnolia
manzanita
maple (except red maple)
Mediterranean laurel
mesquite (remove all thorns)
mimosa
Norfolk Island pine

nut trees (except chestnut
and oak)
palm
papaya
pear
pecan
pine
poplar
pussy willow
ribbonwood
rose (remove thorns)
sequoia spruce
sugar maple
sweet gum
sycamore
thurlow
tree fern
umbrella tree
vine maple
walnut (except black)
white alder
willow

The following woods are toxic and should never be used for bird perches or chew toys:

apricot
avocado
box elder
boxwood
cedar
candelabra tree
cherry
chestnut
chinaberry
crown of thorns (and
other *Euphorbia*)

driftwood
eucalyptus
hemlock
holly
Kentucky coffee
locust
mountain laurel
oak
oleander
peach
pencil tree

plum
prune
rain tree
red maple
redwood
snow on the mountain
spurges

The wood from any tree that has a pitted fruit—peach, apricot, cherry—is likely to be toxic as well.

your avian veterinarian about this.) It is relatively inexpensive, although it might be hard to find. It comes in both white and gray, which will make examining the droppings difficult. This material can be composted, if you are a gardener, and it is safe for septic systems.

PAPER TOWELS

Paper toweling can also be used for the bedding on the bottom of the cage because it is inexpensive and absorbent. It can be ingested, just like any of the other beddings, possibly causing problems. Like newspaper, you can see the droppings, but because it is so lightweight, it can move around and become useless when a bird flaps his wings.

PELLETED BEDDING

Pelleted bedding is a relatively new concept and is made from either paper or grass. Both are chemical free. This type of bedding is heavier, so your parrot won't be able to make it go flying easily. It is hard to examine the droppings with this material, and in some cases it can develop mold or fungus. Some avian veterinarians feel that because it looks like pelleted food, the bird may try to eat the bedding material.

WALNUT BEDDING

Bedding made from finely crushed walnut shells is also new to the market. It is not treated with any chemical, so it's safe in that regard. It is heavier than wood shavings, but it may still be tossed everywhere. Once again, birds like to chew and taste their environment. Walnut shells can be ingested and may cause crop impactions or bowel obstructions.

PERCHES

Besides the cage, the single most important accessory is the perch (actually perches). Improperly sized perches can cause foot problems, such as arthritis, so size really is important. Your bird needs to be able to sit comfortably on the perch. His feet shouldn't wrap all the way around the perch but rather rest on the top half of the perch.

Perches in varying diameters help exercise a bird's feet, which improves strength as well as dexterity. To further help keep your parrot's feet in good shape use a few types of perches as well and not just one type. Most cages come with wooden dowels; they are cheap and easy to clean but do not exercise a bird's feet because they are just one size. You can use them provided there are other types in the cage.

Although it is important to use several different types of perches in the cage, don't go overboard and crowd it with perches. Your bird needs to be able to open his wings without

Never use sandpaper perches or sandpaper perch covers because these are too rough and can cause sores on your bird's feet.

Therapeutic perches have a rough surface that helps wear down a parrot's toenails.

banging them into
a perch.

PERCH MATERIALS

Perches come in many materials, although natural branches work best. This is because not only do they have varying diameters, but they provide a source for a parrot's natural chewing instinct. Most parrots enjoy removing the bark and chewing the branches, so these types of perches tend to be replaced often.

If you are using natural wood from trees, make sure that they have not been sprayed with any chemicals. Before you use them, clean the branches in a 10 percent bleach in water solution (10 parts water to 1 part bleach). Leave this solution on the branches for 10 to 15 minutes and then rinse well. Seasoned

109

branches are safer, but they may contain insects. To kill these insects, bake the branches for 30 minutes in a 350°F (176.7°C) oven. (This sometimes produces a funny odor—okay, it really stinks.)

Manzanita perches are a hardwood perch, perfect for larger birds. Manzanita is the eighth-hardest wood in the world. It has naturally occurring curving and irregular shapes, which help with a bird's foot health. Hardwoods have a tendency to crack, but this is normal and won't affect your bird's health or safety.

Avoid trees that have a high sap, pitch, or tar content. Check the branches for insects, and avoid those with fungus or moss on them. Also avoid branches that have fallen on the ground; instead, you will need to cut them fresh. Sand down any rough areas on the perches to prevent injuries.

Rope perches are wonderful, but they need to be checked to make sure that little strands of rope don't get wrapped around toes, feet, or even tongues. Because they move when a parrot walks on them, they mimic the swaying of branches in nature. Some rope perches can even be put in the washing machine when they need to be cleaned.

THERAPEUTIC PERCHES

Cement perches are generally used for therapeutic perches. They help keep the nails rounded and trimmed down and come in a variety of colors and sizes. Place one as the highest perch in the cage or near a favorite food dish. This way it will be used, resulting in a reduced need for nail trims.

Water Bottles and Food Cups

Most cages come with water bowls and food cups; these may or may not be appropriate for your bird. Even if they are fine, you will want to have extras on hand to simplify cleaning and offering some foods separately from others.

WATER BOTTLES

Water bottles hold an advantage over water dishes. Most birds like to dunk their food in water. Not only will water bottles keep their water clean, but wet food that falls to the bottom of the cage could be a breeding ground for bacteria and molds. Some birds may poop in their water, creating a health risk if they drink it.

Water bottles are wonderful for keeping the water clean, but they still need to be changed daily to keep the water fresh. Buy two bottle brushes of different sizes to clean inside the water bottle so that slime won't build up.

Bowl Cleaning Tip

Cleaning crocks and water bottles can be simple. Have extras on hand so that you can put the dirty ones in the dishwasher. I usually use a sanitizing cycle on my dishwasher to make sure that the crocks and water bottles are really clean.

Training your parrot to drink from a water bottle instead of a bowl will cut down a little on your cleaning chores.

One brush will be for the inside of the bottle and the smaller brush will be for the nozzle.

When you first use a water bottle, make sure that your bird is drinking from it. Start out with the water bottle directly above his water dish. He will start to peck at the water bottle nozzle and get some water out of it. Eventually he will figure out how to drink from it. Never remove the water dish until you see your parrot drinking from the water bottle. In the beginning, you may need to keep checking to make sure that he is drinking.

FOOD CUPS

When selecting a food dish, make sure that the crocks or cups are size appropriate. For example, don't give your macaw a dish meant for a cockatiel; he'll have trouble fitting his head in it and will likely just destroy it.

There are many different styles of food dishes available. Some will fit right into the holder in the cage, others hook on the side, some will need to be screwed on, and still others snapped in. There are even crocks that have a hooded shield that will prevent some seed throwing. (Don't use one of these if you have a parrotlet because these birds will starve before they put their heads inside one of these dishes.)

How many food dishes should your bird have? There should be at least one crock for the seed or pellets, one for a dry treat such as air-popped popcorn or toasted oat cereal, and one or two for the wet foods. If you don't feel like washing dishes all the time, buy more so that you can just pop the dirty one into the dishwasher and put a clean one full of food in the cage. You will need more dishes if you don't use a water bottle. Don't mix wet and dry foods together.

Avoid certain crocks that aren't intended for birds. These may have lead in the paint used to decorate them. Although they may look fancy and beautiful, they could end up killing your bird.

Ceramic crocks usually come with the larger cages. Most of these cages have a guard to prevent a bird from dumping the entire crock. These crocks are breakable. If your bird is able to remove them, replace them with a crock that isn't going to shatter into hundreds of pieces. These pieces not only could cut your bird, but he could ingest them as well. Also, the crock will need to be replaced if it is chipped or cracked. Even hard plastic crocks can be chewed or cracked by larger beaks. The bolt on the ends can be snapped off by a macaw beak. I usually put some heavy toy over the bolt so that my macaw can't get to it.

If you get a metal crock for your bird, make sure that there is no zinc or lead in it. Both are toxic to birds. Stainless steel dishes are the safest choice.

Toys

Parrots need toys to help stimulate them and prevent boredom. Without toys, birds can develop behavior problems, such as feather plucking, screaming, and biting.

Many parrots, such as rainbow lorikeets, will lie on their backs when playing with their toys.

Cages and Other Equipment

Toys are made from a variety of materials, including wood, leather, acrylic, and plastic. There are quite a few toys you can make yourself from these materials, as well as from paper, cardboard, and other things. But knowing what kinds of toys are right for the different species requires both common sense and asking the right questions. Always provide a wide variety of toys. Include several different types: chew toys, puzzle toys, noise-making toys, etc.

Ring toys need to be species appropriate; otherwise, a bird could get stuck in the rings. Always make sure that the rings are large enough for your bird to fit through easily.

Include swings and ladders because these offer some exercise. Don't place the ladder directly underneath a perch because it will quickly become dirty. Parrots will chew the ladder if it is a wooden one, and it will need to be checked and replaced if necessary. Some acrylic ladders are dishwasher safe.

Simple and inexpensive toys can include paper towel rolls and cardboard boxes. Wooden clothes pins (without the metal spring) will also make a fun toy. A friend of mine wraps boxes in newspaper and gives them to her cockatoo, who spends hours unwrapping them. Her cockatoo will then play with the boxes, going in and hiding and having great fun with them.

Kids' Toys for Parrots

Check out your local toy store for toys for your bird. You will be surprised at what you find. My macaw's favorite toy is his Baby Busy Box, which he has had for 16 years now. He spins the knobs, moves levers, and spends a lot of time playing with it.

TOY SAFETY

Make sure that the toy you buy is species appropriate. Don't just assume that because the toy is labeled for a particular species that it really is okay for that type of bird. Toys that are meant for big birds can injure a smaller bird, and a toy meant for a smaller bird can injure a larger bird. Check the toy thoroughly before buying it. If in doubt, don't buy that toy.

Check the toy attachments first. The safest attachments are C-rings or quick links. Although larger birds may be able to open them, they are safe to use for all parrots. If the toy you are buying doesn't have one, you can buy C-rings at a hardware store and just replace any unsafe attachment with this instead. The most dangerous attachment is the keychain type of ring. Birds can get toes and tongues caught, and there have even been birds who had this type of attachment pierce their beaks. If you see one on a toy, either replace it or don't buy the toy. Also, avoid clips and split rings—these types are just as dangerous as the keychain ring.

Good Parrotkeeping

Toy Tips

- Do not put toys where they block your bird's food or water.
- Get a variety of toys and not just one type.
- Rotate toys often to prevent boredom.
- Check toys often to make sure that they are still birdie safe.
- Avoid toys that have been painted because the paint may be toxic.
- The toys that can be washed either in the dishwasher or washing machine should be cleaned often.
- Avoid natural woods that are toxic to birds.
- Make your own toys. Be creative, but think about safety. Pick up things with which you can make toys at pet stores and bird expos.

Check to see how the toy is put together as well. Is the toy on a chain or something else? If there is a chain, make sure that it is a closed-link chain. Open-link chains can catch toes and cause injuries. Whatever is holding the toy together must be strong enough for your bird. Also, the closed-linked chain you are using should be the right size for your bird—too small and he could get a toe trapped inside of it.

Toys to avoid include any type of jingle bell because these have slits in them that can trap toes and beaks. Also, avoid any toy that contains zinc, which is toxic to birds. Stainless steel is a safe metal.

TOY MATERIALS

ACRYLIC

Acrylic toys are wonderful and easy to clean. Make sure that the toy is strong enough for your species. Although these types of toys do not give a bird a chance to chew, many are puzzle-like and have places to hide treats. These puzzle toys are wonderful, and they help stimulate the bird's intellect and relieve boredom. The bird has to manipulate them to get either a treat reward, a noise they like, or some other reward. Best of all, most are easy to clean.

BUNGEE CORD

Bungee cord toys are a favorite among parrots. When buying the bungee cord, ensure that the bird can't get entangled in it; it needs to be the proper size for the bird.

FABRIC

Fabric toys are used more and more lately, and they can provide a bird with hours of entertainment. Like rope toys, these are good for feather pluckers, and you will need to check these toys regularly for dangerous strands.

LEATHER

Leather toys are also enjoyed by parrots, although they may be hard to clean. Make sure that no toxins were used to treat the leather. There are no laws yet that require this information to be put on labeling, but if you buy the toy from a reputable bird store, the staff will have checked this out ahead of time. If in doubt, ask.

PLASTIC

Plastic toys are only good for smaller birds because big beaks can crack the brittle plastic easily. Some of these toys may contain little lead weights inside. If they have any lead parts inside, make sure that your bird doesn't get to them. The plastic shouldn't be too brittle because it could break and be swallowed or broken.

WOOD

With wooden toys, natural woods are best because they do not have any dyes in them. Because birds see in colors, they are attracted to colorful things. The dye used to treat the wood must be nontoxic. Wooden toys are good for parrots because they provide an outlet for chewing.

ROPE

Rope toys provide a bird with the opportunity to preen the toy by pulling little strands of rope off. These toys need to be checked often to make sure that the bird can't get little rope strands wrapped around toes. Some can be washed in the washing machine and others can't. If the rope toy you use can't be washed, replace it as soon as it becomes soiled. Sisal, hemp, and cotton ropes are considered to be the best types of rope to use. These are good toys for feather pluckers.

INTRODUCING TOYS

Some parrots are like little kids: The second they see a new toy, they want it. Other birds may take time to get used to the toy at first; this is often true of African greys. Start with bringing the toy close to your bird, stopping if he seems nervous. Once he accepts the toy where it is, move it a little closer, stopping once again if he gets nervous. Keep repeating these steps until you can put the toy in his cage. It could take a few hours or a few weeks; just be patient.

Use only closed-link chains and c-rings, such as those above, to hang toys. Other hangers may be unsfae.

115

AN EASY-TO-MAKE TOY

Here is a toy that is easy to make, inexpensive, and great for a medium to larger bird. I call it the coconut toy.

You will need the following:

- 1 coconut shell (halved and scooped out; you can let your bird eat the coconut meat)
- 1 closed-link chain or sisal rope
- 1 or 2 C-rings
- 1 heavy, large bead that is appropriate for your bird (you can use anything from a chunk of wood to hard plastic keys)
- 1 drill

Making a T-Stand

This T-stand is simple to make, and it can be taken apart for traveling. Your bird will get a lot of use out of it

Tools Needed

drill   screwdrivers
hammer   sandpaper

Materials Needed

heavy wooden base around 1 to 2 inches (2.5 to 5 cm) thick and 18 to 24 inches (45.7 to 61 cm) square

4 wheels

1 handle (whatever type you like)

PVC piping around 1 inch (2.5 cm) in diameter: 1 piece that's 4 feet (1.2 m) long and 2 pieces that are 9 inches (22.9 cm) long

flange to fit the PVC pipe

male adapter for PVC pipe

T-connector for pipe

2 endcaps that are the right size for the pipe

22 wood screws

2 food cups

2 bolts (for food cups)

2 eye hooks (for attaching toys)

optional: 4 sheets of stick-on tiles (makes cleaning the base easier) sisal rope

To make the toy, drill a hole in the top of the coconut shell. Thread the closed-link chain through the hole and add the bead, which must be bigger than the hole. Attach the C-ring to the end, or if using rope, tie it off. On the other end of the chain, attach the other C-ring and hang in the cage.

Hanging Beds

Many parrot species love to sleep inside something. It gives them a sense of security. You can buy different types of hanging beds in pet stores, or you can even make them on your own. Some look better than others, and some of them can be taken

Construction

1. If using the stick-on tiles, attach them to the board. If need be, use small tacks to attach securely.
2. Flip the base over and attach the 4 wheels with 16 of the wood screws (4 to each wheel); put one in each corner.
3. Attach the handle with the 2 wood screws (any place between the wheels on the bottom).
4. Flip the base over once again, and in the center of the base attach the flange with 4 wood screws. Make sure that it is firmly attached.
5. Attach the male adapter to the flange.
6. Push the 4-foot (1.2-m) PVC pipe into male adapter.
7. Attach the T-connector to the 4-foot (1.2-m) pipe.
8. With sandpaper, rough up the two 9-inch (22.9-cm) pieces of PVC; this will allow your bird to grip them firmly.
9. On each 9-inch (22.9-cm) PVC pipe, drill a hole big enough so that you can add the bolts for the food cups. Add the bolts. (You may have to drill the hole through the entire PVC pipe.)
10. Push each 9-inch (22.9-cm) PVC pipe into the T-connector with the bolt facing upward.
11. Drill a hole in the end of each endcap big enough for the eye hook and nut.
12. Attach the eye hook, and screw the nut firmly in place.
13. Attach the endcaps onto each end of the 9-inch (22.9-cm) PVC pipe.
14. Attach food cups to the bolts.

You can substitute natural wood for the PVC crosspieces. Make sure that they are snug in the T-connector and that they can't fall out and injure your bird. If the perch is still too slippery for him, you can wrap sisal rope around it.

For even more stability, use a metal pipe that can fit inside the PVC. Make the pipe just a shade taller than the PVC. This will be covered when it is attached to the T-connector.

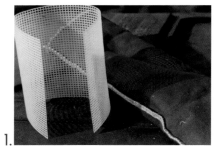

1.

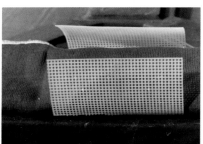

2.

3.

4.

apart for easy washing, while others can't. Some hanging beds are vertically oriented, so a bird can snuggle up against the bed rather than going inside. Not all birds enjoy these beds, and you should see which your bird prefers. Some birds may be more frightened by them, so they should be avoided.

To make a hanging bed on your own, you need the following:

- Good fake fur fabric that doesn't shed much. This will line the inside and outside of the bed.
- Plastic, canvas, elastic, and C-rings for hanging.
- A tube- or oval-shaped item for the body of the bed. Wire mesh works well for larger birds, such as macaws. Large PVC pipes or cardboard tubes (such as an old oatmeal container) work well for small to medium birds.

Start by cutting the fake fur so that the material is big enough to line the inside and cover the outside, with enough left over to fold over the ends. Temporarily pin the fabric inside out. Form a tube with the canvas, and wrap it around the fabric. Once you have the size right, you can temporarily put the plastic canvas inside to get an idea of where to place the elastic straps. Attach these straps. At the top end of the straps, fold the strap over so that you will have a place to attach the C-rings. You could also use Velcro on the ends and attach the two right straps to the left straps. Once you have the amount of fabric right, you can sew the fabric together and neatly finish the outside edges.

Carriers

Most dog and cat carriers are suitable to use for birds because they are easy to carry, safe, and solid. There are plenty of holes for the bird to breathe, and they can even look out through the front. You can attach a perch inside of them by drilling a hole on both ends of a dowel or natural branch and drilling a hole in the side of the carrier. Make sure that it is firmly attached and that it doesn't move around. Don't place the perch too high because

Some of the steps for making a hanging bed for your parrot are shown to the left. 1. Sew the fake fur lining together to form a tube. 2. Wrap the mesh body of the bed around the center of the fur tube, leaving some fur sticking out beyond the mesh. 3. Fold the fur back over the mesh body and sew into place. 4. Sew or otherwise attach straps for hanging the bed to each end of it.

This pair of eclectus makes use of their hanging beds.

you don't want your bird to be hunched over, but don't place it too low where he can't grab hold of it.

There are also several different acrylic carriers available. These are usually just made for birds, and they already have a perch attached. They are easy to clean and are usually taller rather than longer.

Playpens and T-Stands

Playtime is essential to a bird's well-being, and playpens and T-stands are a safe place for your bird to play. Playpens for smaller to medium parrots are nice because most of the time you can move them anywhere—you can even take them with you on trips, which will give your bird a comfortable place to be.

If you want to take your larger bird places, a collapsible T-stand is a must. Some of the larger stands are on wheels so that you can also move them around the house. Make sure that this is a feature when you buy one.

When buying either a playpen or T-stand, make sure

It should be noted that with some birds of breeding age, full-spectrum lighting may cause breeding behavior. If this happens, stop using the lights for a few weeks and then try again. If it continues to happen, you may not be able to use full-spectrum lighting for a long time.

Although your parrot needs enough toys to keep him busy, don't go overboard and crowd the cage with them.

that there are food cups attached; your bird will be spending a lot of time on his stand and will need to eat and drink. On some stands there is even a place to attach toys. Some stands come with ladders and a swing, but the larger ones usually do not.

Air Filters

Dust is everywhere, no matter how much we clean. With birds, this dust seems much worse. HEPA (high-efficiency particulate air) filters help reduce not only the dust but also bacteria, mold, and other particles in the air.

There are many types of HEPA filters available for all sizes of rooms. There are some that even attach right to the furnace, although these are much more expensive. Some of the more expensive HEPA room models will also remove odors and microscopic particles, and these are especially useful if you have a powder bird. The filters must be changed as per the manufacturer's instructions. You will be surprised at the amount of stuff that they remove.

Full-Spectrum Lighting

All birds need some natural lighting. Without it they can develop dull-looking feathers, health issues, and even behavioral problems such as feather plucking. However, as natural light goes through a window, the benefits it has to offer are lost. If your bird never gets to go outside into the natural sunlight, it might be a good idea to invest in full-spectrum lighting, which is special lighting designed to closely mimic natural sunlight. These sometimes go by the name "bird lighting." If you can't find these made specifically for birds, use those labeled for birds and reptiles. Do not use the reptile-only lights, as these may have too much UV for birds.

The bulbs should be placed no more than 2 to 3 feet (61 to 91.4 cm) away and no closer than 1 foot (30.5 cm) from the cage. Any closer and your bird could get to the bulb and get burned.

How many hours you provide your bird with full-spectrum lighting depends on the species. All African species (greys, poicephalus, lovebirds, etc.), eclectus, and cockatoos receive no more than four to six hours a day. All other medium to large species should receive no more than two to four hours a day. Small species such as budgies should receive one to two hours a day.

The bulbs should be placed on a timer because your parrot should have the same duration of exposure each day. The lights should also be used when the sun is normally at its highest point; this will mimic what the bird would experience in the wild.

Cage Covers

Most birds should be covered at night. (The exception is a bird who suffers from night fright—covering him will make his night fright worse.) Covering the cage at night helps establish a bedtime ritual, and your bird will learn that this is the time he should stop playing and settle down for the night.

Covers don't have to be fancy or expensive. You can use an old sheet or lightweight blanket to cover the cage. Some covers will perfectly fit the cage, but these are intended for smaller enclosures. If you have a sewing machine available, you can even make a cover yourself. This way it will fit the cage perfectly and you can pick a pattern you and your bird will like.

Whatever cover you use, check it often for strings that could get wrapped around toes. If any string appears, remove it immediately. The cover also needs to be checked for holes so that your bird doesn't get a wing or foot trapped.

Wash the cover at least monthly *without* any fabric softeners or strong-smelling detergents. I also recommend a second rinse cycle.

Shower Perches

Shower perches are great for bathing your bird. Unlike a mister, a shower perch not only keeps the water in the shower but also gives him a more thorough shower—and your hand will be saved from all the pumping of the water bottle.

Some shower perches are available in stores, but I feel that the suction cup types don't work well for larger birds. Some shower suction devices are very good, but these are hard to find. You can make your own shower perch cheaper than you can buy a good suction device. Natural wood perches do not work well in the shower because they will warp and harbor bacteria. PVC or similar materials work better.

MAKING A SHOWER STAND

Making a shower perch is not too difficult and can be much less expensive than purchasing one.

This red-bellied parrot waits on his play stand while his owner cleans the cage.

121

Good Parrotkeeping

You will need PVC piping that is the appropriate thickness for your bird to perch on. Cut this into 8 equal pieces to fit depth-wise into your shower. (Half of these are for the base and half for the top.) Make sure that you cut the PVC into the right size, taking into account that 4 3-way connectors need to fit width-wise into your shower or tub. You also need 4 pieces of PVC pipe cut to around 3 to 4 feet (91.4 to 121.9 cm) in length; this will be the vertical height of the stand. Lastly, you need 8 3-way connectors and T-connectors. You should also use cotton or sisal rope to wrap around the perches so that they won't be slippery. The bigger the base, the more stable the stand will be.

STEP 1
Place the 3-way elbow connectors at the ends of the PVC that fit depth-wise into the shower. (This is the base.)

STEP 2
Push 2 of the pieces of PVC into the 3-way connector.

STEP 3
Push the T-connectors into this PVC.

Quaker parakeets and other water-loving birds often enjoy shower perches.

122

STEP 4

Push the 3- to 4-foot-length (91.4- to 121.9-cm) PVC into the T-connectors.

STEP 5

Push the 2 elbows onto each end.

STEP 6

Wrap the crosspiece of PVC with the sisal rope or something that will allow your bird to have a good grip on the perch.

STEP 7

Push this wrapped crosspiece of PVC into the elbows.

Birdie Harnesses

These are great for taking your bird outdoors safely. However, you need to make sure that you put the harness on him properly and that it is the right size for him. If it isn't, your bird may be injured.

Not all parrots like a harness, and it may take some time for yours to get used to it. This can be accomplished with a lot of patience. First, get your bird used to the appearance of the harness by just putting it near him. Once he accepts that, move it closer. If he allows that, start touching him with the harness. Do this slowly and talk to your bird, reassuring him and offering praise. Next drape the harness on him, not putting it on yet but just allowing it to rest on his body. Remember to offer praise; you can also offer a treat as a reward at this point. If he accepts this, start putting the harness on him. By going slowly and allowing him to accept it at his own rate, he will feel less threatened and may actually enjoy the harness. Never push!

Setting Up the Cage

Now that you have all of the necessary equipment, you need to set up your bird's home. Cage placement is very important. Birds should be made to feel a part of the family, so keeping them in a room away from human interaction isn't good, nor is placing them in a high-traffic area. Some birds like looking out the window, but this may make others nervous. You will have to see what is best for your bird. I like placing the cage in an area where there are people and the bird can interact with his human family while not suddenly being surprised by people showing up. Do not place the enclosure near a stove, where hot oil or boiling water could splatter on your bird. The living room or family room is probably the best choice,

Harnesses should never be confused with leg chains. Leg chains are cruel and barbaric and should never be used. They are a remnant of the Dark Ages of birdkeeping.

123

but it will vary with your bird and your household.

Start with the perches. Because birds have a natural instinct to go to the highest point in the cage, place the therapeutic perch at that point. Make sure that your bird can stand naturally and not have to hunch over to stand on it. Place a second perch width-wise across the cage. This perch should be slightly below where the food and water is. Do not have a perch above the dishes because your bird will end up pooping in them. If space allows, add another perch.

Next, add swings, toys, and ladders, but make sure that the cage isn't so overcrowded that your bird has to wade through the toys to get anywhere. Ladders should be placed where they can't be pooped on. Place a hanging bed so that it's high in the cage and easy for your bird to access. You may need to adjust the height to his preference.

Cleaning the Cage

Cleaning the cage can either be simple or complicated, depending on how you go about it. How often should you clean the cage? Normally, clean on a daily basis, but if you have a lorikeet or lory, you should do it twice a day. Remember, birds are messy. There is a reason for this. In the wild, when food drops to the ground, it helps feed other creatures, and the seeds help spread the next generation of plants. But in captivity, the combination of droppings and food is an excellent growing ground for bacteria, molds, fungi, and even creepy crawlies.

Food dishes and water bottles should be cleaned daily, and if possible, in the dishwasher on the sanitizing cycle. This is one reason why it is always important to have extras on hand.

WEEKLY CLEANING

Wipe the cage down every week with warm soapy water and then rinse. If there are any droppings on the perches, scrape them off. If the bars have fecal material on them, clean it off. Clean the bottom grate, removing all fecal matter and stuck-on food. If you have lung issues, wear a mask while you clean the cage. Wipe down all toys and remove any fecal matter.

MONTHLY CLEANING

Monthly cleaning is more involved, but if you have extra perches, toys, food dishes, and water bottles, it won't take as long. It also works best if you have a play center for your bird to sit on while you are cleaning. Although similar to weekly cleaning, monthly involves a little more scrubbing and more thoroughness. Every single thing in your bird's cage should be cleaned. While cleaning, you should also check the bars for roughness and make sure that everything is still safe.

OTHER CLEANING CHORES

Once to twice a year, the cage requires a premium cleaning. If possible, take the cage outside with you. If you have a small cage, either put it in the bathtub or even break it down and put it into the dishwasher. This cleaning is even more thorough and involves much more than just a wiping down. During the warmer months, I bring the cage outside where I pressure wash it, which makes the cleanup time much shorter. This doesn't mean that you have to run out and get a pressure washer to do the job; instead, more elbow grease is required.

Now is the time you should sanitize the cage. There are sprays in pet stores that will help with the cleaning of the cage; make sure that the one you choose is bird safe. Grapefruit-seed extract is an excellent nontoxic cleanser. This is relatively new to the market and can be found in many health food stores. It is an antibacterial, antifungal, and antiseptic agent. If you don't want to use this, use a bleach solution (1 part bleach to 9 parts water).

Remove toys and perches before you start cleaning. After you have scrubbed the cage with warm soapy water and cleaned off any fecal material, spray it with your chosen disinfectant—bleach, grapefruit-seed extract, or some other product. Then let it air-dry, preferably in the sun. Follow this with a thorough rinsing. Let the cage air-dry again.

Check the enclosure for areas that may have paint chewed off or that have become rusted. You can use a steel-wool pad on rusty areas. Make sure that little spaces have been cleaned of seed and debris.

Placing the cage in the sun is always the best way to dry it. While the cage is drying, check perches to make sure that they don't have fecal matter on them and that they aren't chewed up. Check toys for continued safety and cleanliness. If possible, put the toys in the dishwasher with the food dishes and water bottles. Throw the fabric toys in the washing machine. If anything can't be cleaned or is very chewed up, replace it.

Because the cage has been moved, you can thoroughly vacuum or wash the floor underneath it. Now is also a good time to wipe the wall down or scrape off any dried food or fecal matter.

After everything is cleaned, rinsed, and dry, reassemble. Place your parrot back in his spic-and-span home, knowing that it will be messy again in about 30 seconds.

Chapter Four

AVIAN SAFETY

Keeping your bird safe is extremely important. As a responsible owner, there is a number of things that you can do to ensure his safety. Because most parrots are like two-year-olds in their pursuit of mischief, you must approach your bird's safety in the same way you would for a human two-year-old; in fact, it is just as important to birdie-proof your home as it is to child-proof it. Like a human child, parrots are curious. They also love to explore by tasting their environment, just as young children do.

While the number of possible dangers to your bird may seem overwhelming, most of keeping your bird safe comes down to common sense. If it's bad for you, it's probably worse for your bird. If it smells strong to you, it is probably too strong to be around your bird. Once you get the hang of how to keep him safe, it will be easy to do so. Does this mean that you have to get rid of everything in the house? No. Once again, use common sense. So how do you protect your bird from household dangers? Careful supervision whenever he is out is the number-one way to keep him safe. If you train your bird to stay in his cage or in his playpen, you can keep him safe easier than if he is allowed free run of the house.

Safety In and Around the Cage

Although I mentioned the dangers of cages in another chapter, it is worth discussing here as well. Check the cage to see if there are any rough spots, as well as areas with lead solder. Make sure that the cage isn't painted with a toxic paint. Decorative designs could injure your bird by trapping his toes.

Placement of the cage is also important. It shouldn't be placed near pictures that he could pull off the walls; glass fragments could go flying when these shatter on the floor. If this does happen, change the food and water immediately. Thoroughly vacuum the cage and the area around the cage. If your bird likes to chew on the walls, place Plexiglas over the walls to prevent this.

TOYS

Check toys often for wear. Make sure that you use quick links or C-rings and not the key-ring type of fastener. Avoid anything with a spring because your bird could easily pop the spring out. O-rings that snap together are also dangerous. Chains should never be the open-linked chains—only use closed-linked chains. Closed-linked chains must be the proper size for your bird, or he could trap a toe or toenail in the chain. Rope toys become frayed easily, so remove any strands that could wrap around his toes.

Toys must be cleaned often, and any debris on them needs to be removed. Otherwise, the toy will become a breeding ground for bacteria. Playthings also need to be species appropriate. A toy that's too big can injure or trap a bird. A toy that's too small is a choking hazard; your bird could even swallow it, causing an intestinal blockage.

MITE PROTECTORS

Although sold as a product for birds, these little cans that attach to the cage are actually dangerous. They contain the chemical paradichlorobenzene, which is the same chemical used in mothballs. It is not only toxic to your bird but is also proven to cause cancer. Mite protectors should never be used around any bird.

Other Pets

People who have cats or dogs often enjoy seeing their pets playing together. This does not work well with birds and other pets. The slightest scratch from a claw or even a tooth can kill your bird. Other pets, whether another bird, dog, cat, or whatever, should never be left alone with each other. It doesn't matter how friendly or gentle the other pet is. It only takes a second and your bird could be injured or killed. Also, some birds enjoy terrorizing the dog, cat, or other pet. For example, my friend's cockatoo would get down on the floor and chase the cat under the bed, keeping him there.

The saliva from a dog or cat can be deadly to birds. Even the slightest scratch could kill him. This is because of the bacteria in their mouths. This does not mean that if your bird touches a dog toy he will die, but you must watch him carefully to make sure that he doesn't become ill afterward. If your bird does get scratched or bitten, take him to an avian veterinarian right away, no matter how minor the injury

Careful supervision is the best way to keep your bird safe from household dangers.

Safe and Toxic Plants

Any plant can potentially be toxic. Some parrots may be allergic to what is commonly thought to be a safe plant. Always use caution with any type of plant.

The lists below are nowhere near complete. There are thousands and thousands of plants around the world. Most are not kept as houseplants, but as horticulture is becoming more advanced, new plants are popping up all the time. Many common garden and landscaping plants are toxic. If you are uncertain whether a plant is safe for your parrot or not, consider it unsafe.

Toxic Plants

Assume all parts of these plants are toxic; if only a specific part of a plant is toxic, that part follows the entry in parentheses.

acorn
amaryllis (bulbs)
angel's trumpet
autumn crocus (bulbs)
avocados
belladonna
black Locust
bleeding heart
boxwood (leaves)
buckeye
buckthorn (bark)
bulbs (most plants including daffodil, jonquil, and hyacinth)
caladium

calla lily
castor oil plant
chinaberry tree
Christmas cactus
Christmas rose
clematis
coral plant
daphne
delphinium
devil's ivy
dieffenbachia
dumb cane
Dutchman's breeches
eggplant (fruit is ok)
elderberry (fruit is ok)

elephant ear
English ivy
euonymus
euphorbia
foxglove
golden chain
hellebore (all species)
heliotrope
hemlock (all species)
holly
honey locust
horse chestnut
hydrangeas (flowers)
Japanese laurel
(*Aucuba*)

jasmine
juniper
lily of the valley
lupine
milkweed
mock orange
monkshood
morning glory
nightshades (all species)
oleander

pennyroyal
philodendron
poinsettia
poppy
potato (eyes, green skin, leaves)
pothos
red maple
rhododendron
sage

spindle tree
spurges (all species)
tansy
tomato (fruit is ok)
tulip
vetch (all species)
Virginia creeper
yew (all species)

Safe Plants

These indoor/outdoor plants are believed to be safe. Make sure that there are no chemicals or insecticides used on them. They should be cleaned before placing them anywhere near your bird. Always consult your avian veterinarian before giving your bird any plant. Remember that even though the plant may be safe, your bird could still have an allergy to it.

African violets
aloe
ash
aspen
bamboo
beech
bird nest fern
Boston fern
bougainvillea
chickweed
Christmas holly
coleus
corn plant
cottonwood
crabapple (avoid seeds)
dracaena
elephant foot tree
elm
figs (most species)

fir
firethorn
gardenia
grape ivy
guava
hawthorn
hibiscus
jade plant
larch
madrone (and other *Arbutus*)
magnolia
maidenhair fern
manzanita
marigold
mother-in-laws tongue
nasturtium
Norfolk Island pine
palms

passion flower
peperomia
petunia
ponytail palm
poplar
prayer plant
rose (remove thorns)
schefflera
snake plant
spider plant
Swedish ivy
sword fern
toyon
umbrella plant
wandering Jew
white clover
willow
yucca
zebra plant

Some birds love to bathe, but they could drown in the water, so you must cover fish tanks. Exotic pets, including ferrets, snakes, lizards, rats, and rabbits, should never be left out together with a parrot. Ferrets, snakes, and most lizards are predators and will view your bird as food. Other animals may frighten your bird or vice versa, causing aggression. Do not allow your pets to mix.

Children

Never leave small children alone with a parrot. Parrots and older kids can be a wonderful combination, but very young kids are not always the best match. Young kids move quickly and suddenly, and this can frighten a parrot. Also, young children don't always remember to close the door or to put things away. Children need to be able to respect the bird as well as be gentle when handling him. While older children can certainly help with parrot care, an adult still needs to make sure that the bird is getting food and fresh water daily.

For the sake of both your kids and your parrot, carefully supervise their interactions.

Dangers on the Floor

Many birds, especially cockatoos, like to get into all kinds of mischief. They love to climb down to the floor to explore their surroundings. This is fine if you can carefully supervise your bird, but it is not okay to let him do this on his own. There are many dangers lurking on the floor.

CORDS AND OUTLETS

Electrical cords are particularly inviting. Although your bird can be electrocuted when biting into these cords, they are more likely to start a fire instead. (A bird's mouth is dry, not moist like a human mouth, so electrocution is less likely.) Place all cords and electrical wires inside PVC pipes.

Install outlet protectors. There are two types available. The first is just a plug-in type, and some of the larger birds could remove these. This type is for outlets not in use. The second type covers both the outlet and the plug, and it is harder for a bird to access.

OTHER HAZARDS

Dog toys, furniture, and human feet are other dangers that parrots confront while roaming the floor. Parrots are likely to find dog toys inviting to chew, but they contain dog saliva, and due to the bacteria on the toys, this could be dangerous to your bird. Put away dog toys, or only let your parrot down on the floor in a dog-free zone.

A parrot's love of chewing can cause him to view the treated leg of an expensive dining room table as a delicious treat. Also, some furniture is made of cedar or cherry, both of which are also toxic to your parrot. If you have a ground dweller on your hands, use thick PVC to protect the legs of your tables and chairs.

Always remember that your parrot is out on the floor because all it takes is a split second for you to step on him. Being stepped on is one of the more frequent causes of parrot death and injury. Make sure that everyone in the house knows that he is out and in which room.

An important step you can take to keep your bird safe is to teach him not to go down on the floor.

Dangers on the Ceiling

Stucco ceilings were once very popular, although they seem to be going out of style now. Tall cages may allow a bird to reach up and nibble on the stucco ceiling, which is dangerous because the paint could either be toxic or cause crop impactions or bowel obstructions. If you have a stucco ceiling, make sure that your bird can't get to it by either getting a shorter cage or removing the stucco on the ceiling. I knew a woman whose green-winged macaw died a painful death from being allowed to chew the stucco ceiling. Of course, chewing any type of ceiling is not good for your bird, and you must prevent this behavior.

CEILING FANS

Many birds have been injured or killed by ceiling fans. Their owners had the fans on and the birds were flighted, resulting in them getting battered by the fan. Don't use a ceiling fan with a flighted bird.

Windows, Doors, and Mirrors

Keep drapes or curtains closed when your bird is out. This will prevent him from mistaking the glass

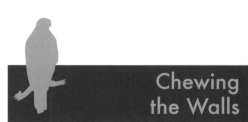

Chewing the Walls

You can protect your walls and keep your bird safe at the same time by installing acrylic corner protectors on all corners inside your house. These are the most likely places a parrot will chew.

Ceiling fans are very dangerous for parrots, especially flighted ones.

window as an opening to the outdoors. Parrots have been killed from flying full speed into a closed window. You can also install window decals, which will not only prevent your bird from flying into the windows but will also prevent wild birds from flying into your windows from the outdoors. When using drapes or curtains, make sure that your bird's nails are well trimmed; otherwise, he may get snared on them.

Flighted birds can escape through a window, door, or skylight, and screens are only partly effective at preventing escape. Many birds have gone right into the screen, popping it out, and then escaped into the wild. A bird who escapes may never be recovered and is likely to die a slow and painful death. If you have screens on the windows, they must be strong and safely secured. Check them on a regular basis for holes or weakness.

Mirrors can be a hazard, particularly with flighted birds. Many a bird has become injured by directly flying into a mirror. Place stickers on them or cover them when he is out.

Many of the dangers from windows, doors, and mirrors will be lessened by clipping your bird's wings. This will prevent most escapes. Keep in mind that some birds, such as cockatiels, are strong fliers and even with clipped wings can still fly to some degree.

BLINDS AND CURTAINS

The blinds used in windows also present a danger because they can contain lead and dust. Imported blinds tend to contain higher amounts of lead than the domestically produced ones. Even the dust on these blinds can cause problems. Because many birds enjoy chewing, the blinds should be tested for lead. Lead test kits are available at many stores.

Curtains sometimes contain weights to help keep them hanging straight. These should be removed, especially if your parrot tends to explore on the ground often. The weights are usually made of lead and are toxic.

Dangers in the Bathroom

Bathrooms are always a dangerous place for birds. They can easily open cabinets where medicines, colognes, and other toiletries are kept. They could also fall into the toilet and drown. Put child-proof locks on all cabinets, and make sure that the toilet seat is always down. Put all chemicals away so that your bird can't get to them.

Some birds have even figured out how to turn the water on in the sinks. There are child-proof devices that can prevent this as well, although you may need to change your faucet to accommodate them. Of course, the best idea is to not let your bird in the bathroom without close supervision

Some people use the bathroom as a sick room for sick or injured birds. This isn't the best idea. When a toilet is flushed, small amounts of bacteria become airborne and spread throughout the room. A sick bird already has a weakened immune system, so this will further endanger him.

Dangers in the Kitchen

Kitchen dangers are many and include the stove, vents, cords, refrigerator, freezer, kitchen cleaners, nonstick cookware, and many others.

If you are cooking, do not take your bird into the kitchen with you. You may think that he is safe on your shoulder, but accidents happen. He could jump or fall off your shoulder and into the boiling water and be scalded or even killed. A bird can become seriously burned from splattering oil or grease while you are cooking. Aside from being scalded, he could also drown in a

Birds Like Bling, Too

Many of us wear jewelry, and because birds are attracted to shiny objects, this can cause problems. Remove earrings, especially if you have pierced ears, whenever you handle your bird. Otherwise, you may end up with new piercings. Your bird could also pop the diamond out of your expensive wedding ring in no time at all. These small items are choking and gut-obstruction hazards. Keep your jewelry and your bird safe by removing it before playing with him.

Keeping your fish tank completely covered will protect both your parrot and your fish.

pot or sink full of water.

My friend went to the refrigerator with his bird one time to get a can of soda. He didn't see his bird jump into the refrigerator. Luckily, he realized what had happened as soon as he closed the door. However, birds have died by jumping into the freezer or refrigerator because their owners didn't notice right away. Parrots have also jumped into ovens, clothes dryers, dishwashers, and similar items. Keep your bird away from these appliances.

Use child-proof locks on cabinets and cupboards because your parrot could get into these things as well. This will prevent him from accessing dangerous chemicals, sharp utensils, and inappropriate foods.

POTS AND PANS

Throw away all of your nonstick pots and pans. Nonstick pans can release polytetrafluoroethylene (PTFE). The most common brand sold is Teflon. It is also found on some cooking bags. It was once thought that if it reached a temperature of 500°F (260°C), PTFE would start producing dangerous and deadly fumes. Now, there have been cases where temperatures as low as 285°F (260°C) have caused deaths in birds. These fumes are odorless and invisible, but just a few minutes of exposure will kill your bird. He doesn't even have to be in the room for this to occur. Lung damage is irreversible and causes a very painful death for birds.

Remember that items like clothes irons, woks, pancake grills, waffle makers, cookie sheets, griddles, bread machines, curling irons, space heaters, drip pans, deep fryers, ironing board pads, blow dryers, some heat lamps and their bulbs, and other items can also be coated with a nonstick surface. Check with the manufacturer if you aren't sure.

Overheated plastic pans and pot handles can be toxic. Many higher-end pots and pans have a very high temperature tolerance. There are also pots and pans that use an anodized aluminum surface, which is close to

There is now some evidence that PTFE fumes can also be toxic to humans, causing flu-like symptoms.

nonstick. This is much safer to use around your birds, but these pans are expensive. You can also use stainless steel, ceramic, or even cast iron, all of which are safe.

Open pots and pans are also a hazard, so cover them whenever you can.

OVERHEATED OIL

There have been many incidents of birds dying suddenly from the fumes of overheated oil. This is another reason why birds should never be kept in the kitchen. Keeping the vents open when you are cooking is mandatory.

Drowning Dangers

Bird can drown quickly in only a few inches (cm) of water. Keep the lids down on all toilets. If you have an indoor hot tub or Jacuzzi, always cover it when not in use. If you have an indoor pool, make sure that your bird can't get anywhere near it. If you have other pets, keep your bird away from their water dishes. Tiny birds, such as budgies and parrotlets, could even drown in a drinking glass. Once again, keeping the wings clipped will prevent most drowning accidents.

Insects

In the wild, birds eat insects and their larva, so it is not unnatural for them to eat these things in the house. Make sure that they do not eat bees, wasps, or hornets because of the stingers. Also, do not use any bug spray near or around your bird. Sometimes the spray doesn't kill the insect right away, and your bird will spot this dying insect and eat it. Because of the spray, your parrot will die as well. If you must kill the creepy crawlies, use a newspaper or other swatter.

Household Chemicals

Always put any household chemicals (bleach, soaps, kitchen cleaners, furniture polish, jewelry cleaners, drain openers, antifreeze, other car-care products, ice melt, etc.) away immediately after use in an area that has been birdie-proofed. As was mentioned, parrots are curious, and they will get into things you don't want them to get into.

Household cleaners and air fresheners can be toxic to parrots. They have sensitive respiratory systems, and these fumes can cause them to become ill or die. Remember to read the label of any chemical you buy. Keep in mind that if it smells strong to you, it will be much worse for your parrot.

Antifreeze is fatal not only to birds but to other pets as well. A safer type is available, but regardless, it too should be kept away from all animals and children.

So what can you use to clean your house? Good old-fashioned things, such as baking soda, work great. Baking soda can be used as a freshener on your carpeting and can be used to clean your oven. If you have linoleum floors, you can use white vinegar in hot water to clean them; use ½ cup

Kissing Your Bird

Many owners kiss their birds or allow their birds to eat right out of their mouths. This isn't good or healthy for birds because of the bacteria in our mouths. If you must kiss your parrot, kiss him on the top of the head instead.

Molds

Molds are toxic to birds, so if you live in an area where it rains a lot, check around the windows and doors. If you see any mold growing, clean it off.

(118.3 ml) vinegar to 1 gallon (3.4 l) of water. A more thorough discussion of bird-safe cleaning occurs later in this chapter.

Scents, Smokes, and Fresheners

Birds' lungs are very sensitive. They will suffer the ill effects of airborne toxins long before a human will—remember the canaries in the coal mines? A number of products that people routinely put in the air can be harmful or even fatal for parrots.

SCENTED CANDLES

More and more people are using scented candles, but these have been linked to many parrot deaths. The oils in them are toxic to birds. However, there are some parrot-safe candles that are sold online. Still, you must take extra precautions to make sure that the hot wax or flame doesn't injure your bird.

AIR FRESHENERS

The same goes for air fresheners—the oils that are used in them are extremely toxic to your bird. Once again, many deaths have been linked to them. Plug-in air fresheners also use oils that are toxic to parrots. *Never, ever* use these around parrots.

Although there is now a trend toward holistic medicine, do not burn essential oils near your bird because the fumes can either make him ill or kill him. Tea tree oil produces fumes that are extremely toxic to parrots. Essential oils of any kind should never be added to the water in humidifiers.

CARPET FRESHENERS

Carpet fresheners also have chemicals in them that make them unsafe to use around parrots. The labels on many state that they are pet safe, but the pets they are referring to are dogs and cats, not birds! Don't be fooled by the labels unless they state on there that they are parrot safe.

POTPOURRI

Many people use potpourri, which can be enticing to parrots, but the oils used in them will kill your bird if ingested. Throw them away to prevent any problems. Wax potpourri can also kill your bird within 12 hours if ingested. To prevent problems, do not use these items near your bird—better yet, throw them away!

OTHER SPRAYS

Never spray any kind of aerosol spray around your bird. This includes hairspray, leather protector, and oven cleaner. Either remove the bird from the room, or in the case of the leather spray, take the item and spray outside to use. You can spray certain sprays onto a paper towel or rag in another part of the house before using them. One poor man I talked to at a bird show told me that he used leather spray on his new jacket and then went to sleep shortly later. When he woke up in the morning, all five of his beloved birds were dead.

SCENTED TISSUES

Another danger that can cause problems in birds is scented toilet papers and scented tissues. Many owners, not thinking that there was a danger with the toilet paper rolls or empty tissue boxes, gave their birds these things to play with only to discover them dead shortly thereafter. Any scented product is probably dangerous for your bird.

Small birds can drown in a tiny amount of water. Clean up drinking glasses before letting your parrot out.

GLUE GUNS

When heated, glue guns produce fumes that are toxic to birds. If you must use a glue gun, do it far away from your parrot. I suggest using it in the garage so that your bird won't be at risk.

FIREPLACES

Don't place your bird near a fireplace. Fumes from the wood or other fuel can kill him. Make sure that your fireplace is well ventilated, and have your chimney cleaned yearly. When you use your fireplace, remember that you will be drying the air out, so you will need to provide extra humidity. Many birds develop dry, itchy skin during the winter, which can lead to feather plucking. Never burn plastics or synthetics in your fireplace because the fumes could be toxic to your bird—and you.

Always make sure that you have a good working smoke/fire detector as well as a carbon monoxide detector. Not only could these save your bird's life, but they could save yours as well. It is also wise to invest in a fire extinguisher.

TOBACCO

If you are a smoker, do your bird (and family) a favor and smoke outside. They are just as prone to lung cancer as we are, if not more so. Also, make sure that you properly dispose of the cigarette or cigar butts because these will kill your bird. Ashtrays are available that close and lock. This is also true for marijuana; your bird can die from breathing in that smoke.

Lamps

Lamps are also dangerous to birds. Have you ever touched a lightbulb after it has been on for a while? It's hot! Some flighted parrots have landed on

Keep all electrical cords out of your parrot's reach or he may decide that they're good chew toys.

lampshades, and some have even misjudged their landing and fell on top of the lightbulb instead, severely burning themselves. The best way to prevent this is to clip the wings.

Electronics

As a general rule, keep your parrot away from all electrical devices. He is likely to chew these items, resulting in their destruction and injury to himself. Television remotes or remotes of any kind are also fun for a parrot to chew. If you don't like trying to figure out what button is what, keep the remote away from your bird.

Computers and parrots do not mix. My friend went through so many keyboards that she started buying them by the caseload. Finally, she ended up making a special keyboard for her grey, and everyone was happy. Her grey loved to pop the keys off the keyboard and then bite off the little prongs that would snap into place. As discussed earlier, keep all cords inside PVC pipes. Be aware that certain printers may be coated with Teflon to prevent sticking. Laser printers can heat up, especially when printing many pages, possibly releasing fumes.

Phones and phone cords are also a favorite item to chew. If you keep these out of reach, you will be fine. A parrot won't get electrocuted by biting into a phone cord, but you won't be able to make a call.

New Carpeting

When buying new carpeting, check with the manufacturer regarding its construction. Some carpeting can contain substances that can cause respiratory problems, not only in birds but also in humans. If possible, have the new carpeting aired out for several days before installing it. The padding should be made of natural fibers. You can ask that the carpeting be unrolled at the store and aired out for several days before you buy it. Explain that you have birds and that this needs to be done. Carpeting made from a low-volatile organic compound (VOC) material such as wool is safer than traditional carpeting

There have also been some problems with fabric protectors, such as Stainsafe. Some deaths have been associated with it even though it is supposed to be pet safe. If you are buying any furniture, check to see if it has been treated.

No Birds in Bed

Never sleep with your bird. Many parrots have been crushed to death by their owners. Always make sure that your bird is safely in his cage at night. Some birds have the habit of going under covers or even hiding in the laundry. To prevent accidents, you should always know where your bird is.

Kissing your bird on the beak isn't a good idea. He could get sick from the bacteria in your mouth.

Mousetraps and Flypaper

Glue-style mousetraps are very sticky and should be removed from your bird's area to prevent him from getting stuck on them. Flighted birds also run into another danger with flypaper, which should never be used near your bird. Not only can the bird fly into the paper, but he will get stuck like a fly. Birds can severely injure themselves trying to get off the flypaper, and the chemicals in it are toxic and will kill them if they ingest it. It's also difficult to remove the sticky stuff from their feathers. You will probably end up plucking many of these feathers, which is very painful to a bird. To prevent this, clip those wings. If your parrot should happen to get stuck to flypaper, take him to an avian veterinarian. It could be painful and very stressful to your bird to have this removed. The avian veterinarian will be able to do it with minimal pain or stress.

Temperature Issues

Although birds can withstand colder temperatures than we have given them credit for, drafts will make them ill. Check your windows and make sure that the weatherproofing seals are working correctly. Don't put your bird directly over the air vents or in front of the air conditioner. When we had a power outage in the Seattle area during the winter, it lasted a week. My house dropped to 50°F (10°C), and yet my birds did fine.

Cold tends not to bother parrots as much as heat does. Even though most parrots come from areas that are very warm, the trees shelter them from direct contact with the sun, and frequent showers cool them down. Never leave your bird directly in the sun. If it is very hot in your house, mist him often. Never leave him in the car, even if you have cracked the windows open.

Bird-Safe Products

I realize that the number of items that are toxic to your bird can be overwhelming. You may wonder what you can use to keep your bird safe.

Some of the best cleaners and odor fighters are the old-fashioned and inexpensive ones.

MULTI-PURPOSE CLEANERS

Baking soda can clean just about anything. You can use baking soda as an oven cleaner. Just spray your oven first with water and then sprinkle on the baking soda. You need to use a steel wool pad to finish scrubbing, along with a little elbow grease. It is great for sprinkling on your carpeting to remove odors. It can remove stains from carpeting too.

Baking soda is great for cleaning aluminum, chrome, plastic, silver, stainless steel, and even jewelry. Pour it down your drain to remove odors. It is great as toothpaste as well. It can also be used to put out fires! Try adding it to your bathwater for a nice relaxing soak, but don't take your bird with you into the tub.

Borax can be used to clean, disinfect, and deodorize many things. You can mix 1/2 cup (118.3 ml) of borax into 1 gallon (3.4 l) of hot water to make an all-purpose cleaner.

Vinegar can dissolve mineral deposits, remove soap scum, remove mildew, deodorize, and even remove wax buildup. Use it in coffeepots to remove the metallic taste, or use it in a water solution to shine windows. Clean linoleum floors with 1/2 cup (118.3 ml) of white vinegar mixed with 1 gallon (3.4 l) of hot water. White vinegar with salt is a great all-purpose cleaner.

Cornstarch is useful as a window cleaner, a furniture polish, and a shampoo for carpeting and rugs. You can even use it to starch clothes. For cleaning most surfaces, use a ratio of four parts water to one part cornstarch. For cleaning windows, use 1 ¼ cup (0.3 l) white vinegar, 1 quart (1.1 l) water and 1 tablespoon cornstarch. For shampooing your carpeting, mix together 1 cup (0.2 l) baking soda, 1 cup (0.2 l) cornstarch, and 1 teaspoon vinegar. Sprinkle this all over your carpet and let it sit overnight. The next morning, vacuum the carpeting. This will leave behind a fresh scent.

Grapefruit-seed extract is great for cleaning surfaces around the house. It can even be used to clean fruits and vegetables. You can most likely find it in health food stores.

Lemon juice can be used as a deodorant and

Poison Control

If you believe that your parrot has been poisoned by a plant or any other substance, you can call the ASPCA's emergency hotline at the numbers below. They do charge a fee but provide 24-hour access to information on what to do if your pet is poisoned.
The numbers are:
1-900-443-0000: This number bills directly to the caller's phone.
1-888-426-4435: This number bills to the caller's credit card.

Clipping your parrot's wings keeps him safe from many dangers, including escape and crashing into mirrors.

glass cleaner, and it can even remove stains from clothes, porcelain, and aluminum. Mixing lemon juice with white vinegar makes a good stovetop cleaner. You can make a great toilet bowl cleaner from baking soda and vinegar or borax and lemon juice.

DEODORIZERS

Want to remove odors from your house and make it smell great? Boil some cinnamon and cloves in a pan of water and your house will smell wonderful. Although many essential oils aren't safe to use around your bird, peppermint oil and lemon oil are safe.

If you have a lot of unpleasant odors in your house, try using dishes partially filled with vinegar to get rid of them. Just place these dishes around the house and the odor will disappear; the vinegar will absorb these odors and leave behind a more pleasant smell.

To get rid of odors from garbage cans, use 1/2 cup (118.3 ml) of borax in the bottom of either a garbage can or diaper pail. Along with preventing odors, this will stop mold and bacteria from growing.

CLEANING JEWELRY AND METALS

Have metals that need to be cleaned? Try using a solution of water mixed with some cream of tartar (potassium bitartrate) to clean anything aluminum. For brass, just dip a soft clean cloth into a mixture of lemon juice and baking soda and polish as usual. Baby oil or the shiny side of aluminum foil will polish chrome. If you need to clean copper, just place it in a pot of boiling water that had 1 tablespoon salt and 1 cup (236.6 ml) of vinegar added to it. You can clean gold and silver with toothpaste. Silver can also be polished by boiling it. First, line the pan with aluminum foil. Add some water and 1 teaspoon of salt and 1 teaspoon of baking soda. Place the silver in it and boil.

MISCELLANEOUS CLEANING

Castile soap is wonderful as a shampoo or body soap. This olive oil-based soap is very gentle. Want to use a bird-safe substitute for aftershave? Try using isopropyl alcohol.

Have problems with your drain? Instead of using toxic drain cleaner, try using 1/2 cup (118.3 ml) of baking soda, then add 1/2 cup (118.3 ml) of vinegar. Never do this if you tried using drain opener first because the chemical reaction can cause dangerous fumes.

For a floor cleaner, you can do the following: Just add a few drops of vinegar to clean water. If you want to make that vinyl or linoleum shine, add a capful of baby oil to the water. If you have brick or stone tiles, use 1 cup (236.6 ml) of white vinegar in the bucket of clean water. After you wash the floor with this, you will need to rinse again with plain clean water. Mineral oil and baby oil can be used as a furniture polish or as floor wax.

Windows and glass can be cleaned by the following: rub with newspaper, or you can use a vinegar and water solution, or lemon juice and water, or even cornstarch, vinegar, and water. Also, if you want to prevent streaks, don't wash the windows when it is sunny out.

DEALING WITH PESTS

Rid yourself of ants by sprinkling red chili powder, paprika, dried peppermint, or even borax where they are entering. Borax mixed with sugar

Zinc Dangers

Zinc is becoming one of the most commonly seen causes of toxicity among parrots today. Zinc toxicity causes gastrointestinal, kidney, liver, and pancreatic issues. Some signs of zinc toxicity are excess urine, weight loss, seizures, weakness, and feather plucking. If you suspect zinc toxicity, your veterinarian can do a blood test to check for this.

Zinc sources include padlocks, keys, nails, snaps on bird toys, quick links, plumbing nuts, staples, nuts on some animal carriers, some antirust paints, shampoo, and skin preparations. Zinc is sometimes used as a coating in iron and steel to prevent rusting. If you keep in mind that everything that is galvanized is zinc, you will be able to prevent problems. Use stainless steel or powder-coated items instead. If you aren't sure, ask the company that makes the item if it contains zinc. Most items for birds are zinc-free.

Good Parrotkeeping

will eliminate cockroaches and other insects as well.

Feeding your dog or cat brewer's yeast mixed into their food will prevent fleas. Fleas do not normally bother birds, but flea products certainly will.

For your garden, you can use pyrethrum to control pests. However, this is slightly toxic to aquatic life, so don't use around ponds with fish in them.

You can use sabadilla to control lice, leafhoppers, and other pests. It has a low toxicity rate to wildlife, but it may be toxic to bees. You can also buy soap-based garden insecticides, which are safe to use around other animals. Neem oil also seems to be safe for birds

Water

Fresh water is a necessity of life, and without it, no animal can survive. In your emergency kit, have water on hand before you need it. Make sure that you have enough to give to all of your birds. Not only will they need water for drinking, but you will need it to clean their food and water dishes. If it is hot out, you will also need water to mist your bird. Do not use your tap water until you are told it is safe to do so. After some disasters, the water supply can be contaminated for a time.

Filtered water removes many impurities, but it may not remove all of them. Check with the manufacturer as to what impurities the filter will remove and if the filtered water is safe to drink under the current conditions. Keep in mind that in some filtering systems, it takes twice as much water to produce 1 cup. If there are water restrictions, this could be a problem.

Disaster Preparedness

I have received numerous e-mails over the years about what to do to save pet birds when faced with a natural disaster. I hope that you never have to worry about this, but if you are faced with a natural disaster, these tips may save your bird's life.

Evacuating with your bird is a little different than with a dog or cat. Unlike evacuating with a dog, who you can put on a leash or into a carrier, you may have to use a towel to restrain your parrot to put him into a carrier. Because a bird relies on instinct, he is more likely to bite you or try to escape. Once you have him in his carrier, you can use the towel to cover the enclosure to help keep him calmer.

FOOD AND WATER

Food and water for a disaster must be properly packaged and stored. Keep a supply of bottled water on hand. Do not get anything that requires refrigeration or that needs to be kept in the freezer. In case of floods, waterproof containers are needed. Canned fruit, vegetables, and meats that do not require cooking are best. Make sure that the cans have pull-top lids, or keep a manual can opener handy—and ensure that everyone in the family knows how to use a manual opener. It may sound funny, but most of my kids' friends had no idea how to use one because they only used electric openers.

Seed or pellets need to be stored in airtight containers. Each time you get a new bag of seed or pellets, rotate it with the one in the airtight container.

146

Your bird's carrier should be ready to go at all times so that you won't have to waste time during an emergency.

This way you will always have fresh food on hand. Improperly stored food of any type can become a breeding ground for bacteria, fungi, and molds.

For baby birds you will need to have a hand-feeding formula with pure water and supplies in your emergency box.

POWER OUTAGES

The most common disaster is power outages due to wind storms, ice storms, or whatever Mother Nature decides to throw at us. Since you can't pick when these things occur, you must be prepared at all times.

Believe it or not, birds will do better with the cold rather than the heat. What seems to bother a parrot most is the darkness, especially if this happens in the winter. To make up for the lack of heat, keep three sides of the cage covered, and you may need to use warmer covers at night. Make sure that there is an opening so that air can get into his cage. Also, make sure that your bird is in his cage before it gets dark. You don't want him to get frightened and fly to the ground and get stepped on or even have him fly into something.

Disaster-Preparedness Kit for Bird Owners

Here is a list of items it is smart to have ready for an emergency. Remember to tailor your kit to the type of disasters your area is most likely to experience.

- battery-operated radio or television with extra batteries
- bird first-aid kit
- birdseed and pellets in airtight and waterproof containers
- bottled water enough for all of your birds
- can opener
- canned foods that don't have to be cooked
- emergency telephone numbers
- extra blankets in waterproof bags
- extra food dishes
- extra towels in waterproof bags
- extra water bottle
- flashlights with extra batteries
- snack foods
- spray bottle
- syringes for hand-feeding
- travel cage or carrier

Items especially for flood-prone areas include:

- extra empty gallon (3.8 l) milk jugs
- nylon rope
- inflatable rafts or pool toys that are big enough to hold a carrier

Make sure that your parrot is eating. It will be hard to feed him fresh fruits or veggies if you don't have power (you probably won't have refrigeration), but you might be able to feed dried fruits and veggies. You just need to add water to rehydrate.

If the power outage occurs during the summer and it is very hot out, mist your bird often to prevent heatstroke. You may need to give him extra liquid during this time. Apples and oranges can be kept out for a few days without refrigeration and are one way of getting some extra liquid into him.

Investing in a generator if you have many power failures will help. Generators cost anywhere from a few hundred dollars to several thousand dollars. They are a good investment. Before you need to use the generator, buy a ceramic space heater or other type of space heater. Remember that some space heaters have a nonstick coating on them. Take the heater outside and burn this off for a few hours before using it inside. The generator could also run a fan or air conditioner to help keep you cool in the summer months. But do not put your bird in front of them.

Never bring your barbeque grill or propane gas into your house. This will kill not only your bird but can kill your family as well. More people die from carbon monoxide poisoning than they do from the cold or other storm-related problems. Countless animals have also died.

If you can safely boil water on top of your grill, you can add dried fruits and veggies and reconstitute them and serve them warm for your bird. Do not put the barbeque grill too close to the house, however. The fumes from the grill could still kill your bird.

If you are thinking of going to a hotel, see if it will take pets. Many do, especially in emergency situations. If there are areas that have power, you can also check with your friends to see if they will take in your parrot.

FIRES

In certain areas, fires are always a threat. Wildfires, when they strike, move fast, and you have to react just as fast. Birds cannot tolerate smoke, and even a short duration of exposure may kill your parrot. Some symptoms of smoke inhalation include depression, refusal to eat, sitting on the bottom of the cage, and problems with breathing and the respiratory tract generally. If your bird was exposed to smoke and it is safe to do so, take him to an avian veterinarian right away.

The first rule is that if you can get your birds and yourself out safely, do so. Although it is hard for me to say, a human life is more important than the birds. A parrot is going to be frightened and may try to bite you as you are trying to save him. Always keep a large towel along with his carrier near his cage, but if you can't, you'll have to use something else, such as a pillowcase or burlap sack. You may have to grab your bird and just throw him in and then get out as quickly as you can. Make sure that there are some holes for him to breathe or he may suffocate. Remember that birds chew, and they may escape.

Parrots may scream, panic, and behave strangely shortly before bad storms, earthquakes, and similar events.

Breeders with outdoor aviaries are faced with another problem. They have to capture fully flighted birds. Also, they may have many birds they have to capture. Many breeders had to make the very difficult decision to open the cage doors so that their birds could escape rather than die in the fire. During the California wildfires of 2006, many breeders did just this. Although they lost several birds, they were also able to recapture others, mainly because they were microchipped.

If your parrot escapes, you may need a ladder to get him down from a tree.

FLOODS

Because most of us do not have an ark in our driveway, you need to have some supplies on hand to not only save yourself but maybe your parrot as well. Of course, the best plan is to get out before the flood hits. Follow any evacuation orders the authorities supply.

Floatation devices are necessary. You could use empty plastic gallon (3.8 l)jugs or even inflatable boats or pool toys to help keep you afloat. Bird carriers can even be rigged with plastic gallon (3.8 l)jugs to keep them afloat. Keep your disaster kit nearby so that you can grab it immediately. Jugs can be attached to this as well to keep it afloat.

When floods hit, they will hit quickly. Get to the highest point. Secure your family members and pets together with nylon rope so that you can all stay together. Remember, family first, then pets.

Keeping warm is a problem most of the time, as well as not having fresh, clean water. You should have warm blankets in your disaster kit that are kept in waterproof packaging. You will be able to keep your bird warm this way. Put any food in waterproof and airtight packaging.

Even though there is water all around, it isn't safe to drink. Make sure that you also have plenty of water for your birds, which includes for drinking and cleaning their dishes.

HURRICANES AND TORNADOS

With hurricanes, you usually have advanced warning so that you can prepare a disaster kit. With tornados, you never know where they will hit. When there is a warning about a tornado being likely, start preparing immediately.

The high winds in both a hurricane and tornado can leave behind an incredible path of destruction. Birds can sense these storms coming way before you can. Your parrot may start to thrash around or appear very nervous or jumpy. Talk to him as calmly as you can, which may help calm him down.

For hurricanes, board up all of the windows and secure your house as much as possible. Put away anything outdoors that can blow away or bang into your house. Not only will things banging into your house frighten you, but it will really scare your bird. Because high winds and rain occur, there is also a possibility of flooding as well. Have supplies handy in case a flood does occur. In addition to water, make sure that you have plenty of seed or pellets and treats for your bird.

When tornadoes occur, they strike quickly and move on. Windows need to be opened or they may implode. This will help equalize the pressure. Going to the basement or storm shelter is wisest, and bring your disaster-preparedness kit with you. Put your bird into his carrier and bring him into the basement with you. Do not leave him loose because he may panic during the storm and become injured or bite you. Bring a working radio or battery-operated television with you, as well as a flashlight.

People with outdoor aviaries should start to take precautions before hurricane season. Check the outdoor flights to determine how secure they are. Bolting down the flights to concrete bases may help.

EARTHQUAKES

Earthquakes are unpredictable. However, many pets, especially birds, may be able to predict these quakes. During Portland's Spring Break Quake, my cockatoo, Toby, started screaming at the top of her lungs at 4:30 in the morning while things were still dark out. It took me 20 minutes to calm her down. She was terrified and frantic. Ten minutes after I finally calmed her down, I heard the rumbling and felt things shaking. I checked on my kids first, who slept through it, and then my birds. Several of them had broken blood feathers due to the fact that they all thrashed around during the quake. My Amazon was the only one unfazed by it all—he seemed more upset that I woke him than from the quake.

A panic reaction is normal for birds. Calm your parrot down as best as you can. If he has broken a blood feather, take care of that as soon as possible (See Chapter 7). Birds can't afford to lose a lot of blood. Remember that with earthquakes there will be aftershocks afterward, and your bird may react to them each time.

Check for gas leaks, and turn off the gas if there is one. Check for other damage next. Get out of the house if it appears unsafe. Keep your bird in his carrier. If there are trees nearby, make sure that they are sturdy and won't fall on your house. Bring your disaster-preparedness kit with you. Do not use tap water until it is safe to do so, and make sure that you know where your water shut-off valve is. Remember that water lines may break during quakes.

Remember, things fall during quakes and aftershocks. If you live in an area where there are quakes, do not put your bird's cage directly under anything that may fall, including pictures, lamps, mirrors, etc. Secure tall furniture to the walls for extra safety. For cabinets, use childproof locks to help keep them from opening up and dumping their contents all over.

If your bird's cage has wheels, it may move during a quake. Place blocks of wood or cement under the wheels to prevent it from rolling. Also, keep your bird away from windows, which may shatter, and for safety, close the curtains or shades. If the window does shatter, this will prevent the glass from flying everywhere.

What to Do if Your Bird Gets Lost

It's summer and very hot outside. To cope with the heat, you open the windows and doors. Your bird is out and playing on the top of his cage. Suddenly he takes off and flies through the open door or window, perhaps right through the screen. His wings are unclipped, and he has flown out of your sight before you could react. This unfortunately is a common scenario. Each year thousands of birds escape, and only a lucky few are recovered.

What can you do to recover your little feathered friend? Here are some steps to take.

1. Keep calling to him, and if you see him, try to coax him down with a favorite treat or toy.
2. If your parrot is in a tree, you can climb on a ladder and then use a long dowel or toy ladder for him step up on. This is where that step up command comes in handy. (See Chapter 8:Taming and Training)
3. Place your bird's cage outside with his favorite food and toys in and around it. If weather permits, place a securely caged "bait bird" in

another cage right next to the other cage. The bait bird's chirps may call the escaped bird back. This works best if they are friends or mates. (Make sure that the bait bird isn't exposed to direct sunlight or the heat/cold. You want to keep him safe.)

4. Prior to losing any bird, make a recording of his voice. This tape will allow you to place it on a continually running tape, which may work to get your bird home. If you don't want to place the bait bird outside, you could also make a recording of this bird's voice.

5. Stay close by the outside cage when you do either Step 3 or Step 4. This way, if your bird does come back, you will be able to get him in the cage once again.

Always travel with your bird in a carrier or travel cage; it's dangerous to let him loose in the car.

6. Have your family and friends walk around the neighborhood calling to your bird.

7. Contact your neighbors, and have them keep an eye open as well. Leave your home telephone number, as well as your work and/or cell number.

8. Post signs throughout the neighborhood. These signs should have a photo of your bird, his name, your name, and telephone numbers. If you don't have a photo of him, find a photo that looks like your bird. Go to several different neighborhoods. Remember that birds can fly miles (km) away from home.

9. Contact the humane societies, local animal shelters, the Audubon Society, etc. Many people who find a lost bird will bring him to an animal shelter or group.

10. Contact different veterinarians in the area and let them know that you are looking for your bird.

11. Call the radio stations. In some areas, radio stations will announce a lost pet on the air.

12. Place notices in supermarkets, convenience stores, hardware stores, etc. Place notices at many different places where a lot of people can see them.

13. Contact your local bird clubs, which can alert members about your lost bird. They have a great network for contacting many people. There are now Internet forums for lost birds, and these can mobilize many bird lovers to help you.
14. Contact local churches, youth groups, rotary clubs, or any place where a large group of people congregate.
15. Put ads in the local papers with a brief description of your bird, but don't just mention the species. Most people wouldn't know the difference between a cockatiel and a cockatoo.
16. Don't give up hope. Birds have been returned to their owners months or even years after they were lost. This has happened when the bird had been microchipped prior to escaping.
17. When someone calls to let you know that they have seen your bird, write down as much information as you can. Find out where the person may have seen your bird.
18. Offer a reward. Money always seems to make people look harder.

If your bird escapes, try luring him down to you with some of his favorite treats.

PREVENTING BIRD LOSS

It is far easier and less stressful to prevent your bird from escaping than it is to find him after the fact. The best way to prevent this is to clip his wings and check them often. Remember, feathers will grow back, so you must check them. If you leave your bird's wings unclipped, you should probably not take him outside.

Microchipping is a must. If your bird escapes or is stolen, there is no other way to absolutely prove that he is yours. Anyone can claim that the bird is theirs. Many veterinarians now routinely scan animals to see if they are microchipped. Because of this, many owners have been reunited with their birds. (See Chapter 7: Avian Health for more information on this topic.)

Traveling With Your Bird

Whenever you take a trip with your bird, he must be as safe as you would keep your kids. Some type of carrier or cage is needed. Pet kennels with a fixed perch are the best means of transporting your bird safely.

TRAVELING KITS

If you travel with your bird, bring along enough food and water for your trip. Grapes, oranges, and apples are good snacks to bring along because they are high in water content, as is watermelon. Because it may be difficult to give your bird water in the car without it spilling all over the place, these fruits are an excellent option. Bring along a cooler with ice in it to keep the fruits fresh.

You should also bring along a first-aid kit for your bird, including a towel. (See Chapter 7: Avian Health.) This is especially true if you are going on long trips. Accidents can happen, and it is wisest to be prepared.

TRAVELING BY PLANE

Airlines usually require health certificates for any animal that is traveling, whether it goes on the plane with you or into the cargo hold. Some airlines will allow you to bring your bird on the plane as long as the carrier will fit under the seat. Airlines usually only allow one pet in a section, and there is a fee, which varies among airlines. You need to have a special ticket for your bird if you plan to take him on the plane with you.

If your bird is going into cargo, provide extra fruits, especially those high in water content. Remember, flights can be delayed, so extra food and water may be needed.

I also recommend making sure that your bird's wings are clipped. If he escapes, he won't be able to go too far. Fully flighted birds have been known to escape.

Remember, you need to bring along food, water, something with which to cover the carrier, and a favorite toy, etc. If you plan to stay in a hotel, you may need a travel cage (one that collapses) or a stand of some kind, perches, food cups, and whatever else your bird likes.

TRAVELING BY CAR

Most parrots like to go in the car and see new places. Others don't. If you have one who doesn't like to travel, car travel will be too stressful for him. Find a way to leave him behind with someone to take care of him.

A loose bird in the car is an accident waiting to happen. This is because a loose bird can jump down under the driver's feet, under the brake pedal or accelerator. A startled or frightened bird may grab for anything handy, whether it be the seat, your arm, or your ear. If you slam on the brakes, he could go smashing into the windshield and get seriously injured. A bird who is secured safely in a pet kennel will be safe from these possibilities. If you love your bird, keep him safe.

When traveling with a bird, you'll need to make extra stops along the way. Some parrots will not mess up their carriers with droppings and will need to be taken out to go poop. It isn't fair to keep him in the carrier for hours on end. Let him get out to stretch his wings, so to speak. This will mean extra time along the way, so schedule in these extra stops and add time for all of the people who will be coming over to check out your bird. Most importantly, make sure that your bird's wings are clipped so that he can't fly away.

If you plan to travel far, you may need to stay at hotels along the way. Some will take pets and others won't. Call ahead so that you won't run into any unpleasant surprises.

Never leave the bird in a locked car in the summer, even if you leave the windows cracked open. Birds cannot sweat, and they become overheated easily, which can lead to death. If you must take your bird with you when you go shopping or to the store, try going early in the morning and just for a short time. Mornings are usually cooler. If you go out to eat, bring your food to the car and eat it there. Open all of the windows or doors, and park in the shade to keep things cooler. When you go for lunch or dinner, park the car in a shaded area. Because fast food is the norm on road trips, eat your meal in the car with

Buy the sturdiest carrier you can find. Parrots have been known to chew through thier carriers.

156

Helpful Hints for Traveling With Your Bird

- Make sure that your bird's wings are clipped before going anywhere.
- Get your bird used to traveling in the carrier before taking any trips. Try taking shorter ones first.
- If you are traveling out of state, know the state laws. Certain states have laws concerning bringing birds or certain bird species into the state.
- Make sure that you have a health certificate for your bird before you travel. Some states may need this. Airlines usually require this as well.
- Check with hotels or the people you are staying with, letting them know that you are bringing a bird along. Make arrangements as early as possible.
- Plan ahead if traveling by car, and make frequent stops.
- Bring along your bird's favorite toys and sleeping hut. This will help ease some stress.
- Bring along either a collapsible travel cage or a collapsible stand.
- If you are keeping your bird in a travel cage while traveling, remove all toys and swings. These can injure him because they do move all around. Just put them back when the car isn't moving.
- Don't forget the first-aid kit.
- If you plan to stay more than a day or two, find the telephone number of a veterinarian close by in case of an emergency. Have the number of your regular veterinarian as well.
- Never leave your bird unattended.
- Avoid large crowds unless your bird enjoys them and loves to show off.
- If you plan to visit places on your trip, such as large theme parks, make sure that they have facilities that will take your bird.
- Bring along plenty of supplies (extra dishes and water bottles, newspaper for around the cage and inside, cage cover, towels, etc.).
- Bring along some cooking mixes that only require you to add hot water. Some motels have microwaves in the room that you can use as well, but all motels have coffeemakers that you can use for heating water. If you have a baby bird, bring along enough hand-feeding formula and supplies
- Spend extra time with your bird reassuring him. This will help relax him.

your bird with all of the windows or doors open.

If you plan to travel with your bird during the winter, warm your car up before bringing him inside the vehicle. This is especially true if you are taking a sick bird to the vet.

HOTEL ARRANGEMENTS

Make any hotel arrangements well ahead of time. Ask if there is a fee to keep your parrot in the room. Some hotels will charge and others won't.

Let the housekeepers know that you have a bird in your room. Explain that certain cleaning agents shouldn't be used near him. To make things easier on the staff, try to either be there when the staff is cleaning or remove your bird from the room before it's cleaned. Remember, some people are afraid of birds, or your bird could be afraid of the housekeepers.

Try keeping things as clean as possible so that the staff doesn't have a lot of extra work. Bring along one of those small handheld vacuums to clean up. Put newspapers under the cage to catch seed or pellets and droppings. Some hotels have stopped taking pets because of the mess.

What about meals? Room service or bringing something into your room to eat is the best option. This way, your bird doesn't have to be in a strange place alone. When my family went on a trip, we took my macaw, Tiny. Because we kept things nice in our room when we called for room service, they would put extra fruits and veggies in our order just for Tiny.

Bring along either a stand or a collapsible cage, and don't forget the toys, perches, and whatever else your bird usually uses. Having at least one or two familiar things could reduce his stress levels.

Motion Sickness

Yes, parrots can get carsick or airsick, just like people do. Some birds may do fine until stressed. My macaw gets carsick every time we go to the vet, but when we travel to places other than the vet, he is fine.

If motion sickness is a problem, talk to your avian veterinarian and see if she can give your bird something that will help. Never give your bird anything unless your avian veterinarian tells you that you can.

Traveling Without Your Bird

If your bird doesn't travel well or is high strung, it may be best to leave him home. However, it is important that you find someone who can take care of him while you are gone.

Never leave your bird home alone with what you think is enough food and water. Accidents happen, and many owners have come home to find that their birds have starved to death or died from thirst.

PET SITTING

If you are hiring a pet sitter, check out her references first and make sure that she has had experience with birds. Keep a list of your bird's idiosyncrasies and

A play stand that collapes or comes apart easily is handy to have when traveling with your parrot.

habits, and mention things such as your bird is afraid of red or of carrots or whatever it is that sets him off.

Have the pet sitter come for early visits so that she will get used to your bird and so that he can become acquainted with her. Show the sitter the proper way to handle your parrot (if your bird does go to other people).

Make enough treats and freeze them so that all the sitter has to do is warm them up. Give her some money for fresh fruits and veggies, letting her know what your bird enjoys, and ask for the receipt. Let her know that these food items need to be removed after a few hours.

Let your avian veterinarian know that you are going on a trip and that you will have a sitter for your bird. You may need to fill out some forms, including ones indicating financial responsibility.

If you have more than one bird, place name tags on the cages (where they won't be chewed off). Have a profile and care instructions on each bird, and keep them near their cages. Have an extra copy that you give to your caretaker. Make sure that you have clear and concise instructions and that the sitter understands them.

If you are going to have a friend come to your house to take care of your birds, she must also know and understand all of these instructions. If you are lucky, you will have a friend who is also a bird owner.

BOARDING YOUR BIRD

If you can't find a sitter or don't want to have one come to your house, boarding your bird is another option. There are several possible places to board a parrot, each with its pros and cons.

THE VET'S OFFICE

Many avian veterinarians have boarding facilities available. Make sure that these facilities are separate from where sick birds are housed. If not, you should probably look elsewhere for boarding. Check to see if they provide food, and if so, what kind. Your bird will be under stress from being away from home, so changing his diet at this time isn't wise.

Provide your vet with a list of your bird's likes and dislikes. Give her information about your bird. Bring along treats, and see if the staff can give your bird fresh fruits and veggies. You may be able to bring some frozen things along so that the staff can just heat them up and give them to him.

Some vets will have cages for the birds, and others want you to bring a cage. Bring along your bird's favorite toys and sleeping hut.

THE PET STORE

Many pet stores offer boarding, but you need to check the ones in your area thoroughly. Make sure that the store is clean and that the birds are free of diseases. Watch how the staff interacts with the birds. The birds should not be kept on the main floor where customers can poke at them or annoy them. Remember, your bird will be under stress as it is. Also, check out the store's security. You don't want someone to walk off with your bird.

It's a good idea to have your sitter over to meet your parrot before you go away.

Leave the same instructions and lists of what your bird likes and dislikes as you would at the vet or with the sitter. Bring along your bird's toys, sleeping hut, and food (if the store gives a different type). Check with the store to see if it feeds fruits and veggies.

Bring your bird in a few times to get used to the staff and so that they will get used to him. See how your bird reacts. If the store stresses him too much, you may need to make different arrangements.

Also, make sure that the store doesn't have snakes. Most snakes will eat birds and are escape artists. This is a disaster that can be easily prevented.

A FRIEND'S HOUSE

Besides having a friend come to your house to pet sit your bird, bringing your bird to your friend's place is the next best thing, especially if she is a bird owner as well. Your friend probably already knows all about your bird, but it is still best to leave instructions and info with her.

Helpful Hints for Dealing With Pet Sitters

1. Leave clear written instructions, and make sure that they are understood.
2. Place name tags on each cage, and if there is more than one bird in the cage, add a description of each bird.
3. Give information on each bird: their likes, dislikes, fears, etc.
4. Prepare the goodies your bird enjoys ahead of time, and freeze them in daily portions.
5. Go over basic birdie first aid, particularly concerning blood feathers and how to recognize a sick bird or injury.
6. Leave the number of your avian veterinarian, as well as other bird-owning friends, and leave a number where you can be reached.
7. Leave all supplies for your bird in one easy-to-reach area so that your caretaker doesn't have to be searching all over for a specific item.
8. If your bird is an escape artist, padlock any area where he may escape. Leave extra keys with the caretaker as well, and keep an extra set with the supplies.
9. If you are leaving your bird at a pet store, padlock the cage for extra security, but leave two sets of keys with the store.
10. Leave extra money for fresh fruits and veggies, and get a receipt.
11. Tipping a sitter is never a bad idea.

Chapter Five

DIET AND NUTRITION

Poor nutrition is the number-one cause of illness and early death among pet birds today. Birds need more than just seed alone. In a study of nutrition using budgies, it was found that the budgies who were fed a seed-only diet lived an average of three to five years. The budgies fed pellets, fruits, vegetables, grains, and other healthy foods lived an average of 10 to 15 years—three times as long!

Parrots need a varied and complete diet that includes pellets, seeds, grains, fruits, and vegetables.

The Problem With Seed

Most types of parrots feed on a wide range of foods in nature. Although seed is a part of the natural diet, for most species it does not make up even half of the foods they consume. Wild parrots of most species feed on leaves, stems, shoots, vines, fruits, vegetables, flowers, seed, insects, and insect larvae. Once a parrot is in captivity, his dietary needs don't change. Asking him to adapt to an all-seed diet makes as much sense as asking you to do the same.

Why are so many birds "seed junkies?" Fat is the strongest stimulus for avian taste buds. Seed diets are oil rich and high in fat, so birds like to eat them. Amazons, budgies, rose-breasted cockatoos, and other species can become obese because of this type of diet, which can lead to fatty liver disease. Baby cockatoos can even develop pancreatitis due to the high fat in some diets. These high-fat diets have also caused hardening of the arteries in Amazons. Additionally, seed is low in many vitamins and minerals, so feeding an all-seed or mostly seed diet often results in deficiencies.

Appropriate Sizes of Seeds and Pellets for Parrots

Species	Feed Seed Labeled For:	Feed Pellets Labeled as:
African Grey	Large Hookbill	Medium
Amazon Parrots	Large Hookbill	Medium
Bourke's Parakeet	Budgie or Small Hookbill	Mini
Brotogeris	Small Hookbill	Crumble to Mini
Budgie	Budgie or Parakeet	Crumble or Budgie
Caiques	Large Hookbill	Small to Medium
Cockatiel	Small Hookbill	Mini
Cockatoos	Large Hookbill	Medium to Large
Conures, Large	Large Hookbill	Medium
Conures, Medium	Large Hookbill	Small to Medium
Conures, Small	Small or Large Hookbill	Mini to Small
Eclectus	Large Hookbill	Medium
Hawk-Headed Parrot	Large Hookbill	Medium
Kakarikis	Small Hookbill	Crumble or Mini
Lineolated Parakeet	Parakeet or Small Hookbill	Mini
Lories and Lorikeets	None	None
Lovebird	Small Hookbill	Mini
Macaws, Large	Large Hookbill to Macaw	Large
Macaws, Mini	Large Hookbill	Small to Medium
Parrotlet	Parakeet or Small Hookbill	Crumble
Pionus	Large Hookbill	Medium
Quaker Parrot	Large Hookbill	Small to Medium
Ring-Necked Parakeet and Other Psittacula	Large Hookbill	Small to Medium
Rock Pebbler	Large Hookbill	Small to Medium
Senegal and other Poicephalus	Large Hookbill	Small to Medium

In this table, "crumble" means that the pellets will need to be crushed somewhat for this species.

Selecting Seed and Pellets

What seed or pellet is right for your bird? When you buy your bird, ask the breeder or pet store what seed or pellet your parrot is currently eating. Start with that type and gradually change it if you desire

Size is an important quality to consider. Different manufacturers of seed and pellets vary in how they rate the size of their product. Some pellets will be labeled medium and may be intended for birds the size of a Quaker parrot, but another manufacture's medium may be for a cockatiel. Look at the product first and see if it is right for your bird. Read the information on the bag as well because it may list the species for which the seed or pellets are intended.

Look at the protein count in the pellets. If the protein is in the 25 percent or higher

Some parrots are hesitant to try new foods. Be persistent and he will try the item eventually.

range, it may be too high for your bird. Look for more natural ingredients, not those that are chemical based. Also, make sure that your bird will eat it. Some pellets have dyes in them to add color. Talk to your avian veterinarian to find out which pellet she recommends.

CONVERTING YOUR BIRD TO A PELLETED DIET

So how do you switch your bird over to pellets instead of seed? Slowly! Don't cut the seed out cold turkey because some birds will just refuse to eat. Instead, start mixing a little bit of the pellets into the seed. You can also sprinkle pellets on top of your bird's favorite wet food or even put them inside muffins that you make for him. Once you see him eating some of the pellets, start removing more and more of the seed, replacing it with the pellets instead. Eventually you will have all pellets. This could take a month or more, depending on how stubborn your bird is.

Supplements

Are vitamins and minerals necessary? If your bird is receiving a healthy and balanced diet, you probably don't need to add extra supplements and can actually cause problems by giving too much. Check with your avian veterinarian before you add any supplements. Supplements such as spirulina algae, wheat grass, and nutritional yeast are safe to use. Sprinkle these on top of wet foods.

Some Dietary Problems

Vitamin and mineral deficiencies are common in some parrot species. Eclectus and Amazons may require diets higher in vitamin A. Eclectus also have a tendency to develop deficiencies in vitamin E. Another common problem is calcium deficiency, especially in African greys and in egg-laying hens. Lories and lorikeets are prone to food poisoning because their liquid diet can spoil rapidly in hot weather. Diets that are too high in protein, such as some pelleted diets, can cause kidney-related problems such as gout in macaws and conures.

FOOD ALLERGIES

Like humans, birds can develop allergies to certain foods. When birds eat something they are allergic to, they can react in several ways. Some birds will start plucking their feathers, while others may have a change in behavior. These changes could be subtle or very noticeable. Some birds become very quiet, while others scream. Some may stop playing with their toys, and others suddenly become hyper and aggressive. It will vary greatly among individuals. Food allergies are rarer in birds than in humans, and most birds never develop a problem.

What foods are the most likely to cause problems? Those that contain dyes are probably the most common source of allergies. Many foods use sulfites as a preservative, and birds can be allergic to this as well. Feed organic foods instead because they do not use any sulfites or dyes. Pellets are made either from a corn or wheat base, and some birds can be allergic to this as well. Using a high-quality pellet or seed mixes is best because they only use human-grade ingredients; many of these are also organic.

Old Seed

Old seed can contain certain fungi, which produce toxins lethal to birds. When buying seed, buy a small amount at a time and then freeze the rest. This will also cut down on seed moths. When you buy seed from a new source, sprout some. If most of it sprouts, it is fresh; if very little does, it's old and you should find a new source for your birdseed.

Introducing New Foods

How do you get your bird to start eating new food items? This is usually not a problem if you bought him as a baby and he was taught to eat new things right from the beginning. But if you have a bird who wasn't

Bird shish kebabs turn food into a toy, encouraging your parrot to try new foods.

hand-fed or who just doesn't like to try new things, don't worry—there are many ways you can get him to eat.

The key to getting your bird to try new things is to keep offering those items. Don't give up after you offer them once or twice—it could take a long time before your parrot decides to sample something new. Like kids, birds can be stubborn about trying new things. Be patient and just keep trying.

My favorite method is trickery. For example, let's say that I just made macaroni and cheese for my parrot. I will take his favorite seed, pellets, or even chopped-up nuts and cover the top of the macaroni and cheese with that, but I push it down slightly. This way when he goes for that favorite nut, seed, or pellet, he has to get some of the macaroni and cheese with it. Eventually, I add less and less of the seed, nuts, or pellets until all I am left with is the macaroni and cheese. This method works for almost all kinds of food except for dry items. These I just mix together, and my parrot eventually ends up tasting the dry treat.

Sometimes offering your bird new food in a familiar surrounding will get him to eat it. Some birds do not like to try new things when in a noisy and a chaotic environment. Turn off the television or radio and get your family to quiet down, and see if that will help your picky eater.

A friend of mine gets her birds to eat new foods by eating with them. She likes to experiment with healthy cooking, so whenever she makes something new, she will eat with the birds just to get them to try it as well.

If you have other birds at home and they eat everything, they may be able to teach the stubborn one to accept new foods. When I was given an older cockatiel whom nobody wanted, he would only eat seed. So I put him in with the other cockatiels, who would pounce on the new foods like they were starving. It took only two days before he too was eating everything.

Most pet stores have bird-specific food hangers, which are like shish kebab holders. The hangers make a bird's food into a toy. Try putting grapes, melons, cut-up veggies, or other items you want your parrot to eat on that.

Another treat that may get a parrot to start eating better is a pine cone smeared with nut butter and then rolled in nuts, seed, or pellets. In your food processor try making fresh almond butter or even walnut butter—any nut can be used to make nut butter. Remember that peanut butter isn't the only nut butter out there.

How to Prepare Food

You will need to prepare foods differently for different species. Large vegetables such as broccoli or cauliflower need to be cut into small pieces for smaller birds, medium-sized pieces for medium-sized birds, and larger-sized pieces for larger birds. Size really does matter when you are feeding your parrot. Carrots could be shredded and fed to smaller birds, cut into quarters for medium birds, and cut into disks for larger birds. The same holds true for other vegetables and fruits. Use common sense as your guide to the size of food you should be offering.

If your bird is fussy about eating vegetables, try putting them in a food processor and pureeing them. Serve the puree warm. This is a good way to get your bird to eat several different veggies. I put spinach, carrots, broccoli, cauliflower, cooked yams, celery, dandelion greens, and kale into a food processor and puree them. Then I pop the mixture into the microwave to warm it up before I serve it—remember to check the temperature to keep from burning your parrot. You can use whatever veggies you want. This is also good if your bird has a vitamin-A deficiency because you could put veggies in that are higher in vitamin A, such as carrots, sweet potatoes, and leafy greens.

Mashes are also good for your bird, and many enjoy a nice warm mash. For mashes I not only use veggies but also cooked beans and brown rice. I generally get the 15-bean soup mix and cook the beans until they are soft.

Cooking for Your Bird

Yes, I admit it, I cook for my birds. I make them all kinds of wonderful treats. In fact, my birds eat healthier than my own family does. Parrots enjoy a wide variety of foods, and they should receive it daily. Offer fruits; vegetables; grains, such as cereals, pasta, rice, oatmeal, and barley; and beans and other legumes.

There are some wonderful mixes on the market today, so all you need to do is add water and cook. Some are better than others, so read the labels. When you make the cooked mixes, serve them warm, not hot. Make sure that you stir them thoroughly so that there are no hot spots. This is true especially if you use a microwave to cook them. Birds enjoy warm foods, but if they are too hot they run the risk of crop burn. This is especially true with baby birds.

After cooking, I use my food processor and chop them until the mixture has a mushy quality to it. My birds just love this, and they get almost as excited as they do with the pureed veggies.

Fruits can also be put into the food processor and pureed. During the summer, my birds feed on pureed fruits in ice cube-sized popsicles. My macaw picks the ice cube up in his beak, tilts his head back, and lets the ice cube melt while it drips back into his throat. My other birds usually just lick it with their tongues.

Be creative when serving food to your bird. Some like to eat it while it hangs on a shish kebab holder; some like leafy greens clipped to the sides of the cage. They think of food more like a toy that way.

Good Parrot Foods

Obviously, no book can cover every conceivable food that you can feed a parrot. Here is a thorough although not exhaustive discussion of good foods for parrots. Remember to feed the widest variety of items that you possibly can.

Smear a pine cone with any kind of nut butter to make a tasty and fun treat for your parrot.

Many birds enjoy oatmeal, Cream of Wheat, and other warm, whole-grain cereals.

GRAIN PRODUCTS

Whole grains and whole-grain products provide proteins, carbohydrates, and various vitamins and minerals. Whole-grain breads, muffins, and other products are much more nutritious than white varieties. If you have a bread maker, try using different grains such as rice flour, rye flour, corn flour, or graham flour. You can even freeze muffins or breads and take out what you need for the day. All grains and beans should be washed thoroughly and then cooked.

Pancakes, waffles, and crepes are very good as well. Try adding fresh ingredients in them, such as blueberries, strawberries, or even cranberries. Chop up some nuts and add those for a special treat.

Here are some other good choices, remembering that whole-grain varieties of these products are best:

- buckwheat and kasha
- Cream of Wheat (and rice)
- low-salt bagels
- low-salt or no-salt crackers
- low-salt or no-salt pretzels
- low-sugar cereals (such as Cheerios, Life, Chex, Kix, etc.)

- matzo
- melba toast
- noodles and pasta, including spaghetti, ravioli, macaroni, etc.
- oatmeal
- pearl barley
- quinoa
- rice (use brown, wild, or other varieties)
- tortillas
- triticale
- wheat berries

VEGETABLES

Most vegetables are best served cooked, but things like baby corn, corn on the cob, and peppers can also be served raw. Always wash vegetables thoroughly before giving them to your bird, and chop them into pieces of the appropriate size.

You can use canned or frozen mixed vegetables, as well as freshly cooked ones. When using any packaged vegetables, use those with no added salt.

Many excellent vegetables for parrots are listed below. Notes on nutritional content appear after some entries.

- alfalfa sprouts (you can sprout your own)
- asparagus, especially the tips (cooked)
- arugula
- baby corn
- bamboo shoots
- banana peppers
- beans, such as green, pole, wax, pinto, kidney, navy, garbanzo, mung, butter, haricot, adzuki, soy, and others (high in various minerals, vitamins, and fiber) (cooked)
- bean sprouts
- beets and beet greens (very high in vitamin A)
- bell peppers
- bok choy
- broccoli (good source of vitamin A)
- broccoliflower
- brussels sprouts (feed in moderation because could cause thyroid problems if overfed)
- cabbage
- carrots, including the tops (good source of vitamin A)
- cauliflower
- cayenne (contains capsicum, which is good for the digestion; a good source of vitamin A)
- celery
- chard

The Onion Controversy

There are two schools of thought regarding onions. Some people say that you shouldn't feed them to birds at all, while others say that onions are fine to feed to parrots. The issue is that onions contain oxalates, which inhibit calcium absorption. I use onions in some of the dishes I make my birds but only very sparingly and always well cooked. There is a similar controversy in the bird hobby regarding mushrooms.

- chayote
- chicory (high in vitamin A)
- cherry pepper
- chickweed (good source of vitamin A)
- chili peppers (high in vitamins A and C)
- cilantro
- collard greens (good source of vitamin A, calcium, and iron)
- corn
- comfrey
- cucumbers
- dandelion greens (rich in vitamin A and calcium)
- daikon (radish)
- eggplant (cooked and ripe only)
- endive (good source of vitamin A)
- garlic (has antibiotic and antitumor properties; stimulates the immune system and kills parasites; helps to eliminate lead, zinc, and other toxins in the body)
- ginger root
- Indian corn
- jalapeño peppers
- Japanese eggplant (cooked only)
- jicama
- kai-lan (also known as Chinese broccoli or Chinese kale)
- kale (good source of vitamin A)
- kohlrabi
- leeks
- lettuce
- lentils (cooked)
- luffa (also known as Chinese okra;

Like many parrots, this black-capped conure enjoys hot peppers.

cooked)
- mushrooms (cooked only and fed with other foods)
- mustard greens
- okra
- onions (cooked only)
- parsley (high is vitamin A; good for the immune system)
- peas such as green, sugar snap, snow, etc.
- peppers (red, green, yellow, jalapeño, serrano, poblano, chili, etc)
- potatoes (cooked, baked is best)
- pumpkins and seeds (cooked) (Canned pumpkin contains the highest amount of vitamin A of all vegetables)
- radishes
- soybeans
- spinach (in moderation because it can bind up calcium; high in vitamin A; frozen spinach has a higher amount of vitamin A than fresh)
- sprouts
- squashes, such as butternut, acorn, hubbard and others (good source of vitamin A)
- sweet potatoes (good source of vitamin A; feed cooked only)
- Thai pepper (also called bird pepper)
- tomatoes (good source of vitamins A and C; you can use low-sodium tomato paste and canned tomatoes)
- turnip greens (good source of vitamin A and calcium)
- watercress (helps aid the kidneys and is high in vitamin A)
- yams (good source of vitamin A; do not feed raw)
- zucchini

The Parrot Garden

At the start of the summer, I plant my own garden. I never use any pesticides because the veggies in my garden are mainly for my birds.

When I plan out the garden, I include plants that are my birds' favorites, as well as those that are the healthiest to feed them. I plant a wide variety of peppers, especially hot peppers. Broccoli, cauliflower, carrots, spinach, kale, squash, pumpkins, watermelon, other melons, sugar snap peas, beans, and tomatoes are all excellent choices for a parrot garden. Don't forget to include some edible flowers. Marigolds, nasturtiums, roses, lavender, and honeysuckle are all bird-safe flowers.

For a special treat, plant a sunflower or two. I have even planted some apple, pear, and Asian pear trees in my backyard. I also have a walnut tree that will hopefully start producing some nuts in the next year. In addition, I have blueberry bushes, raspberries, blackberries, kiwi, and grapes that I grow for my birds. *Never use any pesticides in your garden, and wash everything thoroughly before using.*

FRUITS

Fruits usually have a higher water content than vegetables do. This may mean that your bird's droppings may be more watery than normal after feeding fruits. Parrots usually do not eat the fruit skins, so peel them off first; otherwise, they will be flung all over the place. Always thoroughly wash any fruit before giving it to your bird.

Below you will find many fruits you can feed your parrot with nutritional notes on some varieties:

- apples (all varieties, with the seeds and stem removed)
- apricots (no pits and the area around the pit removed; dried, unsweetened apricots have the highest vitamin A content of all fruits)
- bananas (remove the peel; good source of potassium)
- blackberries
- blueberries
- cactus fruit (prickly pear)
- Canary Island melon (no rinds)
- cantaloupe (no rinds)
- casaba melon (no rinds)
- cherimoya
- cherries (no pits)
- clementine oranges
- coconuts
- coquitos (mini coconuts)
- cranberries
- crenshaw melon (no rinds)
- currants
- dates
- figs
- grapes, such as red, green, black, etc. (help the kidneys by decreasing

Avoid fruit pits, as well as the flesh right around the pit. Have you ever noticed how the flesh right around the pit is discolored? This discoloration is the toxin in the pit bleeding into the flesh. The pits from certain fruits, such as peaches, contain cyanide. Even in minute amounts this can and will kill your bird. Cut away from this area and make sure that there is no discoloration in the flesh of the fruit you're feeding.

the acidity of urine)
- grapefruit
- guavas
- honeydew (no rinds)
- horned melon (no rinds)
- juan melon
- kiwis
- kumquats
- lychee
- lemons
- loquat
- Mandarin oranges
- mangoes
- nectarines (no pits, and remove the area near the pit as well)
- oranges (good source of vitamin C; frozen, undiluted concentrate can be used for cooking because it contains a high amount of potassium as well as vitamin C)
- papaya (helps aid in digestion)
- passion fruit
- peaches (no pits or area near pit;

dried are higher in vitamin A)

- pears (no seeds)
- pepino melons
- pineapple (good for digestion)
- plantains (good source of vitamins A and C)
- plums (no pits)
- prunes (may cause watery droppings; do not use area around the pits)
- pomegranates (good for the kidneys)
- raisins
- tangerines

DAIRY PRODUCTS

Many parrots do not receive enough calcium in their diets. Even though parrots are lactose intolerant, they can still have some dairy products. Moderation is the key—feed small amounts.

Here are some of the best dairy products for parrots:

- cheese (used in cooking only; any type of cheese fine, although the longer a cheese is aged, the better; Swiss contains the most calcium, parmesan is high in both phosphorus and sodium, and cheddar has the highest fat and calories)
- cottage cheese
- eggs, including well-washed shells
- yogurt

MEATS

Yes, birds do eat meat, and it is good for them. In the wild, most parrot species are seen eating insects and their larva. Meat must be thoroughly cooked and never fed rare.

If you are cooking meat that includes bones, you can give the bones to your parrot, along with the meat. Many species will crack open the bones to extract the marrow, which is high in iron and other nutrients.

Good meats for parrots include:

- chicken
- fish (thoroughly cooked and bones

Some Concerns About Nuts

Birds love nuts, but be aware that certain nuts, such as pistachios, may be dyed. Pecans and some other nuts may even be polished. Avoid nuts with dyes or the high-shine polish.

Peanuts, if old or if they have become wet, may be contaminated with mold, which can be toxic to your bird. As another precaution against mold, only feed peanuts that have been shelled. The shell seems to be the part that most often contains mold.

Peanut butter is one thing that you shouldn't buy at a health food store because of the possibility of the *Aspergillus* fungus. Although commercial brands are monitored for this fungus, most health food brands are not. This goes not only for peanut butter but for peanuts as well.

Macaws need more nuts in their diets than most other parrots.

   removed)
- lamb
- liver (although like kids, very few birds will eat this)
- ribs (okay on occasions, but birds have a hard time digesting pork, so use beef ribs)
- roast beef (no pink showing)
- salmon (water packed, canned is the best for birds; it is high in omega-6 fatty acids)
- steak
- tuna fish (water packed and low in sodium)
- turkey

NUTS
Most parrots really love nuts, which makes them a good training treat. Depending on the size of your bird, you can feed nuts whole or chopped. Use unsalted varieties only. Remember that although nuts have many nutrients, most are high in fat. Feed them in moderation.

Many parrots like to eat at the table with their people. Give yours his own plate; don't let him eat off of yours.

Peanut butter isn't the only nut butter. Any of the nuts listed in this section can be made into nut butters; just chop them up in your food processor to make different butters for your bird (and yourself).

You can feed your parrot the following nuts:
• almonds (have the highest calcium amount of all nuts)
• Brazil nuts (only the large macaws and largest cockatoos can crack these; high in selenium)
• cashews
• filberts or hazelnuts
• macadamia (high in fat and calories; one of the hardest nuts to crack)
• peanuts (really a legume)
• pecans (low in protein but high in calories)
• pine nuts (have lowest amount of calcium of all of the nuts)
• pistachio nuts (high in vitamin A)
• walnuts (have some vitamin A content)

FATS AND OILS

You can use oils, butter, and margarine, but use sparingly when cooking for your parrot. Cooking spray is an excellent substitute.

SEASONINGS AND FLAVORINGS

Most seasonings and flavorings have very little nutritional value in the quantities in which we use them. Fresh herbs are a good way to season food. Make sure that no pesticides were used in growing them. Salts should not be used or used very sparingly to prevent health issues. Most birds enjoy crushed red pepper flakes.

SNACK FOODS

We all crave snacks, and our birds are no different. Junk food isn't healthy for birds (or people, either). Try these substitutes instead:
• air-popped popcorn with no salt or butter added; spray a little cooking spray

on it and sprinkle spirulina, nutritional yeast, or vitamins on it.
- toasted oat cereal, shredded wheat, and grape nuts mixed together
- chopped almonds sprinkled on little mini-bagels covered with nut butter
- freshly made nut butter on unsalted crackers or melba toast
- spray millet is excellent for smaller parrots, but it should be given no more than twice a week

Foods to Avoid

The foods listed in this section should never be fed to your bird because they are toxic. Although some of them may not kill your parrot right away, over time they will.
- Alcohol should never be given under any circumstance. It is abuse to give your bird alcohol just to watch him act drunk. It will destroy his liver.
- Avocados have a toxic pit. This toxin can bleed into the flesh of the fruit, making it toxic to parrots. This warning includes guacamole.
- Caffeine in coffee, teas, and sodas can cause nervousness, hyperactivity, and irritability. It can also increase the heart rate.
- Chocolate contains theobromine, which is stored in the liver. When it reaches a toxic level, the bird will start developing neurological symptoms.
- Fruit pits and the flesh around them contain cyanide, which is toxic. This is also the reason not to give your bird any branches from a pitted fruit tree. Fruits to feed with caution include peaches, apricots, plums, cherries, and nectarines.
- Rhubarb contains oxalic acid in high levels, the highest of all vegetables. This acid binds up calcium and makes in unavailable to the body.

Other Food Warnings

Use sugar only in moderation. Like people, some birds will develop a "sweet beak," but too much sugar in the diet is not healthy. Birds can develop diabetes from a high-sugar diet. Small amounts in things you cook for them are okay; for example, if a recipe calls for 1 cup of sugar, use between 1/8 and 1/4 cup instead. You can also use applesauce as a sweetener in place of sugar. Too much refined sugar can lead to yeast infections, heart disease, and calcium imbalance. It is also linked to feather plucking, irritability, anxiety, and nervous disorders.

Salt should also be used very sparingly to prevent high blood pressure. Parrots do not excrete salt like humans do.

Avoid mayonnaise products, not only because they are high in fat but also because they go bad quickly. Food may sit in the bird's crop for a while and spoil, which will cause problems.

Avoid foods with dyes and sulfites, as these are linked to such problems as cancer, kidney damage, allergic reactions, and chromosomal damage. You can buy sulfite-free dried fruits at health food stores.

PESTICIDES

Today's produce is grown using all kinds of pesticides. Some fruits and vegetables have a much higher amount of chemicals on them than others. The data on the pesticides in produce assumes that the items are consumed how people would typically eat fruits and vegetables—for example, apples and grapes are washed, bananas peeled, etc. Remember that washing does not remove all of the pesticides on the produce, although it may reduce the levels. While peeling most fruits reduces the amount further, many nutrients are in the skin. Organic produce is the best way to reduce the amounts of harmful pesticides.

Recipes

The rest of this chapter contains a few recipes that are nutritious for your bird. Some are good for humans as well!

APPLE-NUT PANCAKES

1½ cup flour
2 eggs (washed eggshells included unless you want some as well)
1½ tsp baking powder
1 apple with the skin removed and coarsely chopped
½–¾ cup chopped nuts
1 cup milk
¼ cup melted margarine
½ cup applesauce

Mix all of the dry ingredients together in a bowl. In another bowl, mix the milk, margarine, eggs, and applesauce together. Slowly add the wet ingredients into the dry ingredients. Fold in the chopped apples and nuts. On a griddle, pour ¼ –½ cup of batter. When the pancake is golden brown, flip it over to cook on the other side. Cook on the other side until golden brown. Serve warm.

BEAN AND TURNIP GREENS MUFFINS

1 can organic vegetarian five-bean soup
1 cup frozen chopped turnip greens, thawed
1 cup whole wheat flour
1 cup brown rice flour
1 tsp baking powder

Pesticide Levels of Common Fruits and Vegetables

This list goes from the highest amount of pesticides found to the least amount of pesticides found. The highest score you can achieve is 100. The data comes from the Environmental Working Group (EWG) study based on the results of the more than 43,000 tests done for pesticides between 2000 and 2005 on produce collected by the United States Department of Agriculture (USDA) and the US Food and Drug Administration (FDA).

peaches	100	cantaloupe	34
apples	96	lemons	31
bell peppers	86	honeydew	31
celery	85	grapefruits	31
nectarines	84	winter squash	31
strawberries	83	tomatoes	30
cherries	75	sweet potatoes	30
imported grapes	68	watermelon	25
pears	65	blueberries	24
spinach	60	papayas	21
potatoes	58	eggplant	19
carrots	57	cabbage	17
green beans	55	bananas	16
hot peppers	53	kiwis	14
cucumbers	52	asparagus	11
raspberries	47	frozen sweet peas	11
plums	46	mangoes	9
oranges	46	pineapples	7
domestic grapes	46	frozen sweet corn	2
cauliflower	39	avocados	1
tangerines	38	onions	1

¼ cup carrot juice
2 tsp oil
2 eggs (washed shells included unless you want some as well)
Preheat the oven to 350°F (176.7°C).

In a large bowl, combine the five-bean soup, carrot juice, eggs (eggshells), oil, and turnip greens. Slowly beat in the flours and the baking powder.

Lightly grease 12 muffin cups. Spoon the mixture into the muffin tins. Bake for around 30 minutes or until a toothpick comes out clean.

BIRDIE TREATS

1 cup of mixed dried fruits from a health food store (no sulfates added)
3 tbs shredded coconut (no sulfates added)
½ cup oatmeal (uncooked)
½ cup raisins (no sulfates added)
¼ cup chopped almonds or walnuts
2 tbs almond butter
Preheat the oven to 325°F (162.8°C).

Finely chop all of the dry ingredients together in a food processor. Add the almond butter and process a few seconds more. The mixture is going to be very sticky. If it is too dry, you can add some applesauce (unsweetened) 1 teaspoon at a time. If it is too wet, you can add some more finely chopped nuts.

Roll the mixture into a small ½-inch ball and place on a lightly greased cookie sheet. Bake for around 18 to 20 minutes or until done. To check for doneness, stick a toothpick in the center and if it comes out wet, bake for another two minutes. Keep checking this way until the toothpick comes out clean.

EXTRA-SPICY GREEN MASH

1 bunch collard greens
1 bunch mustard greens
½ bag frozen turnip greens (you can use fresh but these are sometimes hard to find)
1 bunch radishes, tops included
6 red chili peppers (don't use the dried types)
1–2 zucchini
10 baby carrots
1 yam, cooked
½ bag frozen green beans
1 beet (top included)
1 can corn

½ bag frozen peas
½ bag frozen broccoli
½ bag frozen spinach
1 cup cooked brown rice or bulgur

Coarsely chop the peppers, collard greens, mustard greens, carrots, cooked yam, beets, radishes, green beans, corn, peas, broccoli, spinach, and zucchini in a food processor.

In a large pot, add all of the above ingredients and just enough water to cover. Cook on a medium setting, stirring constantly. When all of the water is absorbed, remove the pot from the burner.

Some birds enjoy this dish just the way it is, and others prefer more of a finer mash. If your bird prefers the finer mash, put it into a food processor and puree.

Serve warm. Once the ingredients are pureed, you can put the mixture into a small ice cube tray and freeze. Pop in the microwave to warm.

CURRIED SPICY NOODLES

This is a great recipe for thinner birds or birds who need more fat in their diets. My cockatoo, Toby, was always a picky eater, and I think that she burned more calories just eating the food than she ever got from the food itself. My avian veterinarian suggested that I give her coconut milk because of the calorie content. But she also likes spicy food, so I came up with this recipe just for her.

1 bag either yolk-free noodles, whole wheat noodles, or multi-flavored pasta
4–8 tbs coconut milk (if your bird doesn't need the extra calories, use low-fat coconut milk)
1–2 tsp hot curry powder
1–2 tbs dried red chili pepper flakes

Cook the noodles until tender. Drain them.

In a bowl, combine the noodles, coconut milk, curry powder, and red chili pepper flakes. Stir, combining well. Serve warm.

This is also a tasty dish for people. Adjust the pepper flakes and curry powder to your taste.

Chapter Six

GROOMING YOUR PARROT

Grooming your parrot isn't just about making him look good— although it does do that. It is about attending to the maintenance of his feathers, nails, and beak. Grooming keeps your bird healthy. If you go slowly and offer rewards, your bird may even come to enjoy grooming.

Parrots preen to keep their feathers in top condition and to remove the sheath from newly grown feathers.

Feathers

Feathers are unique to birds, but they evolved from reptilian scales. (Look closely at your bird's feet, and you will still see evidence of his reptilian ancestors.) Feathers also allow for flight, and their colorful nature allows for both camouflage and for mating display.

All feathers are not alike; each type has its own function. Some serve to insulate, aid in flight, attract a mate, help camouflage a bird, and aid in waterproofing him.

Feathers are about 88 percent protein, and most of that is keratin, which also composes human hair and nails. The number of feathers on a parrot varies between species, size, and where and how it lives. In most birds, a third of the feathers are on their head. Typically, feathers make up around 10 to 20 percent of a bird's weight. Each feather has a tiny muscle that controls it, which is why birds can lift just a few feathers at a time or many.

Feathers grow quickly; they start off as blood feathers, and once fully developed, they are dead, just like human nails. Feathers do not last forever, and once they become worn, they are replaced. This happens once or twice a year, depending on the species. It may seem like the bird is always molting, but he is just replacing older feathers because they do not all grow in at once, nor are they all lost at once.

ANATOMY OF A FEATHER

Feathers comprise two obvious parts. The shaft is the long, stiff center that supports the vane or feathery part.

The quill is the uncolored tubular end of a mature feather. This is the end of the shaft that sits in the feather follicle below the skin. This end is called the calamus and has a hollow base where the blood vessels feed the pulp of the developing feathers.

The rachis is the long, solid center of shaft of the feather that is above the skin. This part of the shaft contains pith, which is made up of air-filled keratin-like cells.

Extending from each side of the rachis are rows of barbs. These barbs are slender filaments that come out of the rachis. They are like a hook system that is similar to Velcro. Each time a bird preens, these barbs hook together again, which is what gives the feathers a sleek appearance. This aids in ensuring that the bird is insulated and waterproofed. The vane is either soft or downy (plumulaceous) or compact and closely knit (pennaceous).

TYPES OF FEATHERS

Contour feathers are the most abundant on a bird. These are the colorful feathers that cover his body. They have a well-developed shaft and either a soft, downy structure or a closely knit and compact structure. They are divided into either body feathers or flight feathers. Flight feathers, or remiges, aid in flight. The primary flight feathers are those long feathers that are at the end of the wing. There are around 9 to 12 primaries. The secondary flight feathers are the flight feathers that are closest to the body, and they are usually more rounded on the tip than the primaries. There are anywhere from

The flight feathers are stiff and sturdy to provide needed lift.

During a molt, your parrot will have numerous pin feathers coming in, as this orange-chinned parakeet does.

6 to 32 secondaries. Retrices are the tail feathers. Both the remiges and retrices are long and strong. Covert feathers are the small contour feathers that cover the bases of both the wing and the tail feathers.

Semiplumes have a long rachis and a soft down vane and provide insulation for the bird. Filoplumes are located close to the follicle of each of the contour feathers. These feathers are for providing sensory information regarding the position of the adjacent contour feathers. These feathers consist of a long, fine shaft with short barbs.

Down feathers serve to keep the bird warm, and they are whitish in color. These are the first feathers present after hatching. They are called natal or juvenile down at this time. In adult birds, the down is sometimes referred to as definitive down. These soft and fluffy feathers cover the entire body. In certain species, they may be absent altogether (e.g., Vasa parrots) or restricted to certain areas.

Powder down feathers are specialized to waterproof a bird. Cockatoos, cockatiels, and African greys have them in greater abundance than do other parrots. These

Some sexually mature birds may confuse scratching under the wings, around the tail, and near the vent with courtship. Pay attention to your parrot's behavior when you preen him. If he seems to be getting excited or more aggressive, stop and just limit the preening to his head and neck.

feathers produce a white, waxy powder that gets spread when a bird preens. The powder can cause problems for people with allergies or lung disease and can also affect the workability of smoke detectors. The dust from my cockatiels set off our smoke detector because it obscured the sensor.

Bristles are another specialized feather that is found on the eyelids, nares, and mouth. Like the filoplumes, they have a sensory function. Bristles have a stiff, tapered rachis that does not have barbs.

Hypopnea are sometimes referred to as after feathers. They have a shaft with only barbs or soft downy barbs.

Molting

Molting is the process whereby old feathers are replaced with new feathers. Feathers tend to become worn out or damaged over time, and they must be replaced. All birds molt. Birds do not lose all of their feathers at once, but instead a molt takes place over a period of time. How long it takes depends on the health and age of the bird, the species, the season, and even where you are located. Although parrots normally replace their feathers year round, there are certain times when your bird will seem to be losing feathers all the time.

Molting can affect your bird's behavior. He may seem less playful, may talk less, and may even be ornery. Emerging new feathers, called pin feathers, can be itchy. Your parrot may not want to be petted like he did before and may not even enjoy the head scratches he once craved. During this time, he may enjoy frequent showers or baths even more. Because molting can cause stress, make sure that he is eating a healthy diet.

Preening

Each new feather is protected by a waxy sheath that protects the feather and its blood supply. When the feather first erupts from the skin, the blood supply extends to the tip of the sheath. As the feather grows longer, the blood supply recedes farther down the feather shaft. The excess sheath is normally removed by a bird or his mate during preening.

Preening is accomplished by scratching, rubbing against objects, or by the bird using his beak and tongue to get to the growing feather. Preening is not feather plucking, and it shouldn't be confused with it; preening is a bird's way

Stress Reduction

Preening your bird is not only enjoyable and relaxing for him, but many owners claim that they love it as much as their birds do. Some birds may even fall asleep while being preened. Just like it has been proven that petting a dog or cat can lower your blood pressure and help relieve stress, so can preening your bird accomplish the same thing.

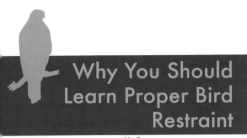

Why You Should Learn Proper Bird Restraint

I once got a call from a woman whose African grey got startled and fell to the ground, breaking several blood feathers. She had never restrained her bird before and didn't know what to do. She was in a panic because there was blood all over the place. She was too far from her vet, and only her husband was there. He was just as panicked as she was. Because she didn't know what to do and was too panicked to follow directions, sadly her bird lost too much blood and didn't survive. Don't let this happen to you and your bird!

of removing the dead parts of this sheath and keeping his feathers in prime condition.

Most parrots possess a preen gland. This gland is located at the base of the tail and is called the uropygial gland. This gland secretes an oil that a bird will then spread onto his feathers to keep them both waterproof and looking nice. Not all parrots have this gland; Amazons and hyacinth macaws, for example, do not.

You can preen your bird, and this is an excellent way for you to bond with him. He may even be preening you when he plays with your hair. Even birds who were not hand-fed can learn to love these preening sessions. What it comes down to is trust. If your bird trusts you, he may allow you to preen him. Go slowly at first, and only do as much as he wants you to do.

Use your fingers or nails to gently scrape off some of the dead sheath. This will flake off easily. Most birds enjoy having these sheaths removed from their heads because it is hard for them to reach there. You can also gently roll the sheath, which will cause the material to flake off. You may need a vacuum to clean up all of the "birdie dandruff" afterward.

Blood Feathers

Learning how to identify blood feathers can help prevent an accident. Blood feathers are those new feathers that are starting to poke through the skin; they look like little pins. As these feathers start to grow out, you will see either a red color inside the shaft (if the feather is light colored) or darkish purple (if the feather has a dark-colored shaft). As the feather grows out, the blood inside the shaft will start retreating farther down until it is gone and only the new feather remains.

You must be very careful around blood feathers. You can take off the dead, waxy substance, but stop before the blood begins. If you go down too far, you may even cause some bleeding.

Restraining Your Bird

Most owners never want to have to restrain their birds. However, sometimes it does become necessary, especially in a life-or-death situation. It is important to know what to do in cases of an emergency.

Why does your bird need to be restrained? This could be for simple procedures, such as cutting nails or trimming wings. Other times, your bird may need to be medicated or even restrained because of an injury or broken blood feather. Restraining him to do a job such as cutting nails or trimming wings usually requires two people.

THE RESTRAINER'S JOB

The restrainer has an important job because she must make sure that the bird doesn't escape and injure himself or someone else. She must also remain aware of the bird's condition at all times.

The restrainer must be aware of the bird's breathing to watch for signs of stress, such as panting or gasping. She must also make sure that the bird isn't getting too overheated. (You can tell by

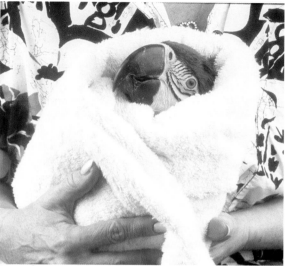

A towel is a useful tool for restraining a parrot while you trim his nails or clip his wings.

his feet, which will feel very hot.) The restrainer must also make sure that the bird's wings are not bent at a strange angle and that blood feathers are not being broken. In addition, the restrainer must position the bird for the other person and keep the bird's beak out of the way at the same time. The restrainer does not need to see everything that is being done to the bird as long as she can adequately monitor his condition. To put it simply, she must keep her head, arms, and elbows out of the way. The person working on the bird needs room to work. The restrainer shouldn't hold the bird too close to her own body either, not only so that the bird won't bite her but so that her body heat doesn't affect him.

When restraining, it is important to know just how much pressure is needed. Too much pressure could cause an injury, such as breaking a bone or crushing the bird. Too little pressure will allow the bird to escape, and he may injure you or himself in the process.

Before you approach your bird to restrain him, make sure that you have all of the supplies you will

Let the Towel Be the Enemy!

Towels allow a bird to bite down and chew on something. The towel becomes the bad guy and not you. When your bird is let loose again, the two of you can take out any frustration on that mean old towel.

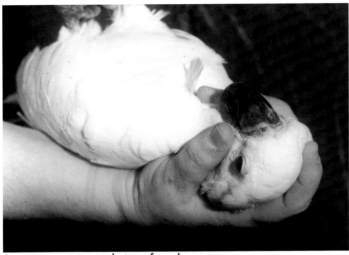

Proper restraining technique for a large parrot.

need ready. These can be things such as a towel, scissors, a dremel, nail clippers, flour or cornstarch as a styptic, medications, and your avian first-aid kit.

RESTRAINING

You need to grasp your bird from behind. This is because birds react in one of two ways: They will either try to escape or they will bite. This is part of a bird's "fight or flight response." With some birds, this response is not as dramatic as it is with others. Some may start to scream at the top of their lungs, they may lunge at you, they may roll over on their backs, or they may even flap their wings and try to get away. Each bird will react differently to being restrained. Even after being restrained, some birds will continue to struggle and fight. Knowing how your bird may react will help you prepare for different situations.

How to Hold Your Parrot

When you restrain your bird, you want to be sure that you are holding him securely enough without suffocating him, crushing him, or allowing him to thrash his wings. You want to hold him tightly enough to have control, not break his bones. This is especially important when restraining a larger bird, such as a cockatoo or a macaw. A bird who is being restrained may be in panic mode, and when in this mode, he may not recognize what he is biting. A large bird who is not properly restrained can grab hold and bite down on anything that is close to his beak. If that object is a finger, you will either kiss it goodbye or at least need plenty of bandages.

When restraining your bird, you need to use some type of protection to prevent him from biting down on your fingers. For a small bird, such as a budgie or cockatiel, you can use a washcloth or even a kitchen towel. Many owners have even learned how to restrain a

Remember not to put pressure on your bird's chest. Birds do not have a diaphragm, and putting pressure on their chests will prevent them from breathing properly, and they may suffocate.

budgie or tiel without a towel. If it is an emergency and you don't have those around, you can even use a paper towel. For medium birds, such as Senegals, you can use a kitchen towel or a bathroom hand towel. For larger birds, use the largest and thickest towel you own. Because he will chew on it, invest in an inexpensive one just for this purpose.

You will need to grasp your bird's head, which will allow you to control the business end of your bird—his beak! With the towel, come in from behind him, dropping the towel over him and carefully noting where the head was. Take hold of the head and then wrap the towel around the rest of the body, being careful of the flapping wings. You can also keep your hands in the middle of the towel and grab his head quickly. Just as quickly, you will need to wrap the rest of the towel around the body before picking up your bird. Never just pick him up by his head alone; support the body. Because the wings will be flapping, wrap the towel gently but firmly around them with your free hand. Wrapping the towel around the wings will prevent them from flapping, thus preventing any problems.

What happens if your bird rolls over on his back and fights you with both beak and nails? You may think that only wild birds react this way, but even the tamest and gentlest of pet birds can do this. If your bird does react this way, you need to be one step ahead of him. Take him into the bathroom to restrain him, but ahead of time place towels in the corners of the room.

When he goes into the corner and flips over on his back, wrap up the towel immediately and then restrain his head. For a bird who does not mind being restrained, you will also need to come in from behind with the towel and take hold of his head to wrap the towel around his body.

Once you have the head, place your thumb and little finger on opposite sides of it, right behind the mandibles or jaws, between your bird's beak and eyes. You do not want to get too close to the eyes because you don't want to cause an injury. Hold below this area but not so tightly that you cause bruising, or worse, injury; just hold tightly enough that you

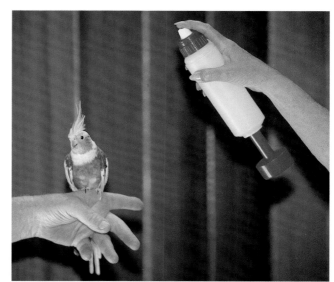

One way to bathe your parrot is to lightly spray him with a plant mister; some parrots really enjoy this.

193

Many parrots enjoy bathing, and you will need to do little to encourage them.

have control and your bird cannot escape. Place your remaining fingers on the top of your bird's head to get more control. Once you have his head secured, as well as the rest of his body, you can either rest your bird on your arm or rest your arm on a table.

Remember that tame or not, some birds may still be fighting, twisting, turning, and struggling in their efforts to escape. Make sure that you have the towel over his wings because with all this fighting, it will be easy for him to sneak out of the towel and start flapping all over again. It takes a lot of concentration to hold a bird securely.

For small birds, such as budgies and tiels, you can restrain in emergencies without a towel. With your index and middle fingers opened up into a V-shape, hold the budgie or tiel's head between those fingers while wrapping the rest of your fingers around his body. For a larger bird, you will probably always need to use a towel for restraint.

Do not use a hairdryer to dry your bird. Never use soap or shampoo on a parrot.

Bathing Your Bird

Why do you need to bathe your bird? Bathing your bird helps remove feather dust, encourages good preening, relieves dry and irritated skin, and reduces the itchy feeling as new feathers start to come in. It also gives the feathers a healthy sheen when they are dry. For some

birds, such as an Amazon or a pionus, it helps reduce that musky smell. Bathing your bird will not only make him look good, but it can make him feel good as well. Just imagine how great you feel after a nice refreshing shower.

It is best to bathe your parrot during the day instead of at night. At night, temperatures drop, and there is more of a risk of a draft than during the day, when the house tends to be warmer.

Some birds (Amazons and macaws) tend to enjoy bathing more than other birds (African greys and cockatoos). But remember that all birds are individuals, so there are some cockatoos who love to bathe and some macaws who hate it. However, even a bird who dislikes bathing still needs a bath now and then, and you can teach him how to enjoy baths, or at least tolerate them.

METHODS FOR BATHING A PARROT

What is the best method of bathing your bird? There really isn't one technique that is better than another. Find out what works for you and your bird, and use that method. If your bird doesn't like one method, try another.

If you have an enthusiastic bather, you may want to place towels or newspaper on the floor so that you don't have to mop up afterward. One owner had even resorted to wearing a raincoat because her bird was really enthusiastic.

What is the best temperature of water used to bathe a bird? Rain doesn't come down hot; it comes down cool to tepid, so this is the best temperature at which to bathe your bird. However, some birds enjoy warmer water. If your parrot seems to shiver when you mist him with cool or tepid water, try a little warmer water instead.

MISTING

A plant mister that has never had any chemicals in it is great for misting your bird. These misters have adjustable sprays. Birds do not like the strong spray setting but rather the

Bathing Do's and Don'ts

- Never force your bird to bathe if he doesn't want to.
- Do not use a hairdryer on your bird.
- Do not use hot water; use cool to tepid water instead.
- Do not bathe your bird if there is a draft or the house is too cold.
- Never bring your bird into a bathtub with you.
- Bathe your bird during the day, not at night.
- Always make sure that your bird has enough time to dry off before bedtime.
- Use a shower perch or shower stand instead of taking a shower with your parrot.
- Try different methods to find which one your parrot likes best.
- Try using a very fine mist for a bird who is resistant to bathing.
- Always offer praise for a bird who is resistant.
- Be patient with a resistant parrot.
- Always keep your bird safe.

Good Parrotkeeping

gentle or fine mist setting. Most birds love getting soaked and will beg for more.

Plant

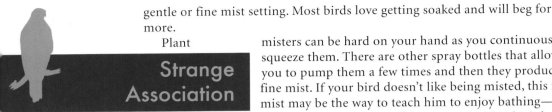

Strange Association

It may sound strange, but for some reason whenever I vacuum, it seems to trigger a bathing response among most of my birds. After talking to well over 100 bird owners, they too have seemed to notice this relationship. So watch your bird carefully whenever you vacuum for signs that he wants to bathe.

misters can be hard on your hand as you continuously squeeze them. There are other spray bottles that allow you to pump them a few times and then they produce a fine mist. If your bird doesn't like being misted, this fine mist may be the way to teach him to enjoy bathing—the spray is so fine that he will hardly notice that he is being misted. This type isn't the best for birds who love being misted because it doesn't seem to get them wet enough.

SHOWERS

Some birds enjoy going into the shower and taking a shower either alone or with their humans. I suggest that they go in alone instead of being on their humans, where they could accidentally slip off and injure themselves or their humans. Several good shower perches are available; just make sure that the one you purchase is appropriate for your bird. These shower perches attach right to the shower wall. You can also use a special shower stand made from PVC piping. Never take a bath with your bird; he could easily slip off you and drown or aspirate water before you have a chance to react.

If you put your bird in the shower, make sure that the water isn't too cool and that it isn't set on too strong a stream. Remember, this should be enjoyable for your bird. Keep him away from all soaps, shampoos, and similar substances.

SINKS AND BIRDIE BATHTUBS

Some owners bathe their birds in the kitchen or bathroom sink with a soft towel placed under the birds. Sinks are slippery, so the towel provides traction. Make sure that the sink is clean and that any chemicals used to clean it have been well rinsed off. You can use a 10:1 bleach solution (10 parts water, 1 part bleach) to clean the sink and then rinse well. This will ensure that the sink is clean and free of germs.

Do not use styptic powder on a broken feather. When a bird preens, he can ingest it, and this may cause crop burn, a serious condition. Use flour or cornstarch instead.

If you are bathing your bird in the sink, make sure that nothing is in reach that could harm him. Only a few inches (5 cm or so) of water are enough for a larger bird. Some birds enjoy having handfuls of water gently dropped over them, while others prefer doing this themselves. Some sinks have a spray attachment, which some birds enjoy as well. Remember, you don't want to

scare your bird, so introduce it slowly.

For smaller birds, such as budgies, you can buy a little budgie-sized bathtub and put a little water in that. You can use a pie tin for a very enthusiastic bather.

A pie tin works best for small- to medium-sized birds. Place a towel under it and put a little water in it, and most birds will love it. Some birds will even roll over on their backs, so don't put too much water in if your bird does this. For birds such as greys or eclectus, you can use a deeper baking tin. Some parrots like to pick up the bathing dish and toss it to the ground. Don't use a glass dish if your bird is like this.

What about the bigger birds, such as cockatoos and macaws? During the summer, I got my macaw plastic kiddie pool. This works great if you have a porch or an area in which you can put a pool and still keep your bird safe. I even put a few plastic pool toys in with him. I make sure to place plenty of towels under it. Do not get an inflatable pool because parrots like to chew, and yours could puncture the pool, causing a flood.

> Extra caution is needed if your bird has a lot of blood feathers growing in. Wild flapping could accidentally break a blood feather.

LETTUCE

No, this isn't a misprint! Wet lettuce is a way that some birds, such as budgies, will bathe. In fact, it may be the only way they will bathe. In the wild, some birds use dew-covered leaves or foliage to bathe. In Australia, where the climate is dry, there are few pools of water in which birds can bathe. Besides, splashing on the ground could be dangerous because it can alert a predator to their whereabouts. But in the early morning when the dew is on the leaves or blades of grass, budgies will rub up against them, getting as wet as they can.

Hang a piece of wet lettuce in the cage and your budgie or other small bird may rub up against it, bathing himself. You can use other greens besides lettuce, such as spinach, collard greens, and kale.

DRYING YOUR PARROT

What is the best way to dry your bird? Normally, it is best to just let him dry on his own. Allow enough time for him to dry before bedtime. Some birds will allow you to gently gather them in a towel and dry them that way.

While I know some owners who use a hairdryer on their birds, this is not recommended at all. Even on a low setting, the warm air could burn your bird. Some parrots have even developed dry skin because their owners used a hairdryer. In most cases, this unfortunately leads to feather plucking. To keep your bird safe, don't use a hairdryer.

RELUCTANT BATHERS

Not all birds enjoy bathing. Although bathing is a personal preference, I have found that birds who come from dryer areas tend to resist bathing more often than birds from wet areas. Birds such as rock pebblers normally don't enjoy bathing, but you can still teach them to at least tolerate a bath. My rock pebbler now loves to splash around in a pie tin. Sometimes jealousy will encourage a bird to bathe. If you have other birds in the house who enjoy bathing, the reluctant one may see how much the other birds enjoy the practice and decide to join in.

Try different methods, and see which one works for your bird. Try a very light mist at first, so light that your parrot hardly notices it. If he seems to accept this, then it is time to start increasing the mist a little more. If he seems too startled or unnerved by it, offer the pie tin containing a little water. If that bothers him, try the lettuce method.

SIGNS TO WATCH FOR

Watch for certain signs that your parrot wants to bathe. Some birds will try to splash water from their water bottle or water bowl. Other birds will fluff up their feathers almost asking to be bathed. They may spread their wings wide open, wag their tail in anticipation of getting wet, or even scream in their demand for a shower.

When you see this happening, it is time to bathe your bird. Remember, never force him to bathe if he is really resistant. If he acts scared, nervous, or starts to thrash around, stop.

Clipping Tips

- Watch out for blood feathers.
- Have all of your supplies ready before you start.
- Have a very good pair of scissors.
- Securely restrain your bird.
- Cut one feather at a time, always checking for blood feathers.
- Know how to deal with a broken blood feather in case an accident occurs.

Wing Clipping

Why should you clip your bird's wings? Clipping the wings allows you more control over him. It prevents him from getting away from you, which in turn prevents him from flying into a window, a wall, or a mirror and injuring himself. He could also become startled and fly through an open window or door, and you might never get him back. It is especially important to have your bird's wings clipped if you take him outside. A pet parrot in the wild usually doesn't survive very long. He may starve to death trying to find food, die from exposure due to the lack of shelter, or be attacked and killed by some type of predator.

Clipping a bird's winds is not cruel, nor does it hurt him if done properly. It hurts no more than it does when you cut your own hair. When done properly, the

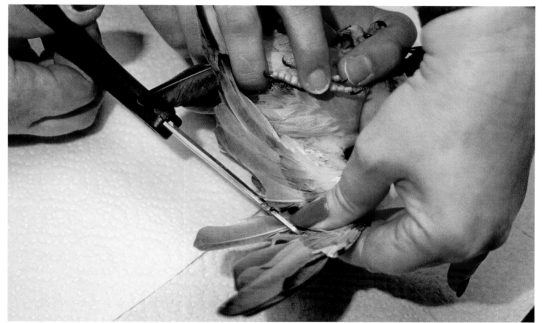

Clipping your parrot's wings requires two people.

wings still look cosmetically beautiful, and the goals of safety and control are achieved as well.

Clipping a bird's wings isn't difficult, but you must be cautious with blood feathers. Make sure that you know how to identify a blood feather before you attempt to clip your bird's wings. If unsure, ask your avian veterinarian to show you what the blood feathers look like and how to avoid them. If you mistakenly cut through a blood feather, you have a potentially life-threatening situation on hand. Know how to stop the bleeding in case you accidentally cut into one.

If you are going to clip your bird's wings yourself, you must be comfortable restraining him. Wing clips require two people. If you don't feel comfortable, your avian veterinarian can do this for you. Some bird specialty stores also offer this service.

CAN HE STILL FLY?

Clipping your bird's wings does not mean that he can't fly. Some birds, especially light-bodied birds such as cockatiels, can still fly slightly with a clip. What the clip does is limit the parrot's flying ability. Clipped birds just glide to the floor.

With patient training, many parrots will cooperate with wing clipping.

If your bird is still capable of flight, you may need to clip a few more feathers. Keep in mind that too severe a clip may throw his balance off, so talk to your avian veterinarian first.

STARTING TO CLIP

You will need someone to help you before you start to clip your bird's wings. Make sure that your helper either knows how to restrain a bird or that she understands how to clip wings. Have all of the supplies handy before you start, including a towel, flour or cornstarch, and a sharp pair of scissors. Some birds have very strong feather shafts, and even with a good pair of scissors, they may be difficult to cut through. Ask your avian veterinarian for a recommendation in this case.

Once you have your bird properly restrained, carefully move the towel away from one side to expose the wing. He may start to flap the exposed wing in an attempt to get away. Take hold of the wing at the top, between the bird's body and where the wing bends. Never try to control a flapping wing by grabbing hold of the feathers.

Once you have the wing under control, separate the feathers to get a better look. Check both sides before you begin. Cut one feather at a time instead of making one straight cut all the way across. This way you can see any blood feathers that you may have missed the first time. If you do see a blood feather, I recommend leaving a feather on either side of it to offer some protection.

TYPES OF CLIPS

Which clip is best for your bird? Ask your avian veterinarian which one is best. Different species may require different clips.

In the most common clip—I refer to it as the "normal" clip—you cut the first five to eight primary flight feathers. If you have a lightweight bird or a bird who can still fly with the first 8 clipped, you can cut up to the first 11 flight feathers. This clip is repeated on the other side. In this clip, you cut slightly under the coverts, making sure that no blood feathers are present.

STOP

Don't cut a toe when you are cutting the nails. Always have a good view of what you are doing before you cut.

The "show" clip is used to give the appearance that a bird has all of his flight feathers when he really doesn't. This clip leaves the first few flight feathers untouched but starts on feather number 3 or 4 and clips up to the 11th flight feather. This clip is sometimes used when showing birds or on birds who appear in movies or on television.

There is even a clip that is used on birds who are more prone to feather plucking. Not many people have heard of this clip; however, some of the older and more experienced avian veterinarians still use it, and it does work. In the "feather plucking" clip, instead of having each feather cut in a straight line, the feathers are notched with a V-shape instead. One of the reasons that it is used so infrequently is that it takes much longer to do and is more difficult. The theory behind this cut is that the V-shape causes less irritation than the normal cuts do. This cut was shown to me by an avian veterinarian who deals with many feather pluckers. She uses it on birds who are more prone to feather plucking, such as greys, cockatoos, and eclectus. Although other birds do not appear to show any irritability when their feathers are cut, some species tend to be more sensitive to it.

In the "every other feather" clip, the bird will still have some flight capability but generally cannot maintain any height or distance. To achieve this clip, just spread the feathers out in the wing and clip every other one.

When trimming your bird's nails, snip off the tips only, being careful to avoid the quick. After trimming, use a nail file to smooth out rough spots.

UNRESTRAINED METHOD

Some birds will allow you to hold out their wings so that you can clip them without having to restrain them. Encourage this by playing with your parrot's wings. (This works best with babies.) Gently open his wings and touch the feathers very gently. By getting your bird used to having his wings opened and held, clipping the wings will be made easier. Offer rewards and praise when your parrot allows this.

Place the cooperative bird in your lap. Hold out one of the wings and check for blood feathers. With a sharp pair of scissors, cut the first feather. Reward your bird. Keep repeating until you have finished that side. Then go on to the other side. If at any time your bird starts to struggle or doesn't want you to continue, you will have to restrain him. However, the nonrestraining method is the least stressful way to clip wings

Nail Care

A bird's nails may grow quickly and become overgrown. Overgrown nails can prevent a parrot from perching correctly, playing with toys, or even climbing or holding food. Overgrown nails can also get caught on things, causing injury to your bird.

Your avian veterinarian or an experienced bird groomer is your best bet for getting your bird's nails trimmed properly. If you ask her to show you how this is done, she will be more than happy to do so.

Cutting the nails isn't difficult, but it can be tricky. You must know just how much to take off and where the quick is, the portion of the nail that contains the blood supply. You can cut too deeply and cause your bird to bleed. Some parrot nails are solid black, and others are almost clear. The latter are the easiest to cut because you can see where the blood supply is.

Before you start, you must have all of the necessary supplies handy. These supplies include styptic powder, flour, or cornstarch to stop any bleeding if you cut too deeply; bird nail scissors; a metal file; a dremel or nail clipper; and a towel.

When cutting the nails, only do one nail at a time. Firmly grasp the nail and only take off the tip of it. The tip is usually pointier and is sometimes sharp feeling. Once you cut the nail, check it to see if it is bleeding. If it isn't, go on to the next nail. If the nail is bleeding, take the flour, cornstarch, or styptic powder and push it into the tip of the nail. The nail should stop bleeding. Go to the next and repeat. When you have finished with one foot, check to make sure that there is no bleeding before going to the next foot.

An avian veterinarian should cut the nails of high-stress birds, like Bourke's parakeets.

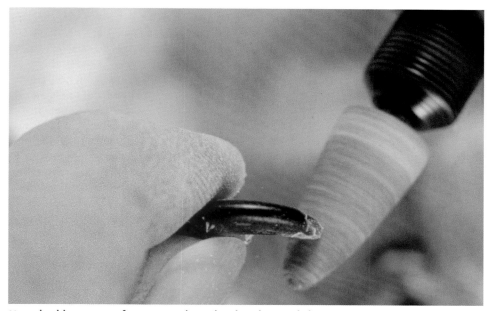

Many bird keepers prefer to use a dremel rather than nail clippers.

CLIPPERS AND OTHER SUPPLIES

For small birds, a little fingernail clipper is fine to use and is safest. This way you don't run the risk of taking off too much. Using the guillotine-type of nail clippers on a small bird is an accident waiting to happen. There have been many incidents of an entire toe being cut off accidentally.

For medium-sized birds, I recommend a bird nail clipper or an emery board or acrylic file. You can also use a mini dremel on medium to large birds. For large birds, you have more choices. You can use a dremel, a bird nail cutter, a dog nail cutter, or a metal file. A dremel has a rough bit that spins at a high speed. This then sands down the nails and tends to make them smoother than a nail cutter would. With some dremels, the high speed may produce heat that will help cauterize any minor bleeding. For home use, there are mini dremels, which work great. Have your avian veterinarian show you the proper way to use a dremel.

The best method of keeping your bird's nails trimmed is by using a therapeutic perch. Do not confuse these with sandpaper perches, which are not recommended. Although a therapeutic perch helps with nail maintenance, using one doesn't mean that your parrot will never need a nail trim. Make sure that when you put the therapeutic perch in his cage, you put it as the highest perch or next to the food cup. That way you know that he will be using it.

The best way to care for your bird's beak is to provide him with wooden chew toys.

PLAY WITH YOUR BIRD'S FEET

It may be easier to trim your bird's nails if he is used to having his feet touched. Start by lightly touching his feet until he is comfortable with it. Then start picking them up and playing with the nails and the feet themselves. Once he is comfortable with that, try using an appropriate nail file on his nails. Start by gently running the file on the tip of the nails. Remember to offer praise and/or rewards when you do so. Just remember that not all birds will allow this. The younger you start, the better chance you have of being able to trim your bird's nails this way.

Beak Care

Look in your toolbox for a handy tool that cuts and grinds, crushes and chops, splits and penetrates, and shreds, peels, and pulverizes. This tool also needs to be very lightweight and able to gently hold things without crushing them. You can't find a single tool that can do all of this? Well, a tool like this exists only in nature. It's a bird's beak.

The beak is sensitive, and it grows continuously. Beaks are used for a variety of activities, including food gathering and transportation, eating, picking, grinding, preening, nest making, feeding the young, turning the eggs, noise, and chewing. They are also used for climbing, playing, swinging, and even self-defense.

Beaks are also excellent for destroying things. But it is this act of chewing wood or other things that helps keep the beak from becoming overgrown. A parrot's beak is his main tool for eating. If there is a problem with the beak, then he may not be eating enough.

The beak is not made of solid bone. It is hollow except for fine bony structures that are like struts. The portion of beak closest to the bird has a blood supply and a number of nerve endings, making it very sensitive. However, the tip of the beak is like our fingernails and doesn't feel pain. The beak, like the feathers, is made of keratin.

BEAK GROWTH

Surprisingly, a parakeet's beak grows at a much faster rate than a larger parrot's beak does. A parakeet's beak grows at a rate of around 3 inches (7.6 cm) a year. At the same time, a larger parrot's beak may only grow at a rate of around 1 inches (3.2 cm) a year. This is because a larger parrot's beak is thicker and heavier than a budgie's.

However, there are times when the beak grows faster than it can be worn down. When this happens, it is time to get outside help. Do not try to trim the beak yourself; instead, take your bird to see an avian veterinarian.

What Is That Hole?

This is a question that many new bird owners have. I know of one owner who thought that his bird was injured when he saw the hole under her beak. However, this hole is perfectly normal. If parrots' beaks didn't possess this space, they wouldn't be able to eat or drink normally.

PROBLEMS WITH THE BEAK

Several medical conditions can cause overgrown, malformed, or rapidly growing beaks. These conditions need to be diagnosed by an avian veterinarian.

One of the more common problems with beaks is a deformity known as scissor beak. "Scissor beak" is the term for the upper beak being off center. This condition is more commonly seen in larger birds, such as macaws, cockatoos, and greys. It can be caused by calcium deficiencies, bad position in the egg, trauma to the beak, improper feeding techniques, genetics, improper incubation temperatures, and vitamin D3 toxicity.

Scissor beak can be corrected, although the most successful method seems to be surgical. In this procedure, the vet uses a dental acrylic to build up the lower beak, forcing the upper beak back into position. It works best on younger birds. The sooner you recognize this condition, the sooner you can have it treated. This is why that early trip to an avian veterinarian is so important.

CARING FOR THE BEAK

As an owner, you don't have to do much to care for your bird's beak. You never want to try to trim the beak yourself if you think that it is overgrown.

Rules for Exercising Your Parrot

- Go slowly, and gradually build up the amount of time for the exercise.
- Never force your bird or push him too fast.
- Exercise with him. Make it fun for both of you.
- Weigh him weekly to check for progress.
- Do not withhold food even if he is overweight.
- Offer praise, letting him know how good he was.
- Make sure that your bird isn't panting excessively; if he is, it could be a sign of stress or illness.

A beak, while lightweight, does contain blood vessels, and you could easily injure it. Your avian veterinarian may decide to use a nail file to file away rough areas or remove beak overgrowth. A dremel is sometimes used as well, but it really needs to be used by an experienced person. By providing toys for your parrot to chew, you will help keep his beak trimmed naturally. Make sure that the toys you provide are of different textures, such as soft and hard woods.

The Ears

Yes, parrots do have ears; they just don't stick out visibly. A parrot's ears are located behind and slightly lower than his eyes. Look at your parrot's head and you will see some feathers that don't look like the other feathers—they will seem too thin. Behind these feathers are where the ears are located. The ears have a small flap of skin that covers them, called the tympanum. Parrots don't hear in the same range as we do, but they hear sounds in greater detail.

Exercising and Your Parrot

As with humans, exercising is important to your bird's health. A lack of exercise, along with a poor diet, can shorten your parrot's life span. In the wild, birds get their exercise by flying from tree to tree and by foraging for food. Companion birds have it easy because everything is given to them. Most companion birds have their wings clipped, so they don't get any exercise by flying. Not only don't they get flying exercise, but they don't have to forage for food either because it is conveniently placed right next to their perch. As a result, many of our feathered friends tend to be on the chunky side. By exercising daily, a parrot will feel better and be healthier in a short time.

PLAY IS EXERCISE

Birds need toys to provide them with the motivation to play. Toys such as bungee cords, ladders, and swings are necessary because these are a great way for your bird to play while getting exercise. Play centers are usually equipped with a ladder and/or swing, and many allow you to attach other toys as well.

WING FLAPPING

Because most of our pet birds no longer fly, they must exercise their pectoral muscles as well as their lungs. This is an exercise that both you and your bird must do together.

Your bird needs to be comfortable with you placing your thumb on top of his feet while on your hand. You don't have to put so much pressure on his feet that you are hurting him but just enough so that you have some control.

To begin, lift your bird higher in the air and start walking very fast or running. Your bird will need to keep his balance, so he will start to flap his wings. Remember to praise him when he does this. Repeat this for a few minutes a couple of times a day. Eventually, you may end up running with your bird for five minutes or longer. If your parrot seems out of breath or is having trouble doing this for more than a minute, start off with 30 seconds first and then increase the time every couple of days.

When I do this with my green-winged macaw, I have to take extra precautions because of his large wing span—sometimes he hits me in the face. His long tail also has a tendency to get me. So with the larger birds, you need to make sure that they have enough room to flap their wings freely.

You can also encourage your bird to flap his wings while sitting on a perch. When you see him flapping or stretching his wings, offer immediate praise and say "wings" or "flap" or whatever else you prefer.

CLIMBING

Another great exercise for your bird is climbing. This is a very simple one, and all it requires is two ladders, a short one and a long one, the longer the better. This works on most birds because they normally want to go to the highest point. Ladders are commercially available for most birds, although finding one for a large macaw could prove challenging.

Place your bird on the floor (make sure that there isn't anything nearby

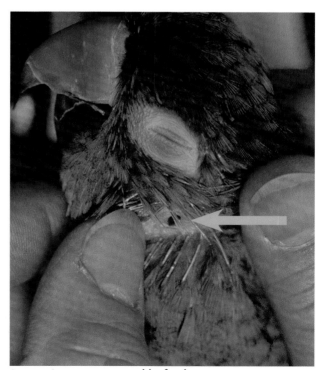

A parrot's ears are covered by feathers.

that would be fun for him to get into) and then put the shorter ladder in front of him. These short ladders usually have around five to six rungs to ascend. When he reaches the top, praise him. Repeat. Start with him going up the short ladder around two to three times at first, and then work up slowly to six to ten. Some birds have short attention spans and may lose interest in doing this too many times. If this is the case, do this exercise several times a day. You can also go to a longer ladder. Remember, start out doing a smaller number of climbs and then work up to more. Never force your bird to do these, but offer praise and encouragement instead.

RUNNING
Another exercise that you can do with your bird is to get him to run to you. This will give you some exercise as well because you will keep changing positions. This game shouldn't be played on the floor because you run the risk of stepping on your bird—you want to make sure that he is always safe.

This game is great played on a table or a bed. It's a fun one to watch because some birds look so comical when they run.

To begin, call your bird while he is on the table or bed. Tap to get his attention if he doesn't come to you when you call him. Once he comes to you, reward him with praise, affection (head scratch or cuddle), or even a healthy treat. Then move your position and call him again. Eventually, you can be running and changing positions so that you end up getting almost as much exercise as your bird.

THE WHEEL
This is great for any bird who is budgie sized or smaller. Your parrot will be exercising on a hamster

Small parrots, such as lovebirds, may enjoy running on a hamster wheel for exercise.

wheel, which needs to be open and not the type that is hard to get into. I have attached this wheel inside my Bourke's cage, and he loves to get into it and run as fast as he can. My budgie goes slowly in it but loves it all the same.

FORAGING FOR EXERCISE

Foraging in nature provide both physical exercise and mental stimulation. This may be lacking in the captive situation. But you can set up your bird's cage where there are spots that he can forage for his meals.

Buy some toys that have spots for hiding nuts, cereal, or other treats. Try rolling some treats in newspaper, and place them all over the cage. I even use small little boxes or paper towel holders that my birds have to work to open. All of my birds enjoy this little exercise because not only do they have fun trying to find the treat, but they also get the treat they worked so hard to find.

Wing flapping is good exercise for your parrot.

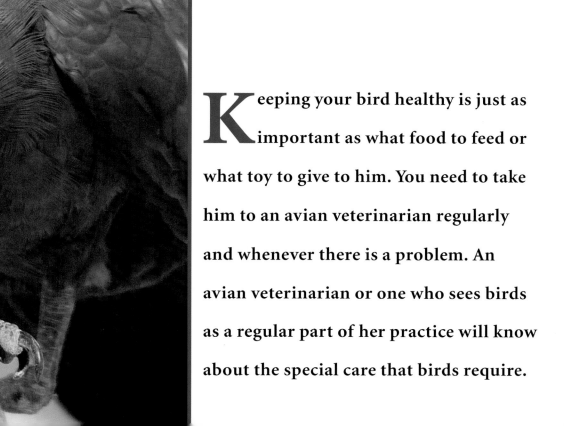

Chapter Seven

YOUR BIRD'S
HEALTH

Keeping your bird healthy is just as important as what food to feed or what toy to give to him. You need to take him to an avian veterinarian regularly and whenever there is a problem. An avian veterinarian or one who sees birds as a regular part of her practice will know about the special care that birds require.

Only an avian veterinarian can accurately diagnose and treat a parrot's health issues.

Avian Veterinarians

Choosing an avian veterinarian is just as important as choosing a doctor for yourself. Where do you go about finding a good avian veterinarian? See what vet your bird's former owner recommends. You can also talk with other people who own birds to see where they take them. Another place you can ask is at bird clubs.

STEPS FOR CHOOSING AN AVIAN VETERINARIAN

- Find out how far away the veterinarian is. Distance can make a big difference in an emergency.
- Chose a veterinarian who will answer your questions in a way you can understand.
- Find out about the fee structures. Is the vet willing to take payments if needed?
- Observe how the veterinarian and staff relate to both you and your parrot. Do they have a good cageside manner?
- Check out the conditions of the clinic. A clean hospital is most important. Avoid those with funny smells or obvious signs of poor sanitary conditions.

Some clinics are members of the American Animal Hospital Association (AAHA). These clinics have different standards than those that do not belong. However, just because a clinic isn't a member doesn't mean that it isn't a good clinic.

- How quickly can you get in to see the veterinarian? With birds, a day's wait can be fatal.
- Find out how emergencies are handled. Does the office take after-hours calls, or does it refer you to another clinic? Is there an answering service with a veterinarian on call or just an answering machine directing you to another clinic?
- Is the veterinarian a member of the Association of Avian Veterinarians (AAV)? Is the veterinarian board certified in avian medicine?
- Does the veterinarian continue attending educational courses in avian medicine? Avian medicine is growing with leaps and bounds as new information becomes available.
- Does the veterinarian have the equipment to treat birds?
- Does the veterinarian take the time to explain about nutrition and the care of your bird?
- Does the veterinarian have birds of her own?
- What are the clinic's hours? If a clinic closes early, it may be difficult to get in if you work.
- Ask members of bird clubs if they can recommend an avian veterinarian. If the avian veterinarian has great references, then she could be the vet you are looking for.
- Does the veterinarian make house calls? This may be necessary if you have many birds.
- Does the office offer services such as boarding or microchipping?
- How many birds does your veterinarian see weekly? If she sees maybe one a month or so, she may not be the vet you should use.
- Does your veterinarian routinely hospitalize, medicate, anesthetize, inject, or do surgery on birds? If she rarely does, find another vet.
- How many veterinarians are in the practice, and how many see birds?
- Is the vet familiar with the species of bird you own? Birds such as linnies or rock pebblers are not that well known, so some vets have never seen that species.
- Are you comfortable with the vet's knowledge and how she treats you and your bird?

QUESTIONS THE VET MAY ASK YOU

Your vet may ask you several questions as well. This is especially true if you have an older bird.

Do you know how old the bird is? Older birds have different health concerns than younger birds, so this information will help with a more thorough exam.

Do you know the sex of the bird? If you don't, it is nothing to worry about. Your new vet may ask if it is important to find out what the sex is and order a DNA test.

Where did you obtain your bird? Let the vet know if you got him from a breeder, pet store, bird rescue, or from an ad in the newspaper. If the bird has had previous owners, this may explain some behavior issues. If the vet knows of certain problems common to babies from the store or breeder you used, she can be on the lookout for those problems.

What are you feeding your parrot? Let the vet know what you are feeding and if you give any supplements. Also, tell her how much you feed and how often.

The Emergency Clinic

Many veterinarians refer their after-hours clients to an emergency clinic. If your vet does this, you will need some information about the clinic before an emergency occurs. Get a business card or the phone number and address of the emergency clinic. Put this card, along with your avian veterinarian's card, on your refrigerator so that you won't have to look for it during an emergency. To be really prepared, get directions to the clinic ahead of time and keep them near the phone number.

How much time does your bird spend out of his cage? This will help explain his routine. If he is in his cage most of the day, this may alert the veterinarian that the bird needs more interaction or is in his cage too long.

What is his typical behavior like? Is he active, playful, quiet, noisy, or sedentary?

If your bird is a secondhand bird, the vet may ask if he was seen by any other veterinarian. This will let her know if she needs to send for records from that veterinarian. It will also let her know if there was anything she should be watching out for.

QUESTIONS YOU MAY WANT TO ASK THE VET

- Is my bird on a proper diet?
- Does he need any supplements?
- Is he a good weight?
- Does he need his wings clipped?
- Does he need his nails trimmed?
- Can you determine my bird's sex?
- Can you microchip my bird?

You can also ask about any behavioral concerns. If your bird is doing anything that causes you concern, ask about it.

If the vet runs tests, ask exactly what the tests are for and when will you get the results. Be clear on

You should take your parrot to an avian veterinarian yearly and whenever a health problem occurs.

any treatment plans for illnesses. Additionally, ask your vet for suggestions on how to make your sick parrot more comfortable. Ask if you need to quarantine or isolate him from any others you have in the house. Find out if your other birds need to be tested.

VISITING THE VETERINARIAN

Before you go to the vet, prepare a list of questions that you want to discuss with her. Don't rely on your memory at this time. You may want to make notes about your bird's behavior, how he is eating or drinking, and even how he is playing.

Birds are adept at masking signs of illness until it may be too late. Sometimes they may act only slightly differently, even if they are gravely ill. Being aware of what is normal for your bird could save his life, and by establishing routine visits with your vet, she will also learn what is normal for your bird. This information will help your vet identify any current or potential problems. I like to bring along a pen and a notepad so that I can write down any instructions or advice the vet has to offer. You do not want to leave this to memory.

If possible, try to bring your bird to the veterinarian in his own cage. (Remove the toys, swings, or any dangling objects for traveling.) This is usually only possible with smaller birds—you can't do this with a macaw cage, for example. This way, the vet may be able to diagnose potential problems from looking at the cage where your bird spends most of his time. She will look at the substrate you use, the placement of food and water dishes and the type of perches, as well as their locations, etc. Some people with larger cages who can't transport them have taken photos to show the vet. Bring a sample of your bird's main diet so that she can check that out as well.

THE EXAM ITSELF

Most avian veterinarians like to run a fecal test on the first visit because it is an important diagnostic tool for parasites or other abnormalities. Because birds poop often, the vet has an excellent chance of getting a fresh sample during the visit. Let her know what your bird has eaten because diet can affect the color and consistency of his droppings. Some things are normal; for example, loose droppings at the vet are usually a sign of stress and not a problem. Blood, undigested seed or food, and mucus are causes for concern.

Because diet plays a major role in the health of your bird, let your avian veterinarian know what kind of diet he was eating before you got him and what diet you are thinking of putting him on. The vet will also weigh your bird. The scale may have a perch attached, and all that he needs to do is step onto the perch, or he may be put into a little basket where he will be weighed. The vet will feel the bird's chest and keel bone to check muscle development. This will help her more than just the actual weight. Your vet will also let you know if your bird is too thin or too fat. A bird who is too thin or too fat may have an underlying medical condition. (See the chart of normal bird weights in this chapter.)

Your bird will need to be restrained for a thorough examination. The veterinarian will have a technician do this, so you don't need to worry. At this time, if you are interested in learning how to properly restrain your bird, ask them to show you; there is information on restraint in Chapter 6 of this book. It is always good to learn the proper way to do this in case of an emergency.

The physical examination will include checking the nares, eyes, ears, beak, throat, neck, wing, legs, feet, nails, vent, and tail. The condition of your bird's feathers, skin, nails, and beak will tell the veterinarian a great deal about his overall health. She will also listen to your bird's heart and lungs with a stethoscope to see if there is a problem.

Paying the Vet

Know up front that avian care can cost more than dog or cat care. This is mainly because the testing is different, extra expertise is needed, and the equipment is different. Pet insurance is available, although many companies do not include birds; check them out to find one that includes birds. Remember that there will be a monthly premium charge, but if your bird is ill, it will pay for itself. Another option is to set up a bank account just for bird emergencies and put money into that monthly.

Keeping track of your bird's weight will help you spot health issues early.

If your bird needs to have either his wings or nails trimmed, the avian veterinarian can do it after the exam. If this is something that you are thinking about doing, now is the time to ask questions.

As part of your first visit, the avian veterinarian may want to run other tests as well, depending on her findings. Ask when the results will be available, and inquire whether the office calls you with the results or you need to call the office. Blood work may be more expensive on birds than on dogs or cats because each species of birds has its own blood values.

Most likely your bird is in good health. However, if the vet sees something wrong, ask her if she will put it in writing so that you can talk to the place where you obtained your bird. Although not all places will pay to correct a problem, many will. But your first concern should be for your parrot.

The Importance of a Bird's Weight

How much should your bird weigh? As with all animals, there is a range. Keep in mind that males tend to weigh more than females. Also, some birds can be larger or smaller than the average. This is why you need to consider body size and build along with weight. The keel bone is one of the best indicators for

Species	Low Weight (grams)	High Weight (grams)		Species
African Grey, Congo	400	650		Hawk-Headed Parrot
African Grey, Timneh	275	400		Hyacinth Macaw
Alexandrine Parakeet	200	300		Illiger's Macaw
Bare-Eyed Cockatoo	425	580		Jardine's Parrot
Blue and Gold Macaw	900	1200		Jenday Conure
Blue-Crowned Conure	90	120		Kakarikis
Blue-Eyed Cockatoo	500	700		Lesser Sulfur-Crested Cockatoo
Blue-Fronted Amazon	275	500		Lilac-Crowned Amazon
Blue-Headed Pionus	225	260		Lineolated Parakeet
Blue-Naped Parrot	260	360		Major Mitchell's Cockatoo
Blue-Throated Macaw	600	850		Maximilian's Pionus
Bourke's Parakeet	40	50		Mexican Red-Headed Amazon
Bronze-Winged Pionus	200	270		Meyer's Parrot
Budgie	30	55		Military Macaw
Buffon's Macaw	1200	1500		Moluccan Cockatoo
Caiques	145	170		Moustached Parakeet
Canary-Winged Parakeet	60	75		Nanday Conure
Cockatiel	80	110		Noble Macaw
Derbyan Parakeet	240	320		Orange-Winged Amazon
Double Yellow-Headed Amazon	350	550		Palm Cockatoo (*aterrimus* subspecies)
Dusky Lory	150	160		
Eclectus	380	550		Palm Cockatoo (*goliath* subspecies)
Goffin's Cockatoo	250	380		
Goldie's Lorikeet	50	60		Parrotlets
Gray-Cheeked Parakeet	45	60		Patagonian Conure
Great-Billed Parrot	260	360		Peach-Faced Lovebird
Green-Winged Macaw	1200	1600		Princess of Wales Parakeet
Hahn's Macaw	155	170		Quaker Parakeet

Low Weight (grams)	High Weight (grams)
200	255
1250	1600
250	280
180	220
110	130
70	100
325	400
300	350
40	50
350	475
230	250
260	280
100	140
900	1000
670	1045
110	150
115	160
180	200
360	490
500	850
350	1300
28	35
210	300
45	60
90	125
90	150

Species	Low Weight (grams)	High Weight (grams)
Rainbow Lory	120	140
Red Lory	160	180
Red-Bellied Parrot	120	140
Red-Lored Amazon	340	360
Red-Tailed Cockatoo	300	350
Ring-Necked Parakeet	110	130
Rock Pebbler	165	185
Rose-Breasted Cockatoo	275	390
Scarlet Macaw	900	1100
Senegal Parrot	120	150
Severe Macaw	300	400
Sun Conure	100	140
Triton Cockatoo	875	1000
Umbrella Cockatoo	435	750
White-Capped Pionus	180	200
White-Fronted Amazon	200	240
White-Winged Parakeet	65	75
Yellow-Collared Macaw	240	265
Yellow-Fronted Amazon	380	480
Yellow-Naped Amazon	480	680

30 grams is approximately 1 ounce.

this—if you can't feel your bird's keel, he may be overweight.

Make a chart so that you can keep track of your bird's weight. Weight him at least twice a week, and weigh a young bird daily. This will tell you if he is eating, if he is overweight, or if he is ill. Keep in mind that a bird's weight will fluctuate during the day depending if he just ate, just pooped, etc. I like to weigh my birds in the morning after the first morning poop and before they eat their breakfast.

Look for patterns on the chart. If you see a consistent weight drop over a period of three or four days, call the vet. If there is a weight loss of more than 2 percent in a single 24-hour period, go to a vet right away. There should not be a loss of 3 to 4 percent over a several-day period. A 5 percent loss is very serious, and anything more than that can result in death if not treated.

Scales are generally inexpensive, and teaching your bird to step up on one isn't difficult either. There are a wide range of scales you can use, and the prices vary. I like the electronic scales myself. Make sure that the scale weighs in grams and not just ounces; grams are smaller, so the weights are more accurate. For small birds, find a scale that will weigh in hundredths. If you have a large bird, such as a macaw, the scale must go up to at least 3,000 grams. You can add a perch to the scale (remember to zero it out after doing so), and there are even bird-specific scales that come with perches. It's a good idea to teach your bird to step onto the scale perch.

Avian veterinarians are seeing more and more obese birds. Obesity is as dangerous in birds as it is in people, leading to fatty liver disease, heart disease, fatty tumors, respiratory distress, and even egg binding. Other health issues may also occur. So weigh your bird! Aviary and high-stress birds should be weighed only by a veterinarian.

Never diagnose or treat your parrot yourself. This could lead to complications or even the death of your bird. Never use over-the-counter medications unless directed to do so by an avian veterinarian.

Health and Sickness

What is a healthy bird? A healthy bird is alert, has shiny and bright feathers, grooms himself, engages in play, is active, has a good appetite, and talks or chatters as normal for his species. His eyes appear bright, and he takes an interest in his surroundings. His posture is upright, and his feathers aren't fluffed up. His nares are clear, and the feathers around the nares aren't stained.

However, like people, birds can get sick, and it is important to know when your parrot isn't feeling well. Birds are good at hiding illness, so it takes a watchful and observant owner to know when her parrot is ill.

Birds vary in how they display an illness or injury.

By knowing what is normal for your bird, you could save his life. *It is vital to take a sick bird to an avian veterinarian as soon as possible.* Waiting could kill your bird.

Until you can get your parrot to an avian veterinarian, keep him warm and try to get him to eat and drink. When you are transporting him to the vet's office in cooler weather, use a hot water bottle wrapped in a towel and put it in the cage or carrier. This will aid in keeping your bird warm.

SIGNS OF ILLNESS

Each bird is an individual, so it is vital that you know what's normal for your bird. Observe him when he is healthy, taking care to notice his activity level, noise level, frequency and consistency of his droppings, food and water intake, general appearance, etc. When one of these things changes, be aware that he may be ill.

The following are specific signs of illness that you should watch for.

ABNORMAL APPEARANCE
- bleeding
- bumps or swellings
- drooping head
- drooping wings
- fluffed up or ruffled feathers
- head weaving
- inability to fly
- leaning to one side
- loss of balance
- signs of hypothermia that do not disappear with interaction (ruffled feathers, holding up one leg, head tucked behind wing)
- sleepy appearance (not to be confused with normal sleeping)
- sores
- swelled with air (looking puffed up like a balloon)
- wounds or injuries

CERE, NARES, AND MOUTH
- discharge or clogging from nares or mouth
- inflammation around eyes or nares

The stained tail feathers on this cockatoo probably indicate a digestive problem.

- regurgitation (not caused because the bird is happy)
- whitish bumps on the roof of the mouth

RESPIRATORY SIGNS
- coughing (not because the bird has learned to imitate you coughing)
- difficulty in breathing
- rapid or labored breathing
- rattling or clicking noise when breathing
- sneezing (not because the bird has learned to imitate you sneezing)
- thunking sound when stressed

FEATHER CHANGES
- abnormal color or growth
- decreased preening
- drab, dirty-looking feathers
- feather plucking
- lines in the feathers
- loss of feather sheen
- matted feathers around the eyes, nares, or mouth
- missing feathers
- unusually heavy molt

EYES
- crusty-looking eyes
- discharge from the eyes
- eye that won't open
- eyes half closed when the bird is not sleeping or napping
- eyes that are dull and listless
- eyes that have an opaque, milky appearance
- injury to the eye
- kicking or rubbing at eye area
- puffy, swollen, or red eyes
- tearing

BEHAVIOR
- abrupt changes in personality
- convulsions
- dazed appearance
- decrease in activity
- decrease in vocalizations
- decrease or loss of appetite
- dizzy appearance
- flicking of head
- hyperactivity
- inability to perch
- increased appetite
- increased tameness (a bird who was wild one day is suddenly tame)
- lying on the bottom of the cage
- loss of use of a limb
- moodiness and or irritability
- not interested in playing with toys
- regression to baby behavior (only eating when hand-fed)
- shivering on perch
- sitting with feet farther apart
- spending more time on the bottom of the cage than normal
- staggering when walking
- sudden biting attacks (not hormonal)
- swaying or falling
- tail bobbing
- thrashing or night fright (this may be normal in some birds)
- unusual fears (afraid of things he wasn't afraid of before)

DROPPINGS
- blood in droppings
- color changes in droppings (not diet related)
- constipation or a decrease in number of droppings
- diarrhea (not caused by extra fruit

in the diet or diet change)
- matted or stained feathers around the vent
- smelly droppings
- soiled or pasted vent
- undigested seed or food in droppings

CROP ISSUES
- air in the crop
- baggy or overstretched crop
- crop empties too slowly
- crop that doesn't empty

BEAK, NAILS, AND FEET
- beak or nails overgrow and need frequent care
- black color on toes (not the nails)
- overly sensitive feet
- scaly crust on feet
- swollen feet

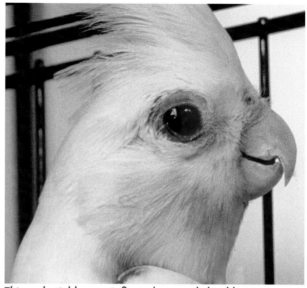

This cockatiel has an inflamed eye and should visit a veterinarian as soon as possible.

Caring for a Sick Bird

If your bird is ill, he may or may not need to stay at the vet. She may suggest that you take your bird home instead of staying at the office or hospital. This can be beneficial because you can give him more TLC than the vet's staff can. Also, your bird will see a familiar face and may eat or drink something because of that. How he feels emotionally could help his physical health.

The most important thing to do is to keep your bird warm and quiet. If you have other birds, quarantine the sick one from your healthy flock. Keep in mind that if your bird is not tame, it may be more difficult to care for him.

THE HOSPITAL CAGE

It doesn't cost a lot to make your own hospital cage. You can use an aquarium, a small cage, a travel cage, or even a brooder. If you have many birds, you might want to invest in a small incubator; these are usually for sale in bird magazines and are nice to have in an emergency. Many of them have both temperature and humidity controls. Whatever you use, you need to have appropriate bedding. Newspaper, paper towels, clean towels, and cloth diapers are excellent, especially if there is an injury. Pine shavings are okay to use if there isn't a wound. Check with your avian veterinarian to see what she recommends.

I like to use a heating pad set on low placed under the sick cage. If you don't have a heating pad, you can use a hot water bottle (placed under the sick cage), but it must be changed often to keep it warm. A heat lamp with an infrared bulb can also be used, but make sure that there isn't any Teflon coating on the bulb. The temperature in the hospital cage must stay between 80 and 90°F (26.7 and 32.2°C). Keep the heating devices away from your parrot so that he can't chew on them or get burned by the bulb. You will also need a thermometer (also kept away from your bird) to monitor the temperature of the hospital cage.

Perches are kept at a minimum in a hospital cage. They are normally at the lowest level possible. If you can't put a very low perch in the sick cage, it is okay to leave the perch out. The sick bird can just stay on the cage floor. There should be at least a small dish of food. I like to use one dish with seed/pellet mix and another with a favorite food. It is a good idea to measure the food and water in the morning and then in the evening to see how much your parrot has eaten and drunk. Toys are normally not put in a sick cage. However, if your bird is comforted by a certain toy, by all means include it.

CHECKING ON YOUR BIRD

Your parrot is sick and needs quiet so that he can get the rest he needs. However, you still need to check up on him often. Extra TLC is important. Talk calmly to him, and give him head scratches if he enjoys this.

Because he may not be on a perch, you must change the bedding often. Take note of the number of droppings and their condition (normal or watery, bloody food in them, etc.). This information is useful to the avian veterinarian.

If he doesn't seem to be eating, try offering warm (not hot) baby food on a spoon. You can also drop a few drops of the baby food with a syringe into his mouth. Don't force anything, though; you don't want your bird to aspirate on the food. Remember to take precautions such as washing your hands or changing your clothes before interacting with your other birds.

MEDICATING A SICK PARROT

If you have to medicate your bird, make sure that you understand the instructions before you leave the vet. Birds require small amounts of medication, and the difference between 0.1 cc and 1.0 cc can mean life or death for your parrot. Write down all of the medication information because you don't want to rely on your

Take Notes

Keep a sheet of paper or small pad with a pen near the hospital cage. Record any information that may be important: your bird's weight, food and water intake, changes in behavior, when you gave medication, his reactions to the drugs, etc. This information could help the vet later. If your bird needs to be medicated, this should be written down and not left to memory.

Mitred conure with a beak deformity. Birds who have beak problems need veterinary attention.

memory. Medicines also need to be given at the proper time. Do not double up a dose if you missed one unless your avian veterinarian advises you differently. Misunderstanding the instructions is the number-one cause of overdoses in parrots. Also, be sure that you know all about the side effects.

Give small amounts of the medication at a time, and don't squirt the entire syringe full of medication into his mouth at once. Doing so could cause your bird to aspirate the medicine.

By knowing that your parrot is indeed taking his medication, you will be able to tell if it is working. If you don't see a change in a day or so, contact your avian veterinarian and let her know. She may need to change the medication. Know what medicine your bird is on so that when you call the vet, you can give her that information immediately.

Common Health Problems

Different species can have different types of health problems. The problems described in this section

If you get your bird accustomed to eating from a spoon or syringe, it will be easier to medicate him should he get sick.

are those that the avian veterinarian sees most often in birds.

NUTRITIONAL PROBLEMS

As mentioned before, a poor diet is the number-one cause of death in parrots. Some individuals can still develop a deficiency, even if given a healthy and balanced diet. The deficiency could be due to another illness, age, breeding, feeding babies, or just because that is how your bird is. The most common deficiencies are vitamin A and calcium. Vitamin deficiencies are usually discovered during a regular veterinary exam. Some can show up as black lines in feathers, or the feathers may no longer look bright and healthy

OBESITY AND FATTY LIVER DISEASE

The most common dietary problem is obesity. This occurs in birds who are not fed properly and who get very little exercise. Obesity can lead to tumors, fatty liver disease, and kidney disease. Diets that are made up entirely of seed are the number-one cause of fatty liver disease.

In fatty liver disease, the liver stores too much fat, so it can't function properly. One of the liver's functions is to convert proteins and carbohydrates into fat. In fatty liver disease, the fat stays in the liver and does not get deposited into other areas of the body. This makes it appear that the bird is losing weight. One study done on poultry showed that choline deficiency can cause fatty liver disease. Some toxins (including chemicals and molds) can also cause fatty liver disease.

Female birds seem more prone to fatty liver disease. Budgies, cockatiels, Quakers, young cockatoos, and Amazons are the species most often diagnosed with this condition. The bird's skin may have a yellowish tinge to it, or his feathers may appear greasy looking.

Your veterinarian will need to test for this. The treatment and outcome depend on how far advanced the disease is. In the later stages of the disease, it is fatal.

PARASITES

Practicing good hygiene is the best way to cut down on parasites. However, even with the best hygiene, there is a slight chance of your bird developing parasites. This is especially true of parrots who are kept in outdoor aviaries.

MITES

The mites that infest parrots look like little bugs when viewed under a microscope but are invisible to the unaided eye. Mites lay their eggs in tunnels they make under the skin, usually causing itching. You will first notice them when they start to hatch because they leave a crusty material around the beak, cere, eyes, legs, and sometimes the vent. Mites are most commonly seen in budgies. Your vet needs to prescribe medication to kill off the mites. If not treated, the beak can become severely overgrown and may even become deformed.

WORMS

Worms can affect any species. Roundworms are long, thin, and white in appearance; these are the most common worms seen in parrots. Birds in aviaries with dirt floors are in the most danger of getting roundworms. If your bird is eating a lot and losing weight, has pasty-looking diarrhea, a stained vent, weakness, or has a pot-bellied appearance, he may have roundworms. This is something you need to see your veterinarian about and not treat yourself. Roundworms can cause liver and other organ damage.

If your bird has worms, sterilize his entire environment. This needs to be done each time you clean the cage and for a period after the worms are gone. All that is needed to test if your bird has worms is a fecal sample. Regardless of being aviary or companion birds, they should have a yearly test for worms.

GIARDIA AND OTHER PROTOZOA

Giardia is a single-celled organism that can infest any bird, although it is

Medicating Made Easy

I feel that it is very important to teach a bird to take food from a spoon or a syringe while he's well. This will make medicating so much easier—a sick bird is already stressed, and having to force medications into him will just add more stress. My oldest bird Charlie loves to be fed his nightly amount of warm oatmeal or baby food on a spoon or in a syringe. All of my birds are fed at least once a week with a spoon or a syringe.

Veterinarians usually anesthetize birds for X-rays, which are used to detect aspergillosis and other health problems.

most commonly seen in budgies and cockatiels. *Giardia* is detected in a fecal exam. This protozoan grows to maturity in the small intestines. Your bird may have it if he has constant diarrhea that smells foul, weight loss or no weight gain, a poor appetite, feather plucking, depression, yeast or bacterial infections in the intestinal tract. *Giardia* could even result in death. Other protozoa can cause similar symptoms, but they are less common than *Giardia*. Be careful interacting with your bird if he has *Giardia*; people can contract this illness.

FUNGAL INFECTIONS

Fungal infections in parrots are normally one of two types: aspergillosis or candidiasis (yeast infection). Other types are possible but rare.

ASPERGILLOSIS

Aspergillosis is caused by a species of *Aspergillus* mold. It affects the respiratory organs, lungs, air sacs, trachea, syrinx, and bronchi. It changes how your bird breathes and vocalizes, causing gasping and wheezing. It is very difficult to treat, and it may take many months of medicating your bird before he is better. The mold can form on peanuts, seed, or even in certain bedding materials if proper sanitation is lacking. Blood work, X-rays, and even cultures are needed to make a diagnosis. If not treated, the bird will die.

CANDIDIASIS

Candidiasis—more commonly referred to as a yeast infection—is also caused by a fungus. Yeast infects the digestive system, especially the mouth, crop, esophagus, and lower intestinal tract. Because of their high-sugar diet, lories and lorikeets are particularly susceptible to yeast infections. This is also true of baby birds. Symptoms can be a slow-emptying crop or even crop stasis. There is weight loss or no weight gain, vomiting, and diarrhea. If the yeast is in the respiratory system, the bird may have trouble breathing.

Testing for Giardia

A new test is now available that uses a DNA probe. This test is extremely sensitive and will detect even the smallest amount of *Giardia*. This is particularly useful to breeders because they can bring in samples taken from several birds.

A culture is usually used to detect yeast, although it can sometimes be seen when there is an excessive amount of yeast on the mucous membranes. It will look white and cheesy and have a foul odor. Supplements such as *Lactobacillus acidophilus* (beneficial bacteria) are sometimes given to baby birds to build up the good bacteria in their digestive tracts. Garlic is another aid, which not only helps digestion but also lowers cholesterol, improves circulation, and helps stimulate the immune system. Birds who are on antibiotics are more prone to yeast infections. Before giving your bird any supplements or medication, check with your avian veterinarian first. Feeding diets high in vitamins A and C helps prevent yeast infections.

BACTERIAL INFECTIONS

Good hygiene and proper food storage help prevent bacterial infections. Bacteria can infect numerous organs and parts of the body, including the eyes, sinuses, and digestive tract. Symptoms include—depending on where the infection is—weight loss, vomiting, diarrhea, loss of appetite, bloody stools, wheezing, sneezing, ruffed up feathers, runny eyes, inflamed eyes, and discharge from the nares. It is best to have a culture done so that the vet will know exactly which bacteria are causing the infection and which treatment is the most likely to be effective.

PSITTACOSIS (PARROT FEVER)

Chlamydia psittaci (now called *Chlamydophilia psittaci*) is one of the few infections that can pass from birds to humans. It is known better as parrot fever or psittacosis. It is very contagious, and it causes damage to the

Peanut shells may contain dangerous molds. To ensure your bird's safety, feed him shelled peanuts.

respiratory and digestive systems as well as the liver and kidneys. It is airborne and found in the dust and droppings of infected birds. Getting a positive diagnosis is difficult on a living bird because there is no single test available that can detect it in all species. Birds who carry the disease may look healthy, but they shed the bacteria in their droppings. Symptoms can include inactivity, loss of appetite, diarrhea, runny eyes, respiratory problems, nasal discharge, green or yellow-green droppings, and ruffled feathers. In humans, the symptoms can range from mild flu-like symptoms to severe and life-threatening pneumonia.

The shed bacteria can remain infectious for several months in the environment and are found most often where there are poor conditions such as overcrowding, cool temperatures, and poor hygiene. If the bird is shipped, the stress can trigger the disease as well. It is all too often seen in smuggled birds.

Although there isn't a definitive test for psittacosis, some tests may be run. The problem is that there are often false negatives for these tests. Talk to your avian veterinarian about which tests she recommends and which is the best one for your situation.

The usual treatment is antibiotics given for at least 45 days. Prevention is the best cure. *Chlamydophilia psittaci* in the cage can be killed with a bleach solution, isopropyl alcohol, and Roccal-D.

VIRAL INFECTIONS

Viral infections are very hard to treat, but the sooner you get your bird to the vet, the better the outcome is likely to be. Similar to bacteria, viruses can cause a wide range of symptoms.

PACHECO'S DISEASE

Pacheco's disease (also called PDV) is caused by various herpes viruses, resulting in acute hepatitis in parrots. Some species such as the nanday and Patagonian conures can be carriers for this disease. Pacheco's is highly contagious.

The mortality rate for Pacheco's is nearly 100 percent. Asian and African species may survive, but they will become carriers. There is no cure; treatments are most effective before symptoms appear. Tests could take weeks to come back, and by then the bird could be dead.

Good sanitation and the use of disinfectant will kill the virus. It is short lived out of the body. Alcohol does not work against Pacheco's, but a bleach solution does. Quarantining will also prevent the disease from spreading. The virus is passed in the droppings within 48 hours after a bird has been exposed. Exposure can be through ingesting droppings or breathing in the virus. Symptoms include regurgitation, yellow to green urates in the droppings, tremors, seizures, imbalance, and finally, death.

Some parrots are more susceptible than others to Pacheco's. These species include the cockatiels, lovebirds, Amazons, macaws, conures, Quakers, rosellas, budgies, African greys, eclectus, and pionus. These birds die very quickly from the disease, although macaws persist longer than other species. Some conures may recover, but they will spread the disease. Any bird who is exposed to Pacheco's and survives should be considered a potential carrier. Blood tests, a cloacal swab, and a test for DNA are generally used to detect Pacheco's.

PROVENTRICULAR DILATION DISEASE (PDD)

Proventricular dilatation disease is also known as PDD and macaw wasting disease. It affects other species as well but was first seen in macaws. The disease is believed to be caused by a virus. The morality rate is near 100 percent. PDD affects the digestive and nervous systems. The bird lacks the ability to digest food, which causes severe weight loss and wasting. Symptoms to look for are undigested seed or food in the droppings, lack of appetite, drastic weight loss, muscle tissue that is wasting away, imbalance, and weakness. Blood work, cultures, and X-rays may be used to make a diagnosis. It is contagious to an unknown degree, so quarantining is essential.

Pacheco's Vaccinations

There is now a vaccine available to prevent Pacheco's disease. Birds as young as four weeks can be vaccinated. Some parrots are very sensitive to the vaccine. Talk to your avian veterinarian about the vaccine, especially if you have a cockatoo, African grey, or blue and gold macaw.

Basic Rules of Avian First Aid

- Place your bird in a sick cage with the perch either low to the ground or missing.
- Keep your bird warm. The range should be around 80 to 90°F (26.7 to 32.2°C).
- Keep your bird quiet.
- Keep your bird isolated from other birds.
- Provide accessible food and water. Make sure that your bird can get to these things.
- Try not to disturb your bird more than is necessary.
- If your bird is injured, stop the bleeding quickly. You may need to check often to make sure that he isn't bleeding once again.
- If your bird has a broken wing or leg, keep him from flapping around.
- Call your avian veterinarian as soon as possible.
- Remain calm.

PSITTACINE BEAK AND FEATHER DISEASE (PBFD)

PBFD affects many different species of parrots. It is most commonly seen in young birds, although older birds can get the disease as well. Symptoms include loss of feathers, abnormal feathers, overgrown or deformed beak, and lesions on the back or feet. In cockatoos, the crest feathers on the head are usually the first to show the disease. It is sometimes confused with feather plucking. There is also a loss of powder down. It is spread from the droppings and feather dust of infected birds. In some species, such as eclectus, the head feathers may appear normal. These parrots may have heavy molts or appear featherless in areas for a time before growing some feathers back.

The incubation period is 21 to 28 days, although the symptoms may not show up for months to several years. The life span of an infected bird is generally six months to one year, although some birds have lived as long as ten years. Because PBFD weakens the immune system, the bird may develop secondary infections.

First Aid

No matter how careful we are, accidents can happen. If an accident does occur, knowing how to handle the emergency can mean the difference between life and death.

THE AVIAN FIRST-AID KIT

Put together an avian first-aid kit as soon as possible. You may never need to use it, but it will be there if you do. Having all of these things in one place during an emergency could mean the difference between life and death for your bird.

A list of items you should include in an avian first-aid kit follows. Items followed by an asterisk are the most important and will help in most emergencies. The other items listed are very good to have; you can add these later to make a complete kit. You can use a crafts box, a fishing tackle box, or even a shoe box to store your supplies. Bird first-aid kits are sold online. However, most are not as complete as one you put together yourself.

Items for an avian first-aid kit include:

- activated charcoal or peanut butter (for ingestion of toxic material)
- aloe vera (for burns)
- antibacterial hand gel (to keep things sterile)
- antibiotic ointment (check with vet as to which one is best)
- bandaging materials (to cover wounds)*
- clotting agent (styptic powder, corn starch, flour, etc.)
- cotton balls (for cleaning wounds)*
- cotton swabs (for cleaning wounds or applying ointment)*
- eye dropper
- eyewash solution (ask your vet what she recommends)
- gauze (for cleaning wounds or covering wounds and burns)*
- gel foam (ask your vet for this; it stops bleeding)
- hand-feeding formula, such as baby foods, baby oatmeal, or rice or barley cereals
- hot water bottle, heating pad, or heat light (to keep your bird warm)*
- latex gloves (to keep things sterile)
- list of emergency numbers*
- magnifying glass (to get a better look at an injury)
- micropore tape, also called surgical tape (to hold gauze in place)
- mild soap or dishwashing liquid (to clean grease or oil from feathers)
- nail file
- needle-nosed pliers or hemostats (for removing blood feathers)*
- Pedialyte, dilute karo syrup, apple juice, Gatorade, etc. (so that your bird won't become dehydrated)
- penlight flashlight (to get a better look at an injury)
- povidine iodine scrub*
- scissors (for cutting bandages, gauze, strings wrapped around toes, etc.)*
- sterile saline solution*
- sterile syringes (to clean out wounds or to give medicine with)*
- sterile water (for flushing wounds)
- thermometer (to check temperature of your bird's environment, not to be used on the bird)
- towel (to help restrain your bird)*
- tweezers (to remove embedded object)*

Don't Do It!

Never do any of the following unless directed to do so by an avian veterinarian:

- Never give your bird any alcohol.
- Never apply oil anywhere on your bird.
- Never diagnose your bird's problem without consulting an avian veterinarian.
- Never give over-the-counter medicines.
- Never treat your bird yourself.
- Never give your bird medication that is meant for humans.

- vet wrap (for broken wings, legs, and holding gauze in place)
- wooden tongue depressors or popsicle sticks (to immobilize broken leg)

BLOOD FEATHERS

The most common emergency is a broken blood feather. If this happens to your bird, you need to address it immediately. Birds do not have a lot of blood, so even a small amount of blood loss could be serious.

It is best to have two people performing this procedure, one person to restrain and the other to either try to stop the bleeding or to pull the feather out. Have your equipment ready before you start. This should include a towel, needle-nosed pliers (or hemostats), and a clotting agent, such as flour, cornstarch, or styptic powder.

With one person restraining your bird, the other person needs to locate the blood feather. First try putting a liberal amount of the clotting agent on the feather, apply some pressure, and wait for a few seconds. If the bleeding stops, keep checking to make sure that it doesn't start again or that your bird doesn't re-injure it and cause bleeding once again. Remember that styptic powder is toxic if ingested, so try other clotting agents—cornstarch, white flour—first.

If the bleeding doesn't stop, then the feather will need to be pulled. With one person firmly restraining your bird, have the second person locate the bleeding feather. Using the needle-nosed pliers or hemostats, the second

Blood feathers on the wing of a double yellow-headed Amazon. Bird owners should learn to recognize blood feathers.

person should grasp the feather as close to the follicle as possible without pinching the skin. Using a steady motion and not a quick jerk, smoothly pull the feather straight out from the follicle in the same direction that the feather was naturally growing. Your bird may squawk in pain slightly or struggle more because it hurts, but you just prevented him from bleeding to death.

Once you pull the feather, check to see if the bleeding stops. If it doesn't, apply the flour and pressure. Hold for a minute or two. Ideally, what happens when you pull the feather is that the feather follicles fold over each other and naturally prevent bleeding.

I Can't Find the Bleeding

What happens if you can't locate the source of the bleeding? Sometimes by applying a small amount of water over the area, you can see

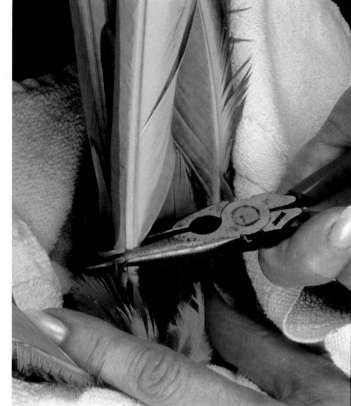

Needle-nosed pliers are useful for removing broken blood feathers.

where the bleeding originated. This can occur when there is more than one damaged feather. You must remove all of the bleeding feathers.

I Can't Stop the Bleeding

What happens if you did everything right and you still can't stop the bleeding? You must get to an avian veterinarian immediately. In very rare circumstances, the follicles do not properly seal up. Don't panic! Call your avian veterinarian even if it is after hours. She may either meet you at the office or direct you to the nearest emergency clinic. If possible, another person can call the clinic and let the office know that you are on your way. This person can give information such as what kind of bird you have and what has been done so far.

Do not drive yourself. You will be worried and scared, so driving at this time isn't a good idea. Apply pressure to the area that is bleeding, but not so much pressure that you break the wing. You do not want to cause further pain and injury to your bird.

Microchip Identification

With today's advances in technology, a bird owner is better able to protect her bird against theft or accidental loss. In the past, if you suspected that your lost or stolen bird was in someone else's possession, you had little chance of proving that he was indeed your bird unless there was something unusual about him. Today, there is microchipping. The largest and the one used most often for birds is American Veterinary Identification Devices (AVID). AVID reads around 98 percent of the chips on the market but can't read the chips on the European market as of yet.

Microchips are the only permanent method of identifying your bird. They are also undetectable except with a scanner. They can't be removed without causing injury or killing your bird. This procedure is relatively inexpensive.

ABOUT THE CHIP

Each microchip is programmed with a unique 13-digit, alphanumeric ID number. This number is stored in a national registry and can be checked to verify ownership. Many animal control facilities and humane societies now have microchip readers available. Because of this, many lost pets have been recovered.

The microchip has a carbon core with a computer chip on half of the core, while on the other half is a copper wire. The chips are encased in solid glass. The reason why glass is used is that it is an inert material, so it is biocompatible and will not cause any reaction from your bird's tissue.

The microchip itself has no power source. To activate the chip, a special reader is passed over the area where it was implanted. The reader is the energy source, and it activates the microchip. The chip's copper wire and the reader's magnetic field produce an electric current. There is no need for concern because your bird can't feel this happening at all.

Microchips rarely go bad. If the chip is defective, it will be defective right from the beginning. How long

Not for Small Birds

Right now, microchips can be implanted into medium to large parrots. Most veterinarians won't chip a bird smaller than a ring-necked parakeet in body size. There are a few avian veterinarians who are implanting chips in birds the size of a canary-winged parakeet, but these are implanted surgically.

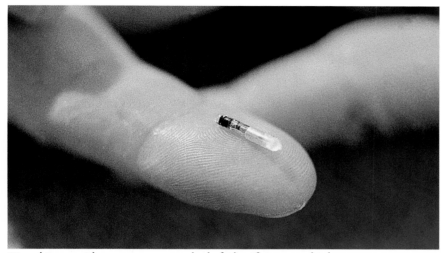

Microchips provide a permanent method of identifying your bird.

the chip will last isn't really known yet. Some birds can live 50 years or more, and there isn't any data available to see if they last that long. In most chips that are implanted into dogs and cats, the manufacturer promises at least a 25-year lifetime.

IMPLANTING THE CHIP

The procedure is simple, safe, and no worse than an injection would be. The chip is manually put into a needle that is slightly larger than a normal needle—this is more upsetting to the owner than the bird. Instead of punching a hole like a normal needle does, it slices a hole. The syringe that holds the needle has a steel pin inside. An assistant firmly restrains the bird while the veterinarian rubs ice on the spot to numb the area. This will also control any bleeding that might occur. (Bleeding is rare.)

The needle is then inserted into the area and the steel pin (plunger) pushes the chip into place. In birds, the chips are always injected into the left breast muscle about 1/4 inch (0.6 cm) deep. Most birds don't make any sound or even struggle when this happens. Once the chip is in place, scar tissue will form around it, effectively disguising it. Because most veterinarians perform this procedure in either a sterile operating room or in a cleaned examination room, infection almost never occurs.

DATABASE

Each chip's ID number is stored in a national database. When your bird is chipped, you will receive a certificate with the number that identifies him.

You will also be asked your address and telephone numbers so that you can be located if your bird is stolen or escapes.

The program has recovered and reunited thousands of owners with their parrots. Keep in mind that you may need to contact AVID if you move, change your name, or sell your bird so that the information will be correct.

Sexing Your Bird

Is your parrot male or female? For most species, this question is not so easy to answer. Many parrot species show little difference (to human eyes, at least) between males and females. To determine the sex of one of these birds, the owner will likely need to consult a veterinarian. There are two methods for sexing parrots: surgical and genetic (DNA).

SURGICAL SEXING

Surgical sexing is the best method for those who wish to breed their birds. It is 90 percent accurate, and it is done under a safe anesthesia. Once the bird is anesthetized, a small incision is made in the abdomen. The vet inserts an endoscope into the incision and views the internal organs. This procedure works best on a mature bird of breeding age. Not only can it tell the sex, but it can also determine how healthy the sex organs are and if the bird is ready to breed.

GENETIC SEXING

Genetic sexing (often called DNA sexing) involves analyzing the chromosomes of a bird to determine his sex. To understand how this is done, you need to know a few basics about bird genetics.

Male parrots have two sex chromosomes called Z chromosomes. The female parrots have one Z and one W. When the sex cells combine to form an embryo, the embryo can only receive a Z chromosome from its father but can receive a Z or a

A veterinarian usually draws blood from a parrot's toe for genetic sexing.

Differences Between DNA and Surgical Sexing	
DNA	SURGICAL
Can't tell if the bird's organs are healthy or if the bird is ready or able to breed	Can tell if the sexual organs are healthy and if the bird is ready and able to breed
The bird can be sexed at any age, even recently hatched	The bird should be older or sexually mature or this method may not be as accurate
No risk at all to the bird	Risk of infection, trauma, or even problems with the anesthesia
99.9% accurate	90% accurate

W from its mother. If the embryo received two Zs, it will be male, and if it received a Z and W, it will be female. This is opposite from humans and most mammals, in which the male determines the sex. In parrots, it is the female who determines the sex.

In DNA analysis, a small blood sample is taken. This can be done during a nail trim. Only two drops of blood are needed for this procedure. It can be done at any age, even on newly hatched chicks because the genes remain constant throughout a bird's lifetime. Then an analysis of the chromosomes is done in a laboratory. This has proven as much as 99.9 percent accurate. The 0.1 percentage of error has always been due to human error, which is usually caused by mislabeling the samples that have been sent to the lab.

An advantage to this method is that DNA sexing can determine abnormalities in the genes. When this happens, it does not necessarily mean that the bird is infertile. If genetic abnormalities are present, the bird may have abnormal sex organs. This can then be investigated further using surgical means.

The Senior Parrot

Birds are now living longer in captivity, mainly due to better diet and advances in avian medicine. As they age, they can go through the same age-related problems that humans do.

Parrots can develop arthritis, heart disease, digestive and respiratory problems, and even senility. Their immune system gets weaker. Like humans, elderly birds need extra care. They may require extra vitamins and mineral supplements in their diet, most notably extra calcium. As a bird ages, his bones may become more fragile and prone to breaks.

You may need to change your parrot's diet because the digestive system of an elderly bird may be more easily upset than when he was younger. He may also need to see the vet more frequently.

You may have to adapt your parrot's cage and environment to meet his needs. A bird with arthritis may not be able to perch or climb very well, so you may have to adapt and lower the perches and possibly provide ramps to help with climbing.

Older birds do not play as actively as they once did. They may sit around quietly much more often, but some exercise is still good for them. Your avian veterinarian will be able to tell you what she thinks your aged bird is able to tolerate.

Handicapped Birds

Birds can develop handicapping conditions at any point in their lives. Some birds are born with a handicap, and others may develop one because of an accident. Minor handicaps like a missing toe may not require any extra care, but birds with more severe handicaps will need extra care for the rest of their lives.

A girlfriend of mine has a cockatoo whose beak was bitten off by a cage mate. She had to hand-feed him for a long time until the surgery to repair his beak healed. Foods were mixed in a blender and spoon-fed to the bird. Feeding a soft diet or hand-feeding is a great way to help a bird with a beak problem.

Blind birds have also proven amazing at getting around. Some owners have trained them to go to food dishes and water bottles by tapping on them. They do this tapping many times a day to make sure that the bird is eating and drinking. One lady who had a blind female cockatoo didn't even know that the bird was blind until her male cage mate got sick. She always wondered why the male would go to the food and water dishes and tap on them. It turned out he was helping her find the food and water.

Birds with foot or leg deformities have a hard time perching, so food and water dishes should be kept low. If you are handy, you can build a nice environment where your bird can get around the cage by ramps. Some perches are necessary, but they can be wider so that your bird doesn't have to grip them as much. Sometimes you may need to help exercise your bird's legs for him, which can also include massage. Your veterinarian will be able to tell you what exercises are best for your bird.

Toys may need to be adapted as well. Your parrot may need toys that are meant for smaller birds because he can't hold or chew the right-sized toys.

Birds with neck injuries and deformities may have trouble getting around, as well as trouble with balance. Certain toys may be needed to encourage play to strengthen neck muscles.

Birds who have seizures may need to have one or two toys (depending on what the vet says), and the cage may require some extra and/or softer bedding material. This will help prevent injury if your bird has a seizure and falls to the ground.

Even birds with one wing tend to get around very nicely; they just can't fly. A one-winged parrot may have some balance-related problems until he gets used to the missing wing, but in time, this problem will disappear.

Handicapped birds require more care, which can be more expensive. You have to decide if the quantity of life outweighs the quality of life. However, everyone I ever talked to who owned a handicapped bird told me the expense was worth it.

For handicapped birds, you may need to eliminate or lower the perches and use a soft floor covering.

When You Can no Longer Care for Your Parrot

Parrots can be long lived—many species can live to be 50, 60, or even up to 100 years old! You need to think seriously about providing for your bird when you are gone or can no longer take care of him.

MAKING A WILL

In many states, it is illegal to leave your estate to an animal. However, you can make provisions for your bird instead. You may want to leave him to your children, a relative, a friend, or a conservation program. Talk with your lawyer and have her formalize your wishes in a legal document.

You may also want to contact bird clubs because they may have information regarding providing for your pet bird. Some clubs have excellent adoption programs that would guarantee your bird a good home. Some seniors who knew that they could no longer take care of their birds have interviewed people to make sure that their bird would be going to a good home.

Don't make this a surprise. Make sure that the person with whom you have decided to leave your bird knows about this. To make it easier on your bird, have that person visit regularly so that he will get to know and accept her. A parrot, like a person, does go through a mourning period, and if he knows the person he is going to, the transition will be easier on him.

TRUST FUNDS

Some people have set up a trust fund for their loyal feathered companions. Although you can't leave your money directly to your bird, you can create a trust fund that will see to his continued care. Do not leave the person that is caring for your bird in charge of this but rather a third party. This is a precaution against the caretaker using the trust for things beside your bird's care. The money can be used to pay for food, toys, and veterinary care or whatever else you specify.

Records for the New Person

Keep copies of your bird's medical records as well as lists of his likes, dislikes, and quirks. Write down what his daily routine is and other pertinent information. If he is microchipped, make sure that you have that number in this important paperwork. Let the new caretaker know where you keep these records so that she will have no difficulty finding them when they are needed.

242

When a Bird Dies

One of the hardest things in life to deal with is the loss of a loved one, whether a human or a pet. Unfortunately, society is sometimes rather insensitive when it comes to the loss of a pet. Comments such as "It was only a bird" or "Just go out and get yourself another one" are heard all too often. People become very close to their pets, and pets are like children to many people. Don't let anyone tell you to get over it or that it was "just a bird." That bird was a very big part of your life.

Losing a pet is difficult for an adult, but it is even harder on a child. A child doesn't understand why the bird died and may not understand what death is. Talk to your child about what happened in terms that she will understand. Let her know that it is okay to feel sad or angry and that it is okay to cry. If at all possible, allow her to say a final good-bye to the bird or maybe even have a small memorial service. These things will help with the grieving period.

As with the loss of any loved one, you need to go through a grieving period. Everyone goes through the grieving period differently. Depression is common. Call your local humane society, and it will be able to put you in touch with a support group. You can also check with your avian veterinarian about a group in your area. Members of these support groups have also lost a pet that they loved, so they know what you are going through. Talking helps, and writing in a journal is also helpful. It allows you to remember your bird and all the joy he gave you.

It isn't only humans who feel the loss of a pet; if you have other pets at home, they may also going through a grieving period. They may not want to eat or play, and they may become very quiet. Try to give them extra attention, stick to your normal routine, and get them to eat. Allow them to go through the grieving period with you.

Don't rush out to get another pet. Not only does this not allow you to go through the grieving period, but you may unfairly compare the new bird with the one who died. Wait, grieve, and accept what happened first before getting

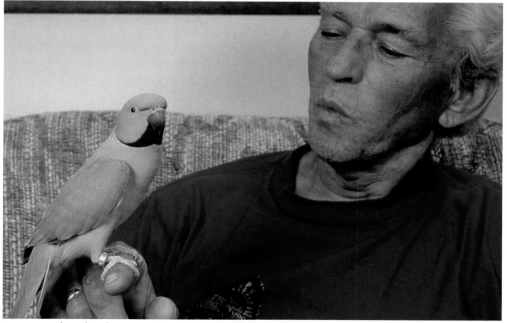

Parrots are long-lived pets, so it is wise to plan for a time when you may no longer be able to care for your bird.

a new one.

EUTHANASIA

If your bird is very ill or seriously injured, your veterinarian may talk to you about euthanasia. Sometimes when a pet has a terminal illness or is suffering, an owner may decide to end his pain or prevent more suffering. Euthanasia is a humane way to quietly and painlessly put an animal to sleep. This is one of the hardest decisions that any pet owner has to make.

Your veterinarian will offer you the option of saying a last good-bye. Some veterinarians will also allow you to be there when they put your bird to sleep. This is up to you, and with some people, it gives them closure. Talk to your veterinarian about what to expect and if it is better to be there.

FINAL FAREWELL

After your parrot passes away, your veterinarian will ask what the final arrangements are. Cremation is an option if you want the ashes back. Many people opt for a backyard burial or even burial at a pet cemetery. Your veterinarian can supply you with the name of a reputable pet cemetery. Other people have chosen to take their pet to a taxidermist and have him stuffed.

If this was a family pet, allow your family to take part in the decision. With a burial, you can have a memorial service, which will also help with the grieving period. If you decide on cremation, you can have a service and scatter the ashes. This will not only help you cope, but if you have kids, it will help them as well.

NECROPSY

A necropsy is an autopsy on an animal. Sometimes it is necessary to determine the cause of death. This is especially true if you have other birds around. Many things can contribute to a bird's death, and a necropsy can help determine the cause. A necropsy is important because if your bird did die of some contagious disease, you may need to treat all of your other birds to prevent them from becoming sick, or it may reveal a situation you need to correct.

As with coroners, veterinarians take great care with the deceased, treating the pet with the same respect as she did when he was alive. She will carefully check the organs for any clue. If there is no visible clue, she may take cultures and body fluids for further testing.

If you can't get to a veterinarian a short time after your bird has died, place the deceased bird in a plastic bag and put him in the refrigerator. *Do not put him in the freezer.* Freezing the bird will destroy tissues, possibly

Tips for Coping With the Loss of a Pet

- Don't be surprised if you feel many different emotions when your pet dies. You will feel sorrow and a sense of loss, but you may also feel guilt, anger, depression, and denial. These are all a normal part of the grieving process.
- Talk about your feelings. Don't deny them. You have a right to feel what you feel. If it makes you feel better, cry, scream, pound on a pillow, and talk out loud. Do what makes you feel best.
- Write down your feelings. Some people write stories, letters, or even poems. You can also make a photo scrapbook or memorial.
- Contact a support group though a humane society, church, hospital, or Internet forum. You deserve support during this time.
- Don't let others minimize your loss.
- Support your children and allow them to grieve as well. Be honest with them about what happened, and answer all of their questions.
- If there are other pets that are mourning, allow them to do so, but provide them with more TLC. They also need to grieve in their own way.

preventing the veterinarian from making an accurate determination of the cause of death.

A necropsy can also put to rest any guilt you may feel over your bird's death. It may let you know that you were not responsible for his death and that there was nothing you could have done to prevent it. I have personally lost a few birds, and I had necropsies done on them. It helped ease my mind knowing that there was nothing I could have done to prevent their passing.

Chapter Eight

TAMING AND TRAINING YOUR PARROT

Parrots are wonderful companions, and with proper care and handling, they can remain wonderful companions for the rest of their lives. You can keep your bird from becoming a monster by establishing clear and consistent rules early on and sticking to them. You need to establish a nurturing, dominant bond with your bird in which you are the one in charge, not him. This must be done in a loving, patient, gentle, and consistent manner so that your bird will not constantly be contesting your authority.

Consistent and gentle training will help you develop a trusting bond with your parrot.

Ideally, this process should start when you first bring your bird home. It is much easier to start off on the right foot than to try to retrain a bird after behavior problems have surfaced. The key to a well-behaved parrot is to buy one who has been properly socialized. Birds who were properly socialized and not force-weaned have fewer behavior problems than those who were force-weaned and not properly socialized.

Holding A Parrot

Holding your bird the right way is a good place to start proper training. When this grip is used properly, it will prevent your bird from flying or jumping off your hand and will give you more control over him. With your hand held out as if to shake someone's hand, your bird should stand with one or both feet on your hand between your fingers and thumb. Then place your thumb over one or both of the bird's feet. You do not need to put a lot of pressure on his feet; you are just holding them gently.

Whether you hold onto one or two feet will depend on the size of your bird. Larger birds may feel more comfortable with one foot on your wrist while you hold onto the other with your thumb. This gives them a wider stance for better balance.

Smaller birds are sometimes shy of hands, and they may object to you touching their feet with your thumb. Be patient and go slowly. Start with barely touching your parrot's feet. Remember to offer praise when you do this. Eventually, it will become second nature to you and your bird. I know that whenever I hold my birds, this is so automatic that I never have to think about it.

By using this grip, you will also prevent a larger bird from climbing up on your shoulder. Remember that a bird on your shoulder is the one who is in charge of the situation and not you. If he is startled or scared, he may fly away forever or he could rearrange your face.

Parrot Body Language

Wouldn't life be so much simpler if our birds could tell us what they are thinking, what they are feeling, and what they want? Our birds do communicate their needs to us through their body language. Some are better

Learning to read your parrot's body language is essential to successful training. Note the raised nape feathers and tiny, pinprick pupils on this blue and gold macaw. These are warnings to back off or risk being bitten.

at communicating through body language than others, but if you know what to look for, you'll be able to understand your bird better. Parrots also communicate through actions such as beak wiping, pushing their human's hand for scratches, and vent rubbing.

BEAK GRINDING

This is a normal behavior that many birds do when they are content and ready to go to sleep. Some species do this more often than others do. Grinding is normal, crunching isn't—crunching likely indicates that your bird is demolishing something. When your bird grinds, you may notice that his eyes are closed or half closed, and his feathers may be slightly fluffed up.

I Want a Bath

Most parrots enjoy bathing, and some don't like to wait for you to fit it into your schedule. These birds will let you know when they want a bath.

A bird who wants a bath will ruffle up his feathers, spread his wings, and maybe start surfing up and down his cage. He may even go over to his water bottle or water dish and try to splash water on himself. He may move his head as if he is throwing water on his back. His tail area may be ruffled up (not spread), and he may wag his tail.

If I can, I mist my birds when they engage in this behavior. I feel that they enjoy their baths so much more if they get one when they want it instead of when it's convenient for me.

BEAK WIPING

A bird will wipe his beak for two reasons. First, he may be wiping food or debris off his beak. Parrots don't like having food all over their faces. Second, if another bird or intruder comes into his territory, beak wiping is a threat or a challenge. You can determine which is the case by seeing if your bird just ate or if someone (person or other pet) entered his space.

EYE PINNING

Pinning, also known as flashing or dilating the size of the pupils down to pinpoints, can be a sign of many different things. A bird could be pinning because he is excited, nervous, or very happy or even as a sign of aggression. If it is accompanied by a tail that is fanning—spreading out the feathers of the tail—this is an aggressive behavior and it means back off.

FEATHERS

Birds can communicate by how they hold their feathers. If your bird is holding his feathers tightly against his body, he's scared of something. If his feathers are fluffed up and he is standing up trying to look larger, he is defending his territory. Fluffed feathers can also be a sign that your bird is cold or sick. Feathers raised on the nape is one sign of aggression.

Cockatoos and cockatiels signal their feelings with their crests. If yours opens his crest, he is excited and happy to see you. If he holds his crest very high, it

could be an indication of excitement or fear. If his crest lies flat while he hisses, he is being aggressive and might attack.

HEAD DOWN, FEATHERS UP

All of my birds ask nicely for head scratches with their body language. A parrot who wants to be scratched will drop his head, close or half close his eyes, and raise the feathers on his head and back. Some of my birds will lift their foot up to their head and almost caress and scratch one area that they want me to scratch in particular.

When you scratch your parrot's head, do so slowly and gently, scratching the top and sides. If he has pin feathers coming in, be extra careful around these. When done correctly, your bird will almost fall asleep.

REGURGITATION

If your bird regurgitates on you, you should feel lucky. This is a sign that he really likes you and you have been accepted as a member of his flock. Your bird will bob his head up and down or even side to side to bring up some food from his crop. He may also move his head from side to side. This is not the same as vomiting; a bird who is vomiting must be seen by a veterinarian. Regurgitation is not a violent act and will occur when your bird is playing with a toy or interacting with his favorite people. A vomiting bird flicks his head quickly and may have semi-digested food stuck to himself.

SHAKING AND FLUFFING

Birds will fluff up, ruffle, and shake their entire body. You will notice that when they do this, dirt and feather dust go flying. This helps return their feathers to a normal position and helps remove the feather dust. Sometimes a bird will do this to relieve tension.

If a bird is cold, he may also fluff up his feathers. If this continues for a long time, he may be ill and will need to be seen by an avian veterinarian.

Head shaking is most commonly seen in birds such as African greys. It may look like they have water in their ears and are trying to shake it out. This is a normal behavior unless the bird is doing it constantly. If so, a trip to the veterinarian is in order.

A blue-crowned conure with his tail feathers spread out. This bird is upset about something.

251

STRETCHING

If a parrot stretches his entire body, standing almost tiptoed with feathers raised and maybe even wings spread and swaying back and forth, it is a sign that he is agitated. You may notice his eyes pinning at this time as well. Some birds will also open their beaks in a threat and may growl or hiss. A cockatoo or cockatiel may raise his crest; he is trying to look bigger and more intimidating.

Quakers Will Quake

Quaker parrots may get the name for quaking behavior. This behavior is common in baby Quakers who have not yet weaned or who have just recently weaned. In quaking, the bird has an almost continuous head shaking, which is sometimes accompanied by rapidly flapping wings that are held close to the body.

TAIL BEHAVIOR

Parrots communicate with their tails. Tail fanning—spreading the feathers wide apart—indicates aggression and that the bird is upset and angry. It can also be a sexual behavior. Tail wagging is sometimes seen when a parrot wants a bath, is bathing, or is happy and content. Tail bobbing usually means that the bird is ill. However, it is normal for a bird to bob his tail when he is talking or singing. It is also normal to do this after exertion or a fright.

WING BEHAVIOR

When your bird flaps his wings rapidly, he is exercising them; he feels good. He may also want more attention or want to play.

Wing flipping—moving the wings in a quick shrug—can be a sign that your bird is angry, annoyed, or in pain. It could be due to a feather that just isn't lying right, or he may be upset about something. If the wing flipping is accompanied by hunching of the shoulders or head bobbing, your bird wants attention or to be fed.

Wing drooping is often a sign of overheating, especially if accompanied by panting. A bird will also do this to dry his wings off after a bath. This behavior is seen in baby birds as well because they haven't learned how to hold their wings right yet.

Displays

Why does a bird display? Birds display for a number of reasons, including courtship, excitement, territorial aggression, and fear. Displaying seems to the favorite pastime of many Amazons. They display with the tail spread or fanned wide, eyes dilating, wings held away from the body, head feathers ruffed up, and the body held in a threatening posture. This means "Do not bother me!" If you do, you will get bitten as you approach him. This is a warning!

Sometimes displaying can also be used in courtship. Instead of a

Military macaw blushing; most macaws will blush when they are excited or angry.

threatening posture, your bird will strut about, and this may be accompanied by vocal sounds. The parrot may still be ready to bite, so leave him alone when he is displaying

Should you or shouldn't you handle your bird at this time? It depends on why he is displaying at the time. If it is due to hormones, I back off because he isn't in control at all. But if the bird is being territorial, I do not allow him to be in charge. Keep in mind that you may be bitten, but it is important that you don't let this behavior dictate when you are able to handle your bird. I use a wooden dowel and have the bird step up on that. Then I talk to him calmly and wait for him to calm down before I make him step up on my hand.

I Need to Go!

Birds give signals when they are going to poop. If you know what these signs are, you will be able to put your bird over a garbage can so that he can poop in that. A bird who needs to go will back up a step or two and shift his weight backward. He may lift his tail slightly as well. Some birds may also squat slightly.

253

Can I Have Some?

Begging is most often associated with weaning or recently weaned babies. The bird will sit low on the perch with his head turned up. His wings will begin to slightly quiver, and his head will bob rapidly. This means "I am hungry; feed me now!" Adult birds also do this when they see a human eating something they also want.

Sounds

Birds can communicate through a number of vocalizations. Some of these can be very loud, while others can be much softer.

CHATTERING AND MUMBLING

These can be signs of contentment, or it could be that the bird is learning to talk. Chattering in the wild takes place in the evening before the flock goes to sleep. Loud chattering may be a way of getting your attention.

CLICKING

Clicking is a sound that some parrots make as a way of saying "Come here; get me; play with me; love me!" The behavior is seen most often in cockatiels and cockatoos. This is tongue clicking and is different from beak clicking. If a bird is making a beak clicking sound and is stretching his neck and raising a foot, he is sending a signal to keep away.

GROWLING

This is also a warning. African greys are particularly known for their growl, which is a warning that precedes a bite. This is especially true if the bird's eyes are dilating and the feathers are raised on the back of his head. If your bird starts growling, take a step back but talk calmly and softly to him. When he stops growling, you can move closer, stopping if he feels threatened once again.

HISSING

Hissing is another way of a bird saying back off. Cockatiels tend to do this more often than other species do. It usually happens when a bird is scared. He will take an offensive posture (crouched position) and start hissing. This hissing could be combined with little spitting sounds as well. Birds who aren't well socialized or who are semi-tame usually do this, while tame birds do not. This is more or less a bluffing behavior and used to intimidate. For a bird like this, be mindful that he is scared and take things slowly. Talk softly and calmly to him. Go down to his height and don't hover over him. By going slowly and calmly, your bird will calm down and you may start to develop some trust with him.

PURRING

Purring is a content sound that lets you know that your parrot is comfortable and happy. (My caique makes a purring sound whenever I cuddle with him.) Watch how a purring bird holds his body. If he looks relaxed, he is comfortable and happy. Some species will make a purring/growling sound when they are annoyed, almost as if they are complaining.

SCREAMING

This is a natural behavior, although excessive screaming is a learned behavior. Normal screaming is done at sunup and sunset, although parrots may also scream a little in the afternoon as well. Normal screaming may be done when a bird is scared or is in trouble of some kind.

Excessive screaming is screaming throughout the day. (See section "Problem Behaviors.")

Training Your Parrot

Training your parrot can be a fun way for the two of you to spend quality time together. It is a good way of establishing a bond while also allowing you to keep control of your bird. For example, just teaching him to step up when you want him to can keep him safe if he is in a dangerous situation, such as trying to chew on wires.

FIRST COMMANDS

The following are the most important commands that you can teach your bird. When used consistently, they will enable you to build a good working relationship with him that will put you in charge, not him.

UP OR STEP UP

The *up* or *step up* command is the most important of all commands. This command is used to establish nurturing control over your bird, as well as to deliver a clear message as to what you want him to do. Use this command the moment you bring your bird into the

Start training your parrot to step up as soon as you bring him home.

255

house. You even use it with baby birds who aren't perching yet. It must be used consistently by everyone in the household who handles your bird. When he responds correctly, praise him as a reward.

No matter what happens, never *hit* your bird!. It is easy to seriously injure a parrot this way, and you will permanently damage your relationship with him.

This command can even save your bird's life; he can step out of danger onto your hand or a perch. Consistent use of the *up* command can reduce biting and injuries due to fights between two birds, as well as help you catch an escaped bird.

Start with pushing your finger or hand (depending on the size of your bird) right above his legs and push slightly upward on his stomach area. When you do this, use the word "up." Keep repeating this step several times a day until your bird starts to step up when you cue him to.

If your bird doesn't step up when you push upward on his stomach area, try lightly tapping his feet with your fingers. Some birds will raise their feet in response to this. If your bird does, slide your fingers underneath his foot, then place your thumb over his foot and raise your hand slowly. Don't forget to use the word "up" along with praise.

If that still doesn't work, you may have to physically lift your bird off the perch and use the word "up." He may protest and try to bite, but more than likely it will be more of a threat than an actual bite.

Down

This is another command that should start the moment you bring your bird into your house. This command is useful in controlling him and getting him to where you want him to go. All of my birds understand this command, and I use it to get them to step back down onto a perch at the vet's office so that they can be weighed. This demands consistency in the use of the word by everyone who handles your bird.

To train it, while you are holding your bird place him slightly above and in front of a perch. Use the command *back* or *down*. When you do, crowd him so that he has to back up. Remember to use praise when he does so.

No

This is very important in controlling unwanted behaviors, such as biting. When used, your voice should take on an authoritative tone. You don't need to yell, just use a firm voice. It can also be combined with that look your parents would give you to make sure that you behaved. My grandmother referred to this as the *look*. Many bird behaviorists refer to it as the evil eye.

COME

A bird who is trained to come can be called away from dangerous situations. The command can also prove helpful if he escapes. Training this requires patience, time, and consistency. I used small pieces of a treat and tapped the spot where I wanted my bird to be. Using the word, I would call him, showing him the treat. When he came to where I wanted him, I rewarded him with the treat. I repeated this several times a day, rewarding each time. Eventually, the reward became a head scratch and praise. Once your bird learns this, you can use it to train cued behaviors.

STAY

I use this command when I put my birds on their play centers or T-stands. Parrots are like little kids, and they like to get into trouble when you aren't watching. I taught them to stay where I put them with this word. To train this, put your parrot on the perch and get close enough to him that he can't quite step up. Then raise your hand, palm facing your bird with fingers pointing upward, and use the word "stay." Wait a few seconds and then reward your bird with a little affection. Repeat, each time stretching out the duration of the *stay*.

Hand-Taming

Budgies are not usually hand-fed, so you will have to hand-tame your bird. These methods will also work on other species. The keys to hand-taming are consistency, patience, and understanding your bird's state of mind. Hand-taming isn't accomplished overnight; it may take a few days to a few months. Some wild-caught birds may never be completely tamed.

Your bird's wings should be clipped before you start to train him. This will allow you better control over him because a bird with clipped wings cannot fly

Training your bird to stay on his play stand will help keep him out of trouble.

257

Remember to reward your bird with praise and head scratches whenever he does something you want him to do.

away from you. Remember that your bird is scared and he could panic, flying out of control into walls, windows, or anything in his way.

The following method of training works best on budgies and other small parrots. Remember to always use praise, and end any session on a positive note. Make sure that you use the *up* command when working with any bird.

Take your bird to a small room with few distractions—a bathroom or spare bedroom will work. Be sure that the room is parrot-proofed before starting. Sessions should last around 10 to 15 minutes, depending on your bird. If he is breathing very hard and rapidly, stop the training session for a while. Remember to use praise and the word "up."

Bring the cage into the room with you and open it up. Your bird's wings should be clipped so that when he tries to escape, he will only flutter to the floor. When he does this, corner him, sitting down on the ground near him and offering him no other escape but your hand. (Be careful not to step on him.) Your bird will probably step up when cornered like this but will immediately jump off. Just pick him up again using the *up* command.

Taming and Training Your Parrot

Eventually, your bird will prefer your hand to the floor. Instincts dictate that the floor is a place of danger—higher is safer! He will start staying on your finger longer and longer. Remember to use lots of praise, and talk in a soft and soothing voice. If your bird tries to bite you, say no firmly and never, ever hit him. (Biting and other problem behaviors are discussed later in this chapter.)

TAMING MEDIUM AND LARGE PARROTS

For medium birds, such as conures, pionus, Quakers, and caiques, you want to limit the taming area even further, and the best way to do this is in the bathtub. Before putting your bird in the bathtub, place a soft, large towel down so that he won't slip or slide. Sit with your back to the faucet and the drain. Be aware that your bird may try to bite you, but more likely, he will try to get away. Wait for him to calm down first. If you rush in while he is thrashing around, not only could you get bitten, but he could injure himself. Talk calmly to him and offer your hand very slowly. Try not to pull it away if he tries to bite; instead, use that firm *no*. Once he has calmed down, he may step up on your offered hand, if only for a second or so. Remember to use praise. Keep repeating. Let the session go for around 10 to 15 minutes. If your bird appears overly stressed, stop the session. Always end any session on a positive note.

You can also tame parrots using a T-stand. The T-stand needs to have food cups on it, which work great in trying to get a bird out of the cage. Put your parrot's favorite food in the food cups, along with his regular food. Remove the food cups from his cage. (Remove them for only a few hours. If he isn't going out to get the other food on the T-stand, you don't want him to starve.) Let him get comfortable with going out to get the treat and food on the T-stand. If he hasn't tried to get out of his cage at all, you have to be a little sneakier. Start with the T-stand as close to the cage as possible; it needs to be close enough so that

Training Reminders

- When your bird shows signs of stress or being overtired, stop that session for the day. Signs may include panting, holding wings away from the body, and seeming frantic.
- Be consistent. Always use the same command for a given behavior.
- Keep in mind that when a larger bird is cornered, he may attack.
- There are no guarantees that you won't get bitten.
- Never hit your bird.
- Taming takes time. Be patient, don't rush things, and have realistic expectations.
- Always use praise and a soft, calm voice.
- Don't react if your bird does bite you.
- End every taming session on a positive note.
- Make sure that the taming session is a safe one.
- Clipping your bird's wings makes it much easier to tame him.

Good Parrotkeeping

A parrot always has a reason for screaming, biting, or other problem behaviors. The trick is to figure out what the reason is.

all he has to do is poke his head through the open door to get the food. Remember, you don't want to ever starve your bird, so after a few hours, put food back into his cage.

Once he is comfortable on the stand, move it away from his cage with him on it. Do so slowly, talking calmly to him. By now you should have an idea what his favorite food is. This is what you will offer as a reward for taming. Start by offering the treat, moving slowly and talking calmly. Once your parrot accepts this, move one arm closer to the stand, but make sure that it is still below his level. Keep offering the treat and try moving your arm closer to the stand each time. Stop if he starts getting nervous or looks like he wants to fly away. If he bites you, don't overreact to the bite. If you do, he will bite more often because he knows that he can intimidate you.

Your hand should now be directly under your bird. At this point, start moving your arm up toward him. Do so very slowly, rewarding and praising your bird with each increment that you move your arm. When he doesn't react to this, you can then move the treat closer to you so that he has to start leaning over your arm to get it. At first it may just be a very slight distance over your arm that he has to lean, but increase this gradually. Eventually, he will have to put a foot on your arm to get to the treat. When he does, don't move; don't react with anything other than calm. Reinforce this behavior with extra treats and praise.

Let your bird become completely comfortable standing on your arm. When you are at this point, move your arm away from the stand while he is still on your arm. Praise him, then put him back on the stand. Repeat this several times, each time letting your bird know that he is safe and that he can still go back to where he feels safe.

In this way, you are building a trusting bond with your bird. It may take some time, so don't be concerned that weeks or months pass before your bird trusts you enough to step up every time you want him to. Remember to use the *up* command when you are working with him.

Discipline

Discipline in birds is different than discipline in humans. A human can understand why she is being disciplined, while a bird doesn't. There is a difference between punishing and discipline. With discipline, you are gently guiding and molding a parrot to achieve the proper behavior. Punishment is usually correcting a problem with force.

Training Don'ts

- **Never hit your bird.**
- **Never grab his beak to stop him from biting.**
- **Never lose your temper.**
- **Never scream at your bird.**
- **Never spray your bird with a hard stream of water as a form of punishment.**
- **Never throw things at the cage to get him to be quiet.**
- **Never withhold food from your bird as a form of punishment.**

"NO" AND THE EVIL EYE

We already touched on one of the best methods of discipline, which is the word "no" followed by the look, or the evil eye. When you are giving your parrot the look, make sure that he is lower than you are. It is hard to use this as discipline if you have to glare up at him. Keep in mind that tone of voice is very important; lower it and use a firm *no*.

My cockatoo Toby understands this look very well, and she figured out how to use it to her advantage. When she is doing something she shouldn't, I use the *no* and the look. Toby will look at me with her big brown eyes and say in a soft voice "I love you, Mama." This is the only time she says it, so it is hard not to give in. I know her well enough to realize that if I give in, she will continue doing what she wants and ignore me.

DISTRACTION

Distraction is another method that is used on a bird who is trying to get into trouble or even on a bird who is nippy. Try offering a favorite treat or toy before your parrot starts to bite or get into trouble. Do this before he is actually getting into trouble. Distraction is tricky because you don't want to use this to reward a bad behavior. This is why you need to use this method before your bird is doing something he shouldn't. For example, if he likes to

If your parrot bites you, try not to overreact because this will just encourage him to bite again.

go off his cage when you need to do something else, try giving him something he likes to play with before you go away to do what you need to do. When you come back into the room and he is still on the cage, reward him with a little affection.

TIME-OUTS AND IGNORING YOUR PARROT

A time-out is putting your bird back into his cage to calm down or think about what he did wrong. For example, if your bird is screaming for attention, he should go back into the cage. When he is in the cage, ignore him, even if he is still screaming. Because your bird wants your attention, by not giving in to this demand, you can shape his behavior for the better. Of course, this doesn't work if your bird wants to go back to his cage.

If he is very agitated or still screaming, cover the cage for a few moments to calm him down further. Do not keep him covered. Once he calms down, remove the cover and let him back out of his cage.

I use a time-out with my macaw, Tiny, when he decides that he wants attention by screaming. All I have to do is give him the look and he runs into his cage and sulks for a few moments. When he comes out, he behaves himself for the rest of the day.

THE WOBBLE

I only use this method if the bird is going to give me a painful bite and then only for medium and larger parrots. If your bird is about to bite you, slightly wobble your hand. Don't wobble so hard that he falls off, though; you never want to do anything that could hurt your bird. It is more like a distraction. When he tries to regain his balance, he will forget about biting you. Use the firm *no* and the look once you have his attention. I like to reinforce the *up* command at this point by making the bird step up several times. Afterward, I reward him with praise but only if he hasn't tried to bite again.

Problem Behaviors

A bird may develop a problem behavior for many reasons, including:

- He wasn't properly socialized.
- He isn't getting enough attention.
- He is confused about the rules (or there aren't any rules).
- He wasn't taught to entertain himself.
- He has hormonal issues.
- He is ill.
- He is overly stimulated.
- He is bored.

   Your job as a bird owner is to prevent behavior problems before they start. Providing toys, a nutritious diet, and proper training go a long way toward this goal. If your bird does develop a problem behavior, you must act quickly to resolve the issue. The longer it goes on, the harder it will be to address.

THE DIARY

When your bird develops a problem behavior, start figuring out why it is happening. The best way to play detective is to start with a diary. Write down what is happening, when it is happening, what happened before, what happened after, who was in the room, if anything new was introduced, and whatever else you think is important. For example, if you were roughhousing with your bird and he bit you, write that down. From this you could probably figure out that he was overstimulated, and unless you want to get bitten again, you should correct the situation by playing in a calmer fashion.

   Other problem behaviors may not be so simple. By studying the diary, you may notice an emerging pattern. For example one woman's cockatoo became

Use the evil eye to help curtail your bird's misbehavior.

263

aggressive when she wore a certain color shirt. Normally her cockatoo was calm and gentle, but if she wore a bright red shirt, the bird would go berserk and attack her. It took her months to figure out that the bird would only do this when she wore bright red. She got rid of the shirt and the aggression in her cockatoo disappeared.

Eliminate the stimulus that is causing the bad behavior to occur. For example, if you jump up and down and start yelling every time your bird screams, you are rewarding a bad behavior. You are giving him a reason to continue screaming. He learns that you put on a show for him when he screams. Ignoring the screaming is the better way to deal with it.

You also need to address behavior problems before they become a problem. For example, if your bird is aggressive when he plays with a certain toy, remove the toy. Problem behaviors that have gone on for months or years will be much more difficult to correct. For every day that the problem has gone on, it will take anywhere from three to five days to correct it.

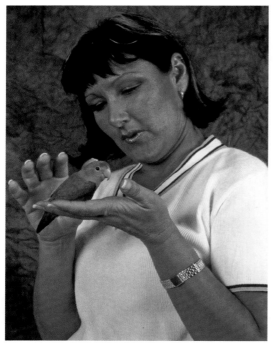

Boredom and lack of attention can cause a number of problem behaviors. Be sure to spend enough time interacting with your parrot.

Consistency is needed! For example, if your bird tries to escape from you every time you go to pick him up and you let him, you will always have a hard time getting him to step up. But if you are consistent with the *up* command and make sure that he does step up when you want him to, he will stop trying to run away and will do what you ask. Have him step up on command daily; this should be a normal part of your routine. Always praise or reward him when he does this.

Never lose your temper because birds do not respond to anger. This will only make the situation worse. If at any point you start feeling frustrated, stop what you are doing. When you are frustrated, you may not be thinking clearly and could do more harm than good.

If you can't figure out what is causing the problem behavior, you may need to have an impartial judge step in and see what you are doing. Talk to your friends at the local bird clubs to help you with this. They can watch to see what is going on. For example, say your bird is trying to step up on your hand and he uses his beak to help him. You may interpret this as a potential bite and move your hand away. As a result, your bird bites you when he steps up. You may not have noticed that you are moving your hand, but an impartial judge may.

BITING

All birds are capable of biting. This is an unpleasant fact about owning a bird. Even a hand-fed baby may bite out of fear, when overly stimulated, or when threatened. If you are aware that any bird—no matter how gentle he may be—can bite, you will not be as surprised when it happens. However, some birds seem to bite for no apparent reason or at least no reason you can think of. Let's first examine what can happen when someone is bitten.

First there is the surprise of the bite and then a reaction. This reaction could be as simple as moving your hand away to jumping up and down

Although any parrot can become a plucker, some species—such as umbrella cockatoos—are more prone to it than others.

screaming and yelling. Remember that birds love it when their humans put on an exciting show for them. Jumping up and down, yelling, and screaming is entertainment. When you entertain your bird like this, he will continue with the unwanted behavior because he is being rewarded for it.

Another reaction that might occur is that the person who was bitten will begin to act differently toward the bird. She may attempt to physically punish him, such as striking him or thumping his beak. Or she may fear the bird and stop interacting with him. In these scenarios, the owner has lost control over her bird. The bird knows that all he has to do is look as if he might bite and the owner will allow him to get away with anything. The bird is in control at this point. As the owner, you must take control back in a way that is nurturing and loving but assertive. Reassert your control will be a gradual process, but you must be consistent in doing so; otherwise, your bird will win.

Decide on a time schedule in which you can work with your bird. These sessions do not need to be lengthy; ten minutes or so will do nicely. Try working at least twice a day with him. If you can fit in more time, that is even better. You will probably get bitten a few more times, but training and the breaking of bad habits take a long time, as well as many bandages.

Develop a trusting bond with your bird by going slowly and not losing your temper. When working with him, use a favorite treat. Offer the treat during these sessions only. Start with just giving him the treat and offering praise if he doesn't bite you. If he attempts to bite, do not give him the treat. Instead, stand as tall as you can, look down on him, and give him the look. Use the word "no" in that special tone of voice. If he doesn't try to bite you, offer praise.

Eventually, you can start trying to get him on your arm again. It is very important that you use the word "up" in an authoritative tone. Use the treat as a bribe to get him on your arm; this is where it is best to use the T-stand and the sweatshirt. Keep reinforcing the *up* command, using praise when your bird responds correctly or the *no* and the look when he attempts to bite. Make him step up over and over, several times in a row. Remember the praise and the treat.

For each success, you will probably have several failures as well. Birds have their own minds, and some of them are very stubborn. It may take months before you can get your bird to come to you without trying to bite.

Sexual Maturity

You are in a completely different situation if your bird is biting due to sexual maturity. He is not completely in control of his actions. You may not be able to handle him during this time, and it is fine to back off. This type of biting usually occurs during the breeding season. You will see your bird displaying more, making funny sounds, or behaving aggressively. My Amazon, Charlie, goes through these seasonal changes and I give him his space during this time. Once the season is over, he is back to his old loving self and everyone in the household can handle him.

Remember, a bird cannot pluck his own head feathers. If your bird is bald and is not being plucked by a cage mate, get him to an avian veterinarian right away.

Biting Significant Others

Some birds will allow certain members of the family to handle them, while they may bite anyone else. They might be biting other family members out of jealousy, or perhaps they see them as a rival. This could be a problem, although with work, your bird may accept the other person.

Start with having the other person do things your bird enjoys. This could be bathing him, giving him special treats, or even changing his cage. Make sure that this person talks calmly to your bird, offering praise and a special treat as a reward. It is best to do some of these things without the favorite person in the room. Although this person may still not be your bird's favorite, he may start to accept her more and no longer attack her.

FEATHER PLUCKING

Feather plucking is a common problem in pet birds. Although some birds are psychological feather pluckers, there are a number of medical conditions that can cause the behavior.

Feather plucking can be caused by medical and psychological issues. An avian vet can help you determine the cause and find the cure.

DETERMINING THE CAUSE

An avian veterinarian will be able to help you determine the cause of the feather plucking. Before your visit, make some notes to take with you. These notes should include when you first noticed the problem, any changes in your household or routine, the type of diet your bird is on, the duration of the problem, his overall history, and anything else that seems to affect the plucking.

Some of the medical causes could be internal or external parasites, nutritional deficiencies, lack of proper lighting, metabolic disorders, hormonal imbalances, allergies, bacterial infections, and viral infections. Stress can also lead to feather plucking. If your avian veterinarian has ruled out a medical condition, the plucking is probably related to a psychological problem.

PSYCHOLOGICAL PROBLEMS

Birds are extremely emotional. Cockatoos, for example, require a great deal of physical contact; they are very tactile. Many cockatoos are bought as hand-fed babies, and when they are first brought into the home, the new owner will spend many hours cuddling with them. As the birds get older, this amount of cuddle time starts to decrease. To them, this lack of attention is like abandonment. They cannot play by themselves, and their emotional needs are no longer being met, so they begin feather plucking out of frustration and boredom. Such a scenario can happen to any species of parrot.

BOREDOM

In this situation, the bird is pulling his feathers out because he has nothing to keep him busy. He was probably never taught to play on his own. There are toys made of rope or yarn that can help simulate the preening behavior and refocus this action in a harmless direction. You need to teach your bird how to play on his own with these toys.

Start with a toy that interests your bird, and move it toward him. Play with it to get him interested. Praise him when he starts to play with it. Go slowly with this game until he starts showing interest in playing on his own. Remember to always praise and reward your bird.

Once he gets used to playing with the toy on his own, start adding new toys to his cage. Remember to do so slowly, gauging his reaction because some birds can be nervous about new toys and start to pluck for that reason.

EMOTIONAL ABUSE

Parrots are extremely sensitive creatures. Neglected or maltreated birds may develop emotional problems that could lead to feather plucking.

My avian veterinarian told me of a case of a macaw who was left

Yelling at your bird when he screams provides him with entertainment and therefore just encourages him to keep screaming.

alone in a cage that was too small with no toys, a poor diet, and no social contact. If the macaw made any noise, the owners would throw things at the cage, scaring him. The owners were scared of the bird even when he was shivering on the bottom of the cage. They called the vet to come out to the house to check on him. The bird only had head feathers, having plucked out all of his other feathers, and his skin was covered with sores from self-mutilation. The vet rescued the bird, but because of the amount of time that the feather plucking went on, the feather follicles were damaged and will probably never grow feathers again. The bird is untrusting of people, and he is cage-bound and fearful. However, his new human is taking it very slowly with him and is making some progress. He will never be a normal bird, but at least he was rescued from that situation. Unfortunately, abuses like this happen all too often and frequently cause feather plucking.

The Vacuum Screamer

It is normal for many birds to scream while their owners use the vacuum. Birds will scream and display while the vacuum is running, and they will stop once it's turned off. If this bothers you too much, consider getting a manual sweeper. It won't make any noise, so your parrot will likely not scream.

OTHER CAUSES

Sudden changes can also cause a bird to start plucking. These changes could be a new baby, a new house, or a new spouse. Birds are creatures of habit, and they enjoy a routine, so make changes gradually. Talk calmly to your bird, letting him know that everything is fine.

Loud noises can also bother a bird. This happens a lot during Fourth of July fireworks displays. Try staying home during this time, and give your parrot extra attention, reassuring him all the time that things are okay.

Lack of humidity can contribute to dry skin, which will cause itching and feather plucking. If you use a fireplace or have the heat on a lot, buy a humidifier to add moisture to the air.

RESOLVING FEATHER PLUCKING

Feather plucking can be difficult to correct. You will likely need the help of an avian veterinarian and perhaps an avian behavioral consultant. Here are some general guidelines that will help, but every situation is unique.

- Don't overreact. Remember, if you overreact you are rewarding a bad behavior.
- Some birds respond to being misted more often. It makes their feathers feel less itchy.
- Birds who self-mutilate beyond feather plucking may need to have a special collar put on to prevent them from plucking.

Tips for Dealing With Behavior Problems

- There are no quick fixes for bad behavior.
- Address bad behavior as early as possible, before it gets out of hand.
- Set guidelines early and stick with them.
- Keep a diary of what your bird is doing because this may help you figure out what is causing the problem. This will help you play detective.
- Do not reward an unwanted behavior. Think before you react. Ask yourself if you are giving your bird what he wants.
- Never hit your bird.
- Never do anything that will make your bird lose trust in you.
- Make sure that you see an avian veterinarian to rule out a medical condition.
- Use distraction.
- Teach your bird to play on his own.

- Some birds may respond to herbal treatments that your veterinarian can prescribe. Never give your bird any medications without your avian veterinarian telling you to.
- Provide toys that encourage your bird to preen those instead of plucking himself.
- Teach your bird to play on his own.

NIGHT FRIGHT

What is night fright and what causes it? Night fright is when a bird thrashes about wildly at night. It could be caused by a noise like a car going by outside, or it can even be caused by a bad dream. It could be a curtain that is blowing in the breeze. It could also be caused by a physical problem such as seizures. If night fright episodes are frequent or are increasing in frequency, have your bird seen by an avian veterinarian. Night fright affects many different species of birds but is most common in cockatiels.

One theory to explain night fright deals with how birds sleep. When a bird goes to sleep at night, his feet lock around the perch so that he won't fall off. It has been suggested that perhaps a noise or movement awakens the bird slightly. Upon this slight waking, his feet unlock and he becomes off balance and disoriented and starts to thrash around because he feels like he is falling. Some experts believe that diet may also play a role in thrashing. Still others think that there is a genetic factor because it occurs more often in lutino cockatiels than the normal tiels.

INJURIES

Injuries can occur during an episode of thrashing. Most common is a broken blood feather, although broken legs or wings can also occur. More serious injuries have also occurred, but these are rare. Make sure that you check on your bird if he does thrash. If he has a broken blood feather, take care of it immediately. If he has a broken bone, keep him warm and get him to a veterinarian as soon as you can.

NIGHT-LIGHTS

Many owners have reported success with the use of a night-light and leaving the cage uncovered. By providing some light, these birds had far fewer episodes, and some even stopped the problem altogether. If you must cover the cage at night, only cover three sides and do not cover it completely. These birds need some light.

PRECAUTIONS

If your bird suffers from night fright, remove toys, swings, and ladders prior to going to sleep for the night. This will help prevent injuries. A larger cage may be necessary so that your bird does not keep crashing into the sides of the cage. You may want to avoid using a bottom grate because wings can get trapped. Providing something soft on which

Cockatiels are more prone to night fright than other species.

your bird can land can prevent injuries too. A softer bedding material on the bottom of the cage is a good idea.

Do not place the cage near a window. Car lights or a cat passing by could be the cause of the thrashing. Draw the drapes or blinds before putting your bird to bed. This will also help block out the headlights of a car or other shadows.

If you are going to go into the room, alert your bird first. Talk calmly to him so that he will know you are there. If he is thrashing, calm him down and check him out to make sure that he isn't injured. This could take a few minutes to an hour or more, depending on the reason he was thrashing. Have a first-aid kit nearby for blood feather emergencies.

If your bird has night frights, make sure that they aren't caused by a medical condition. Have the veterinarian examine your bird to rule out a physical cause. Low levels of calcium can cause seizures that can be confused with night frights.

SCREAMING

One of the most annoying bad habits that parrots have is screaming. Birds scream for a variety of reasons. Some birds will scream for attention, some will scream only during certain times of the day, and others will scream during spirited family repartees. Each bird is different and will have a different reason for screaming.

FIGURING IT OUT

Screaming for attention is one of the most common reasons for screaming. Think about what you do every time your bird screams. Are you reinforcing this bad behavior by running to him, or are you yelling back? Many owners are unaware that they are perpetuating this bad behavior.

Look at things from your bird's perspective. The moment his owner leaves the room, he starts to scream. The owner, annoyed by the screaming, runs back into the room and yells at him to shut up. Some owners may even be so upset that they wave their arms about wildly in the air. Other owners may go over to the bird to pick him up and cuddle with him, giving him further reward for being noisy. The bird has now learned that by screaming, he will get what he wants: attention.

The best way to stop this scenario is not to let it get started in the first place. When your bird starts to scream when you leave the room, do not run back into the room to see what is wrong. First, always let him know that you are leaving the room. If he starts to scream, do not go back in there until he has stopped. When you go back into the room (once he is quiet), reward him for being quiet. He will learn that screaming will get him nothing but being quiet will.

Some birds like to know where their owners are. Remember that you are a flock member and that in wild flocks, members keep in touch by screaming. When you leave the room, you can tell your bird that you are going to be right back and then continue talking in soft, soothing tones until you return to the room.

Distraction is another method of preventing screaming. Save a special treat and hide it in a toy. When you are gone, your bird will play with the toy to get the treat. His attention will be turned to the toy and not focused on screaming for you.

I WANT OUT

Some birds scream because they want out of their cages. As your parrot's well-trained owner, perhaps you run over to his cage and let him out because the screaming bothers you. Once again you are rewarding and reinforcing a bad behavior.

Remember, you are the one in charge—not your bird. Ignore him when he is screaming. If he hasn't stopped after several minutes, cover the cage until he quiets down. Once he is quiet, then and only then should you let him out.

Taming and Training Your Parrot

SUNRISE AND SUNSET

Parrots commonly scream at dawn and dusk. This is an instinctual behavior, and it is normal. Some birds only scream to greet the sun, while others scream in the morning and then again at dusk. This screaming doesn't last very long, and if ignored, it won't become a problem.

Birds do not understand the concept of weekends or vacations, but you can help your parrot out by making it darker in the room at these times. This will prevent him from realizing that the sun has come up. You can also distract a dusk screamer at dusk so that he won't scream. Remember to use a special treat or use that time to play with your bird.

SCREAMING CONTESTS

Your kids are noisy; they are running around the house, yelling and screaming, and soon your bird joins in. Once again, this is normal. His flock is making noise, so he is making noise. Try to quiet your kids, and

In severe cases of feather plucking, a parrot may need a collar to prevent this behavior.

start talking very softly and calmly to your bird. He will calm down because his "flock" has settled down. Your kids don't have to be the sole cause, either; if you are having a noisy get-together with friends or the dog is playing and barking, your bird will join these activities too.

A bird who is overstimulated can also start to scream. Remove anything that could be causing him to become overstimulated, and talk softly and calmly to calm him down.

CLOSING THOUGHT

Did you know that more than 8 million parrots are captured for the pet trade annually, and more than 90 percent of them will die before they ever reach their final destination? Each year more and more species are becoming endangered or threatened because of the destruction of their habitats. Some species are even on the verge of extinction, but because of many caring and dedicated people and conservation groups, they have a chance. Here are five conservation organizations I have dealt with and hope you will consider supporting. Contact information for these organizations is in the Resources section in the back of this book.

Ecotourism can help preserve the habitats of wild parrots (along with other species).

Macaw Landing Foundation is run by a wonderful and caring man, Jack Devine. I know Jack personally, and he is truly dedicated to saving these magnificent birds. The foundation operates solely on donations.

Loro Parque was established in 1994 and is dedicated to the preservation of parrots and their habitat through education, research, responsible breeding programs, and community-based conservation programs. Located in the Canary Islands off of Spain, it has done more to save different species than just about any other organization and has the largest collection of birds in the world. The organization is working to save one of the most endangered species, the Spix's macaw. It needs donations to help continue its wonderful work.

The Rare Species Conservatory Foundation is working with the imperial Amazon, red-browed Amazon, and the red-necked Amazon, as well as other endangered species. It works with government agencies and focuses on education to save habitats and the species within them. Research projects investigate the ecology, behavior, reproductive physiology, and genetics of the different species to develop strategies to save them.

The World Parrot Trust has members in more than 50 countries, and it is working for the survival of parrots in the wild as well as the welfare of captive parrots around the world.

Finally, ProAves has done a lot to save many species. It was ProAves Columbia that rediscovered the Fuertes parrot. Working together with Loro Parque, its efforts have helped the golden-eared conure start a comeback from the verge of extinction.

You too can help. Don't buy any bird unless you know the source. If the price is too good to be true, the bird could have been illegally smuggled. Write to the food companies, cage manufacturers, and parrot toy companies, and ask them to make donations to different conservation groups. Buy only rainforest-safe products, especially wood. Make donations to help different conservation groups. Support ecotourism. Let's help save these magnificent creatures for future generations.

Bird on the Wing

This poem was written by my dad, Bernard Cohen, more than 70 years ago. I thought it would be a good way to close this book.

Fly on, fly on bird on the wing
You knoweth not what morrow brings
You knoweth not today from morrow
You knoweth not grief nor sorrow.

Fly among the clouds so high
You are the masters of the sky
We bow ourselves to you great one
Who flies so high up near the sun

Oh flying, flying so far and wide
Way out among the spacious skies
Oh if a bird I could only be
Flying o'er the land or sea

Making where I would my home
Forever more then would I roam
But for you only are these things
They were not meant for human beings

To you I give the name of King
For you our praised do we sing
For who has better right to be
Majesty of the skies we see

A toast to you I now do give
May you and yours forever live

Good Parrotkepping

Resources

ORGANIZATIONS

American Federation of Aviculture
P.O.Box 7312
N. Kansas City, MO 64116
Telephone: (816) 421-3214
Fax: (816)421-3214
E-mail: afaoffice@aol.com
www.afabirds.org

Avicultural Society of America
PO Box 5516
Riverside, CA 92517-5516
Telephone: (951) 780-4102
Fax: (951) 789-9366
E-mail: info@asabirds.org
www.asabirds.org

Aviculture Society of the United Kingdom
Arcadia-The Mounts-East Allington-Totnes
Devon TQ9 7QJ
United Kingdom
E-mail: admin@avisoc.co.uk
www.avisoc.co.uk/

The Gabriel Foundation
1025 Acoma Street
Denver, CO 80204
Telephone: (970) 963-2620
Fax: (970) 963-2218
E-mail: gabriel@thegabrielfoundation.org
www.thegabrielfoundation.org

International Association of Avian Trainers and Educators
350 St. Andrews Fairway
Memphis, TN 38111
Telephone: (901) 685-9122
Fax: (901) 685-7233
E-mail: secretary@iaate.org
www.iaate.org

The Parrot Society of Australia
P.O. Box 75
Salisbury, Queensland 4107
Australia
E-mail: petbird@parrotsociety.org.au
http://www.partosociety.org.au

EMERGENCY RESOURCES AND RESCUE ORGANIZATIONS

ASPCA Animal Poison Control Center
Telephone: (888) 426-4435
E-mail: napcc@aspca.org (for non-emergency, general information only)
www.apcc.aspca.org

Bird Hotline
P.O. Box 1411
Sedona, AZ 86339-1411
E-mail: birdhotline@birdhotline.com
www.birdhotline.com/

Bird Placement Program
P.O. Box 347392
Parma, OH 44134
Telephone: (330) 722-1627
E-mail: birdrescue5@hotmail.com
www.birdrescue.com

Parrot Rehabilitation Society
P.O. Box 620213
San Diego, CA 92102
Telephone: (619) 224-6712
E-mail: prsorg@yahoo.com
www.parrotsociety.org

Petfinder
www.petfinder.com

VETERINARY RESOURCES

Association of Avian Veterinarians
P.O.Box 811720
Boca Raton, FL 33481-1720
Telephone: (561) 393-8901
Fax: (561) 393-8902
E-mail: AAVCTRLOFC@aol.com
www.aav.org

Exotic Pet Vet.Net
www.exoticpetvet.net

INTERNET RESOURCES

BirdCLICK
www.geocities.com/Heartland/Acres/9154/

HolisticBird.org
www.holisticbird.org

The Parrot Pages
www.parrotpages.com

Parrot Parrot
www.parrotparrot.com/

CONSERVATION ORGANIZATIONS

Kakapo Recovery Programme
www.kakaporecovery.org.nz

Loro Parque Foundation
Avenida Loro Parque s/n - 38400 Puerto de la Cruz
Tenerife, Canary Islands
Spain
Telephone.: +34 922 37 38 41
Fax: +34 922 37 50 21
www.loroparque-fundacion.org

Macaw Landing Foundation
P.O. Box 17364
Portland, OR 97217
www.macawlanding.org/index.shtml

ProAves
www.proaves.org/sommaire.php?lang=en

Rare Species Conservatory Foundation
www.rarespecies.org/

World Parrot Trust (UK)
Glarmor House
Hayle, Cornwall TR27 4HB
Telephone: 444 01736 751 026
Fax: 44 01736 751 028
E-mail: uk@worldparrottrust.org
www.worldparrottrust.org

World Parrot Trust (USA)
P.O.Box 353
Stillwater, MN 55082
Telephone: (651) 275-1877
Fax: (651)275-1891
E-mail: usa@worldparrottrus.org
www.worldparrotrust.org

MAGAZINES

Bird Talk
3 Burroughs
Irvine, CA 92618
Telephone: 949-855-8822
Fax: (949) 855-3045
www.birdtalkmagazine.com

Bird Times
7-L Dundas Circle
Greensboro, NC 27407
Telephone: (336) 292-4247
Fax: (336) 292-4272
E-mail: info@petpublishing.com
http://www.birdtimes.com

Good Bird
PO Box 684394
Austin, TX 78768
Telephone: 512-423-7734
Fax: (512) 236-0531
E-mail: info@goodbirdinc.com
www.goodbirdinc.com

Parrots Magazine
Imax Ltd.
Riverside Business Centre
Brighton Road, Shore-by-Sea,
BN43 6RE
Telephone: 01273 464 777
E-Mail: info@imaxweb.co.uk
www.parrotmag.com

Species Illustrated by Page

Good Parrotkeeping

Good Parrotkeeping

Good Parrotkeeping

Dedication

As always, I dedicate this book to Steve, my loving husband of 32 years, and my two children, Marcy and Scott, for believing in me and supporting me during this endeavor. To my dad, Bernard Cohen, for giving me his love of animals and sense of humor. To Al and Sylvia Lazar, for not only putting up with my dad but for showing that you don't have to be related to be family. I would also like to dedicate this book to the memory of my mother, Harriet Cohen, for always being there for me; to Arnold and Sylvia Deutsch, the best in-laws anyone could ask for; to my grandparents, Nathan and Sarah Cohen, Mildred and Sidney Devorkin; and my beloved uncles, Irving and Morris Kobrin, for teaching me I could achieve anything I ever wanted. To all of my birds for giving me the inspiration and desire to write this book.

Finally, I want to dedicate this book to the memory of my very dear friend, LaDemah Mae "Smiles" Germeau. She freely offered advice about birds to anyone who asked. Her knowledge was extensive and her love of birds unequaled. The bird world will never be the same without her.

About the Author

Robin Deutsch lives in Yelm, WA, with Steve, her husband of 32 years; two children, Marcy and Scott; and three parrots, including a yellow-fronted Amazon she has had for 32 years. Originally from Chicago, she studied biology at Northeastern Illinois University. Robin works as a caregiver for her autistic daughter and helps her run her art business, Critters on Things. Robin has been a bird lover since receiving her first bird at the age of seven and has written several bird care and training books, including *The Healthy Bird Cookbook* and *The Click That Does the Trick: Trick Training Your Bird the Clicker Way*.

Photo Credits

Larry Allan: 91, 113, 234, 251; Joan Balzarini: 40, 45, 51, 76, 87 (right), 90 (both), 92 (both), 93, 177, 204, 248 258, 262, 268; Bomshtein (courtesy of Shutterstock): 87 (left); Katrina Brown (courtesy of Shutterstock): 149, 263; Paul Buturlimov (courtesy of Shutterstock): 183; Erik E. Cardona (courtesy of Shutterstock): 186; Susan Chamberlain: 67, 119, 193; Judy Crawford (courtesy of Shutterstock): 22; Demark (courtesy of Shutterstock): 139; Robin Deutsch: 38, 55, 115 (both), 118 (all), 192, 200; Pichugin Dmitry (courtesy of Shutterstock): 19; fivespots (courtesy of Shutterstock): 1; Susan Flashman (courtesy of Shutterstock): 6, 62 (right), 154, 170; Foxie (courtesy of Shutterstock): 31; Isabelle Francais: 20, 36, 44, 47, 49, 50, 57, 64, 79, 105, 109, 120, 142, 159, 166, 230; Cindy Fredrick: 122, 171; Nicola Gavin (courtesy of Shutterstock): 7, 162, 253, 260; Michael Gilroy: 28, 32, 94, 106; R.L. Hambley (courtesy of Shutterstock): 34, 56, 209; Susan Harris (courtesy of Shutterstock): 184; Barbara Heidenreich: 77, 249; Eric Ilasenko: 10, 13, 104, 111, 201 (right), 243; Eric Isselee (courtesy of Shutterstock): 3, 43, 69, 277; J_S (courtesy of Shutterstock): 276; Bonnie Jay: 12, 71, 74, 132, 160, 173, 178, 188, 191, 201 (left), 203, 221, 225, 228, 235, 238, 264, 265, 267, 273; Andrew Kua Seng How (courtesy of Shutterstock): 26; Joyce Mar (courtesy of Shutterstock): 26; Bobbye Land: 129; Jill Lang (courtesy of Shutterstock): 246; Xavier Marchant (courtesy of Shutterstock): spine; Horst Mayer: 53; Juriah Mosin (courtesy of Shutterstock): 70; Robert Pearcy: 68, 86, 136; George Allen Penton (courtesy of Shutterstock): back cover; Rafi Reyes: 75; Peter Rimsa: 134, 140, 156, 194, 217; Laurin Rinder (courtesy of Shutterstock): 4; Ronen (courtesy of Shutterstock): cover; Vincent Serbin: 271; Lori Skelton (courtesy of Shutterstock): 62 (left); Gina Smith (courtesy of Shutterstock): 30; Ronald R. Smith: 102, 168; Laura Stern: 212; Alexander Sviridenkov (courtesy of Shutterstock): 100, 210; Karl H. Switak: 73; Luis César Tejo (courtesy of Shutterstock): 59; John Tyson: 82, 88 (right), 112, 126, 144, 153, 223, 226, 241; Louise van der Meid: 215; Ashley Whitworth (courtesy of Shutterstock): 274
Illustrations by Marcy Deutsch